# The Making of Hong Kong: From Vertical to Volumetric

With its island origins, skyscraper skyline and world city status, Hong Kong is often likened to New York. However the comparison soon falters with the realization that Hong Kong's skyscrapers are only the more visible aspect of a far more complex urban condition. A steep and contorted terrain has ensured that built-up areas are compact, rich in spatial experience, rarely far from hills and water; and connected by an array of public transport that is second to none.

The three authors of *The Making of Hong Kong* see value in these conditions – a metropolis with a small urban footprint, 90 per cent use of public transport for vehicular journeys, and proximity to nature. Though the compact city is a model that is frequently advocated by urban thinkers, it is one rarely encountered. Here, the evolution of Hong Kong's intense urbanism is traced from the region's pre-colonial walled settlements and colonial shop-houses to the contemporary vertical and volumetric metropolis of towers, podia-and-towers, decks, bridges, escalators and other components of multi-level city living. On a site bedevilled by an acute shortage of flat land, Hong Kong is portrayed as the 'accidental pioneer of a new kind of urbanism' that commands the thoughtful attention of a wider world.

The book's lucid text and over 200 mostly original illustrations, including images of design futures, are an essential package for urban designers, architects, planners, landscape architects and other urban professionals with interests in urban design, density, urban theory, East Asian urbanism and, of course, Hong Kong's built form history and future.

# Planning, History and Environment Series

**Editor:**
Emeritus Professor Dennis Hardy, High Peak, UK

**Editorial Board:**
Professor Arturo Almandoz, Universidad Simón Bolivar, Caracas, Venezuela and Pontificia
Universidad Católica de Chile, Santiago, Chile
Professor Gregory Andrusz, London, UK
Professor Nezar AlSayyad, University of California, Berkeley, USA
Professor Robert Bruegmann, University of Illinois at Chicago, USA
Professor Meredith Clausen, University of Washington, Seattle, USA
Professor Robert Freestone, University of New South Wales, Sydney, Australia
Professor John R. Gold, Oxford Brookes University, Oxford, UK
Professor Sir Peter Hall, University College London, UK
Emeritus Professor Anthony Sutcliffe, Nottingham, UK

**Technical Editor**
Ann Rudkin, Alexandrine Press, Marcham, Oxfordshire, UK

### Published titles

*Planning Europe's Capital Cities: Aspects of nineteenth century development* by Thomas Hall (**paperback 2010**)

*Selling Places: The marketing and promotion of towns and cities, 1850–2000* by Stephen V. Ward

*Changing Suburbs: Foundation, form and function* edited by Richard Harris and Peter Larkham

*The Australian Metropolis: A planning history* edited by Stephen Hamnett and Robert Freestone

*Utopian England: Community experiments 1900–1945* by Dennis Hardy

*Urban Planning in a Changing World: The twentieth century experience* edited by Robert Freestone

*Twentieth-Century Suburbs: A morphological approach* by J.W.R. Whitehand and C.M.H. Carr

*Council Housing and Culture: The history of a social experiment* by Alison Ravetz

*Planning Latin America's Capital Cities, 1850–1950* edited by Arturo Almandoz (**paperback 2010**)

*Exporting American Architecture, 1870–2000* by Jeffrey W. Cody

*Planning by Consent: The origins and nature of British development control* by Philip Booth

*The Making and Selling of Post-Mao Beijing* by Anne-Marie Broudehoux

*Planning Middle Eastern Cities: An urban kaleidoscope in a globalizing world* edited by Yasser Elsheshtawy (**paperback 2010**)

*Globalizing Taipei: the political economy of spatial development* edited by Reginald Yin-Wang Kwok

*New Urbanism and American Planning: The conflict of cultures* by Emily Talen

*Remaking Chinese Urban Form: modernity, scarcity and space, 1949–2005* by Duanfang Lu

*Planning Twentieth Century Capital Cities* edited by David L.A. Gordon (**paperback 2010**)

*Planning the Megacity: Jakarta in the twentieth century* by Christopher Silver

*Designing Australia's Cities: Culture, commerce and the city beautiful, 1900–1930* by Robert Freestone

*Ordinary Places, Extraordinary Events: Citizenship, democracy and urban space in Latin America* edited by Clara Irazábal

*The Evolving Arab City: Tradition, modernity and urban development* edited by Yasser Elsheshtawy

*Stockholm: The making of a metropolis* by Thomas Hall

*Dubai: Behind an urban spectacle* by Yasser Elsheshtawy

*Capital Cities in the Aftermath of Empires: Planning in central and southeastern Europe* edited by Emily Gunzburger Makaš and Tanja Damljanović Conley

*Lessons in Post-War Reconstruction: Case studies from Lebanon in the aftermath of the 2006 war* edited by Howayda Al-Harithy

*Orienting Istanbul: Cultural capital of Europe?* edited by Deniz Göktürk, Levent Soysal and İpek Türeli

*Olympic Cities: City agendas, planning and the world's games 1896–2016*, 2nd edition edited by John R. Gold and Margaret M. Gold

*The Making of Hong Kong: From vertical to volumetric* by Barrie Shelton, Justyna Karakiewicz and Thomas Kvan

# THE MAKING OF HONG KONG
## From Vertical to Volumetric

Barrie Shelton
Justyna Karakiewicz
Thomas Kvan

Routledge
Taylor & Francis Group

LONDON AND NEW YORK

First published in 2011
by Routledge
2 Park Square, Milton Park, Abingdon, Oxfordshire OX14 4RN

Simultaneously published in the USA and Canada
by Routledge
711 Third Avenue, New York, NY 10017

*Routledge is an imprint of the Taylor & Francis Group, an informa business*

© 2011 Barrie Shelton, Justyna Karakiewicz and Thomas Kvan

Typeset in Aldine and Swiss by PNR Design, Didcot
Printed and bound in Great Britain by the MPG Books Group

This book was commissioned and edited by Alexandrine Press, Marcham, Oxfordshire

The right of the authors has been asserted in accordance with sections 77 and 78 of the
Copyright, Designs and Patents Act 1988.

The publisher makes no representation, express or implied, with regard to the accuracy of the
information contained in this book and cannot accept any legal responsibility or liability for any
errors or omissions that may be made.

*British Library Cataloguing in Publication Data*
A catalogue record of this book is available from the British Library

*Library of Congress Cataloging in Publication Data*
Shelton, Barrie, 1944–
The making of Hong Kong : from vertical to volumetric / Barrie Shelton, Justyna Karakiewicz,
and Thomas Kvan.
p. cm. — (Planning, history and environment)
Includes bibliographical references and index.
1. Cities and towns—China—Hong Kong—History. 2. Cities and towns—Growth. I.
Karakiewicz, Justyna, 1954– II. Kvan, Thomas. III. Title.
HT147.C48S5324 2011
307.76095125—dc22
2010024635

ISBN13: 978–415–48701–6 (hbk)
ISBN13: 978–203–83560–9 (ebk)

# Contents

# Acknowledgements

During the preparation of this book, we have been variously on the staff of the Universities of Hong Kong, Melbourne and Sydney, and we are fortunate to have been able to draw on their excellent libraries and research facilities. Likewise, across the three universities, there is a large number of students with whom we have worked and learned, and whose questions, explorations and conceptual propositions have expanded our insights and challenged our thinking. (We have conducted 'Hong Kong' urban design and architecture studios from all three places.)

There are people, mostly postgraduate architecture and urban design students, who have assisted us in our investigations and preparation of graphic material: Bao Wei, Chris Cowell, Ryland Fox, Kam Shing Leung, Angus Ngai Chung Hon, Yu Ka Shing and Andrew Witt in Hong Kong; Matt Choot, Ryland Fox and Leanne Hodyl in Melbourne; and Irene Rui Cheng, Yuji Ji , Rachel Keys and Madhan Sekar in Sydney. Special mention should be extended to Matt and Leanne for their graphic experimention in the earlier stages and to Madhan for bringing consistency towards the close. Also, thanks should go to Yina Sima for assistance with indexing.

Photographs have played an essential and prominent role in our work, and some older photographs can only be described as 'invaluable' for the information they portray. We are especially indebted to K.E. Barker and Maria Kvan Mortensen, who generously searched their respective photograph collections for the decades following World War II, and allowed us to reproduce items in chapters 2, 3, 4 and 7. (K.E. Barker for 2.8, 3.9, 3.14, 3.15, 3.25, 4.1, 4.4, 4.6, 4.7, 4.8, 4.13, 4.24 and 7.33; and Maria Kvan Mortensen for 3.11 and 4.13.)

Three colleagues, whose economic, morphological and wind flow insights must be acknowledged are Frederik Pretorius of the University of Hong Kong, Philip Steadman of the University of London, and Tsou Jin Yeu of the Chinese University of Hong Kong.

Our experience of the Kowloon and Canton Railway Company's Linear City Project (2004–2005) provided opportunity for urban investigation and speculation on Hong Kong's future form that is the foundation for our Addendum. For this we acknowledge the opportunity that Andrew Seah Hann Jen made available when he conceived of this project and the support for our evolving ideas as it progressed.

Each one of us has been recipient of particular assistance or advice. Barrie

Shelton would like to thank Iris Se Hwang, Nick Rae, Noni Ruker and David Tickle for their lengthy discussions and ideas on Hong Kong's volumetric condition and possibilities: also, figures 8.3 and 8.4 are adapted from Iris's work. Barrie would also like to thank his wife, Emiko Okayama, whose deep knowledge of East Asian cultures and languages has been a regular source of reference.

Thomas Kvan and Barrie Shelton would like to acknowledge their co-author's generosity in allowing her remarkable drawings to adorn the book's cover and chapter title pages.

The University of Melbourne has been generous in providing publications assistance for final preparation of the manuscript. Likewise, the Faculty of Architecture, Design and Planning, University of Sydney, supported aspects of the investigation and preparation of the document.

Lastly, we would like to thank Ann Rudkin for her constant attention, critical support, encouragement, and wise advice throughout the entire process.

# 1 A State of IntenCity

Since 1841, Hong Kong has operated effectively as a city-state, first under British colonial rule, and more recently as a Special Administrative Region (SAR) within China. Accepting this semi-autonomous status in the world table of nations, its territory of 1,104 square kilometres ranks 184th by area between Martinique and Sao Tome & Pincipe, 98th by population (6.9 million in 2004) between Honduras and El Salvador, a surprising eighth by the size of its trading economy (Ingham, 2007), and a staggering third on the international ladder of connectivity, ahead of cities such as Tokyo and Paris (Johnson *et al.*, 2008). On the latter point, Chep Lak Kok Airport, which is one of the world's largest and busiest, plays an important role. Most important, however, is Hong Kong's position as an economic powerhouse, and a major logistics and knowledge centre – a member of an elite club of international finance centres, being the world's third largest after New York and London (Ingham, 2007). The latter, **LONDINIVM**, is ancient by comparison; and even 'New World' New York, or New Amsterdam as it was known originally in 1625, was founded two centuries before Hong Kong, and is therefore middle aged.

In other words, Hong Kong has barely left its youth on a city age scale. It was an infant prodigy at the turn of the twentieth century. The city is still not 170 years old, having grown from a small isolated military-cum-trading post on the north side of an inhospitable island just 2 km off the coast of China where evidence suggests more than six millennia of settlement. It is a central place in a vast Asian region that consists of both mainland and islands, and has been dominated by Chinese culture for many centuries. While it is recognized that the area of Hong Kong SAR has a long pre-colonial history, this will feature only occasionally here as our focus is on urban growth and form. Under most of the period of British colonial rule, it grew massively in population but modestly in area. Only once during those 156 years did it lose significant population, and that was during World War II under Japanese occupation. Immigrants have been mainly Chinese, and the place's rapid growth was in part due to its 'pull' as a centre of trade. But it also had much to do with the 'push' from various political upheavals in the region that saw hundreds of thousands of refugees from China and elsewhere pour into the Colony, at times in flood-like proportions. The first major civil unrest in China that propelled people to Hong Kong was soon after foundation: that was associated with the 1850–1861 Tai Ping Rebellion. Within less than twenty years, there were over 100,000 people in Hong Kong, and over a quarter of a million before the end of the nineteenth century. This growth compares with or outstrips that experienced by several cities of Victorian Britain during their most frantic years of industrialization. Thus, the city was quick to become sufficiently populous to ensure a measure of self-sustaining growth. But this growth was relatively minor compared to that experienced from the middle of the twentieth century: few places in the whole history of cities can match Hong Kong's expansion during the years following Japanese occupation and in the years surrounding China's communist revolution: from 1945 to 1951, the population grew by 210 per cent, from 0.65 million to 2.02 million, after which the city continued to grow by between one-half and one million people per five year period until the mid-1960s (Lo, 1992). Only in the early years of the twenty-first century do we see this scale of growth matched in the massive rural to urban migration now underway in China.

At the time of British settlement, Hong Kong island, from which the metropolis grew, was famously referred to as a 'barren rock': it had an area of less than 80 km² whose landform rose steeply from the surrounding sea, and was devoid of any resource to speak of. Even when the Colony 'jumped' Victoria Harbour to occupy a fragment of the Asian mainland, with the acquisition of Kowloon Peninsula (adding a mere 9 km² in 1861), and further extended to embrace the New Territories in 1898, the territory remained small – just 1,070 km² in all – mostly mountain but also with extensive swamp. It is an understatement to say that opportunities for city building were constrained.

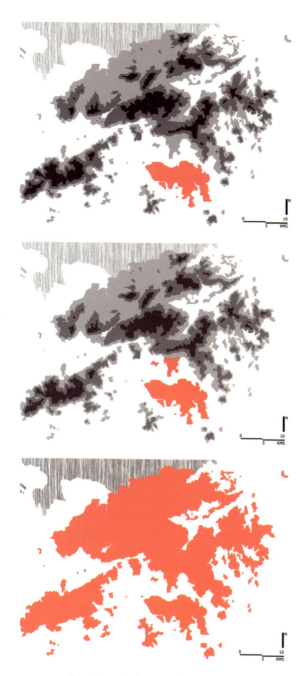

Hong Kong territory. **1.1.** The initial British colony: Hong Kong Island, 1841 (previously part of China). **1.2.** First extension to include much of Kowloon Peninsula, 1861. **1.3.** Second extension to include the New Territories, 1898. In 1997, Hong Kong was returned to China and designated a Special Administrative Region (SAR).

It was against this unusual physical and demographic backcloth, that land became the Hong Kong government's main instrument for shaping the Colony's economy and urban form. And it is one of the ironies of Hong Kong's success that, although wedded to capitalist free-market development, the British crown government held a socialist-like (without the ideology) hold on ownership and control of land, to gain its main revenue from the sale of development rights for subsequently leased land. From within four years of settlement, this was the *modus operandi*, and remains so to this day. No other government in the modern world, communist or capitalist, has been so consistent, effective or comprehensive with such a policy over such a long period of time.

Further, within this framework there has always been a government-controlled programme of land construction through reclamation – from sea and swamp. From the early years, lots that were leased to developers included watery 'marine lots' – filled and developed by private interests within the parameters of government-determined survey. Today surfaces reclaimed from the sea alone represent no less than 6 per cent of Hong Kong's total land area: between 1887 and 2006, some 67 km$^2$ of sea were converted into land (Hong Kong geographic data). If the modest areas of reclamation from the earlier years of settlement are added, the total approximates to the entire island area of the original Colony. Approximately one-third of Kowloon (which is increasingly the heart of Hong

Kong) is on reclaimed ground. And of all developed land in Hong Kong, over 35 per cent has been reclaimed from the sea (Jiao *et al.*, 2005)

In short, the government has not only controlled the sale of land development rights and leased the land, but also initiated and effectively built (or at least determined the 'building' of) much of the ground on which development has actually occurred: in the process, it has built the equivalent of another Hong Kong Island but arguably more useful in its flatness. Hong Kong is like Holland in the reclamation game, although with the latter it was a matter of extending an already flat country, while in Hong Kong it is a case of adding a skirt to a body of hills. Perhaps a better analogy is as a micro-Japan. The latter consists of several large mountainous islands, leaving only 30 per cent of the nation sufficiently flat to readily accommodate urban building: the result is extensive reclamation, particularly for city growth.

To reclamation, we can add another major layer of government-initiated building in the form of public housing. Although the government's entry into this arena was comparatively late and prompted by necessity, it has been huge. In the 1950s, following some catastrophic fires in squatter settlements, a start was made in this kind of urban development. It entered reluctantly but very quickly became an effective and massive supplier of public housing – with much of it on land constructed through reclamation. It was not until 1954 that a public housing authority was set up in Hong Kong: yet within just over a decade (1965), 1 million or nearly one-third of residents were living on public housing estates. By 1981, this had risen to 2 million or almost two-fifths of the Colony's population.

From such circumstances, we would expect dense development to have emerged but the sheer concentration of people and built form in Hong Kong still astonishes most observers. Land construction and modification, the sale of development rights, land leasing and public housing have been combined unwaveringly into policies of deliberate density. Again neither the pursuit of public housing nor density was strongly ideological but as will be seen in later sections, mostly a pragmatic response to circumstances.

Important here is that Hong Kong has evolved into the quintessential high-density small-footprint city – with a population of 7 million on an urban land area of just 120 km$^2$: this gives a concentration of people approaching 600 per hectare – without doubt, at the top of the city-wide average population density table in the world, and rivalled only by Mumbai and Dhaka. Further, densities of 1,000 or more people are commonplace in Hong Kong, and can rise to approximately four times that figure per hectare on particular blocks or lots, for instance in Mong Kok and in some new towns. Thirty-plus storey housing and commercial towers are a ubiquitous sight across the metropolis, with multi-level shopping a general experience. Gross residential densities measure in four figure whole numbers in several places – a phenomenon hardly known at even small spot points in most of the urbanized world. In fact, no matter where you may be standing in built Hong Kong, whether it is the Central District or a peripheral new town, you are likely to be in or between the shadow of towers or other high buildings, yet remain only a few minutes walk to water or mountain (and forest) respectively, most probably both.

**1.4.** Three strip 'ecologies': wooded hill, dense city and polluted sea Towers stand close, slender and tall – *like bamboo shoots after rain*.

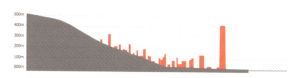

**1.5.** Hill, City and Sea: with the city's narrow section itself divided into two distinct topographical bands – steep foothill and reclaimed flatland. The section is through Hong Kong Central: the tall waterfront building, Two International Finance Centre, stands at 415 m.

It is, writes Peter Rowe, this scale of Hong Kong that 'sets (it) apart from most, if not all, other living environments and offers the prospect of a different way of life'. Further, he adds, these characteristics 'begin to define a difference in the kind of living environment, rather than simply a difference in degree' (Rowe, 2005). In recent discussions of urban *intensity*, it is not surprising to find a play upon the word with it morphing to *intenCity* in more than one arena. It is a valiant attempt to capture the combination of several urban qualities – of concentration, density, complexity and verticality, where the interplay between the quartet brings a level of intensity that is somehow much more than the sum of the parts. While more will be said of this later, it is a fact of urbanism that no city has deserved the term so much and so consistently as Hong Kong.

This was highlighted by material comparing the two cities shown in a recent exhibition at New York's Skyscraper Museum: *Vertical Cities: Hong Kong/New York*. Using 400 feet or 122 m as a height criterion, it showed Hong Kong to be well ahead of New York in the tall building league with 558 skyscrapers compared to New York's 360. It saw both cities as having evolved as colonial ports on small islands aside outstanding natural harbours but recognized that Hong Kong 'surpasses New York in the number of high-rises, hyper-density habitation and efficient mass transit' (The Skyscraper Museum, undated). However, it also acknowledged some very important differences: most of Hong Kong (Victoria, Kowloon and its extensions, and the New Territory new towns) all stand consistently at densities that approximate to what is a central density in New York: and, as noted above, most of Hong Kong exists in walkable proximity to mountain and/or sea. From our morphological and ecological perspectives, these are crucial differences.

Prior to the *Vertical Cities* show, the same museum mounted another exhibition dedicated to New York's emergence as a skyscraper city in the early twentieth century, which included the high-rise city visions of several New York architects of the time: these were not just skyscraper cities but multi-level cities in the sense of having a publicly accessible domain rising through several levels. The assertion is that Hong Kong, became the arena in which some of those visions were later played out; and where relevant, we shall make appropriate flashbacks to these, for it can be argued that it is in Hong Kong that many visions from elsewhere have found their realization.

The final point in this introductory section is that Hong Kong's functioning as a dense city depends on most people making almost all their journeys on public transport or, as is typical of Hong Kong, on publicly regulated private vehicles. The transport system offers a diversity of complementary services that, together, are second to none. It includes train, 'tube', subway or *underground iron*, bus, mini bus, several types of ferry boat, taxi, tram, bicycles and more which give choice in speed and price, plus considerable convenience in changing from one to another. The result is that 90 per cent of journeys are made on vehicles providing public passenger services. In a city in which gross densities of 500 per hectare plus are commonplace, and the unit length of road per registered vehicle is the shortest in the world, public transport is a necessity. In 2008, there were 575,000 vehicles and 2,080 km of road, thus 282 vehicles for every kilometre. The circumstances should not, however, blind us to the achievement, for Hong Kong's public transport is exceptional by any standard – so much so, that urban transport and energy use analyst, Jeff Kenworthy, was able to proclaim Hong Kong's 'remarkably successful transit system and very low car usage' as a model to the world in his 'Model Cities: Asia' paper (Kenworthy, 2001). Amongst several reported statistics, he cited a HK per capita increase in car use over the decade 1981–1991 of just 146 km, compared to 2,584 for Los Angeles. He noted that half of Hong Kong's residents lived within 500 m of a Mass Transit Rail station, and that 70 per cent of users of this intensively used system walked to and from their origin and destination stations when making their trips. Only 3 per cent of passengers used some other form of transport at both ends of their train rides to connect to other places.

To think of Hong Kong's 'public transport' only in terms of conventional vehicles is too limiting and should rightly be extended to include 'public movement infrastructure services', for lifts, escalators and other people movers play crucial roles in the compendium of interdependent systems that keep this city mobile. Their collective capacity, complementarity and convenience is impressive; and each has its own, sometimes very special, setting, configuration and dimensions that will also receive our attention.

Many authors have contributed to our understanding of Hong Kong's form and growth by turning their expert attentions to particular events or conditions: the extreme physical geography, land development as economic policy, reclamation, the territory's refugee history and demography, its West-East hybrid culture, the late but massive public housing programme, variety in public transport, the evolution of specific districts and more. For instance, Owen and Shaw's graphic portrayal of Hong Kong's underlying geology and geomorphology, Edward Pryor's charting of Hong Kong's earlier housing years, Peter Leeds's account of developments in public transport, Frank Leeming's excellent early seventies' street studies, Nuala Rooney's fascinating exploration of Hong Kong people's high-density spatial sensibilities, Alan Smart's challenging commentary on the rise of Hong Kong's housing policy and McDonogh and Wong's highly readable cultural overview of Hong Kong as a colonial and global centre are just a few examples (Owen and Shore, 2007; Pryor, 1972 and 1983; Leeds, 1998; Leeming, 1977; Rooney, 2003; Smart, 2006; McDonogh and Wong, 2005). Such works have provided us with invaluable contextual sources. Our focus is overlapping but different, namely the physical urban form at various scales of resolution from the network of old centres and new towns through to building and spatial detail: thus it includes urban structure; natural and constructed ground; local street, block and subdivisional layouts; building and spatial typologies; infrastructure; etc and their relationships. While we do not ignore the influencing circumstances, we are concerned primarily with the city's form or *morphology*, component *typologies* and physical transformations or *morphogenesis* through time: thus our sights are fixed firmly on the territory's changing landform and built forms that together make up the world's most *concentrated* and *vertical* city.

As an extreme concentration of people and tall buildings, Hong Kong represents a condition of density. Thus our work is both an investigation of the particular city and the broader condition, and associated issues. This is because we live in times when many urban and environmental experts are advocating the raising of densities as urban policy for compelling reasons: an impending environmental crisis that embraces such massive issues as global warming, climate change and rising sea-levels. They are urging planning and development authorities to build our cities more densely to reduce dependence on the automobile for travel, and to use more renewable energy sources to fuel our cities. With similar concerns, Andre Vijoen, his co-authors and many others call also for the development and incorporation of urban agriculture (Vijoen *et al.*, 2005).

However, while cities are commonly cited as major contributors to a deteriorating environment, they must also be advanced as part of a solution. It is clear that high-density cities with good public transport systems and shared infrastructure make fewer per capita energy demands on the environment in a world in which urban transport is a major consumer of energy (Kenworthy, 2003). In this way, Hong Kong's high-density compact form takes on a new significance, and in this context Hong Kong has appeared in such compendia as *Future Forms and Design for Sustainable Cities* (Jenks and Dempsey, 2005). Thus the city's form is a worthy object of investigation in its own right – as a unique and tangible urban fact, and in a broader sense as a representative of dense urbanism. It is important to discover how the place and its components work and extract the underpinning urban design principles, for these can be adapted to guide and inform development elsewhere. With enhanced understanding, Hong Kong emerges as an urban laboratory within which further intensification of an already compact city can be explored. Our work has aspirations in all of these areas: with the understanding emerging from Chapters 2 to 6, and possibilities explored in the Addendum.

We are, however, by no means the first to draw attention to the positive implications of Hong Kong's high densities, compact forms and good connections: for this, we must turn back almost half a century.

## Flashback: The 1960s

In 1963, following fifteen years of the most rapid and chaotic population growth in Hong Kong's history, an article appeared in the *Journal of the American Institute of Planners* that compared aspects of Hong Kong and American urbanism. It bore the innocuous title of 'Implications of Density in Hong Kong' and the author, Robert C. Schmitt, was a little known statistician who had visited the city in the previous year. He had also absorbed Jane Jacobs's views on density in her then recently released *Death and Life of Great American Cities*, now acknowledged as a planning 'classic' (Schmitt, 1963).

At first sight, given the article's bland title and the enormous contrasts that existed in space and wealth between Hong Kong and the USA, it would have been very easy to overlook it as a simple and rather meaningless statistical comparison. It was after all the heyday of the American suburban dream with cities sprawling rapidly outwards in the form of freestanding villas, green belts, culs-de-sac, freeways and car-dependent drive-in 'shopping towns'. By contrast, Hong Kong's tiny territory had been a major destination for refugees from neighbouring China, for over fifteen years, gathering refugees at an average rate of well over 100,000 per year, the population having risen from a half-million at the time of Japan's withdrawal in 1945 to a staggering 3.2 million in 1961. However, the city's footprint had extended only modestly to register the world's highest urban densities, and acquire hundreds of thousands of squatters' huts, both on the ground and above on roof-tops. In fact, Schmitt used his five pages to launch a very important message.

He drew attention to density figures that were unimaginable to most Western professionals. There were eleven whole census districts that recorded densities of over 2,000 persons per gross acre (approximately 5,000 per hectare). (Census districts were not small in terms of people, each having a minimum of 10,000.) Further, there were two areas, each of more than 2 acres, where more than 2,800 people were packed over each gross acre of ground (approximately 7,000 per hectare): in Wan Chai and Sheung Wan. In his native America, it was difficult to find districts exceeding 150 people per acre (375 per hectare), with the highest density districts just topping 450 (1,125 per ha) in parts of only two cities: Boston and New York: the next highest density census patches were in Chicago and Philadelphia reaching 163 and 150 (400 and 375 per ha) respectively.

In the article, he also drew attention to a planning profession that had long been suspicious of high densities, viewing them as intrinsically 'undesirable'. Indeed, for several decades, it had been fixated on spaciousness and greenery as a prerequisite for healthy people and a moral society – as, for instance, in the gospels according to such garden and agrarian city luminaries as Ebenezer Howard, Clarence Stein and Frank Lloyd Wright. Their garden settlements attained averages of 32 people per acre or 79 per hectare, 21 per acre or 52 per ha (in Radburn) and 5 people per acre or 12.5 per ha (Broadacre City) respectively.

It was likely, wrote Schmitt, 'that most orthodox planners … would expect densities of the magnitude found in Hong Kong to precipitate serious health and social problems' with 'death, disease and social disintegration of a scale unparalleled in American cities'. Crime, delinquency, suicide and similar problems would be out of control. But according to Schmitt's dispassionate statistics, nothing was further from the fact, with the notable exception of tuberculosis. The Colony's residents were otherwise as healthy, better adjusted and more law-abiding than their American counterparts, despite the inclusion of several offences in Hong Kong that were not penalized in the USA.

He wrote the paper while observing Hong Kong firsthand, and after reading Jane Jacobs's critique of essentially negative conventional planning attitudes to urban density. Schmitt highlighted her rejection of the notion that 'high densities (were) invariably associated with blight, decay and social disintegration' and her counterargument that they are actually 'needed to maintain diversity and depth of urban services', and would anyway prove inevitable as a simple consequence of metropolitan growth and change. According to his cool quantitative head, urban Hong Kong may have been super-dense and overcrowded but it was rather less dysfunctional than its more spacious and wealthier counterparts in America.

His article stuck essentially to the facts, although he did venture into two related territories, which may be categorized generally as cultural and environmental. In the first, he acknowledged that the tolerance of high densities was tied to a long-established Chinese cultural tradition of close living. And on the environmental front, he made reference to motor vehicles and the fact that Hong Kong people had to share their preciously limited space with relatively few motor vehicles. Although Hong Kong had a high number of vehicles for its length of road, it had very few vehicles for the size of its population, and went about its movement by many other means. In his home country, car-dependence and peripheral urban expansion went hand-in-hand, resulting in the wasteful displacement of prime agricultural land, and expensive and tiring journeys between home, work, school and shopping. While there may have been many other hardships in Hong Kong, at least the city did not suffer these disadvantages in the same way.

His conclusion was that planners should 're-examine' their attitudes to urban density. He even suggested that demographic changes might well force shifts in attitude towards density and bring some aspects of American living closer to those of Hong Kong. In particular, American (and he might well have said Anglo-American) planners had to free themselves from certain preconceptions (prejudices if you like) about urban density and its consequences.

Eight years later, Jon Prescott (1971), a practising architect and contributor to Hong Kong University's Department of Extra-Mural Studies also wrote a refreshing article about Hong Kong's high density. He challenged most planners' attitudes of the time, which ranged from bemused indifference to unforgiving condemnation at the mention of densities of 2,000 per acre. (Prescott gives one figure, presumably a net density, of some 9,000 people per acre.) With a subtle swipe at (garden city) 'idealism … based on small town community life' and its irrelevance to the coming twenty-first century, he wrote: 'there is much to be said in favour of high-density living and it is important not to reject, a priori, (this) modern city form'. While by no means blind to Hong Kong's many problems, he nevertheless concluded in favour of a dense city model that offers 'high accessibility' and 'low time-distance', stressing the importance of communication. He noted that 'no city (had) consciously developed such high overall residential densities in the twentieth century' or placed such emphasis on the minimization of movement of people and things. He further noted Hong Kong's 'nearly constant level of demand for transport over the seven days of the week'. Thus, in his discussion, he was starting to recognize the principles underlying the successful side of Hong Kong's 'uniquely uniform high-density environment such as hardly exists anywhere else'. And because his attitude was one of searching for underlying principles, he was quick to conclude that 'population density alone cannot define a way of life'. For Prescott, 'The movement patterns of an area give a very good indication of the degree of integration of the area, the reliance of one part on another and its relationship to the totality'. It is here that we see shades of thinking about the nature and importance of connection in cities that were sparked particularly by Christopher Alexander (1966) but were still to be developed beyond the conceptual stage. These are important insights for this book and will be re-visited below, with reference to some more recent theorists.

Five decades on, Western cities continue to expand at relatively low densities. Yet there are demographic and environmental changes underway that are forcing a 're-examination' of urban form and density free from the prejudices of the old order, with a renewed emphasis on the nexus between living, work, education, shopping and recreation as flagged by Jane Jacobs in 1961, and a greater emphasis on the related role of connectivity and transportation. Although under the heading of 'permeability', Bentley et al. (1985), again discussed the key role of connection in cities in their 1985 urban design primer, *Responsive Environments*, and offered methods for both analysing and designing it. Bill Hillier (1996) and Stephen Marshall (2005) have since taken the subject to another level of sophistication in their works on urban space configuration and street patterns. These contributions will also be referred to later.

Schmitt's (1963) and Prescott's (1971) articles make a useful point of reference for they draw attention to conditions and reinforce viewpoints that remain relevant, and are central to this work. Both questioned the essentially negative and suspicious attitudes that prevailed towards high urban densities at their time of writing – a period when most cities were either decanting their urban populations into car-dependent low-density suburbs or, if attempting the development of denser forms, building or encouraging towers and slab blocks that stood apart from each other as islands in broad landscapes of green space or hard plazas, traffic ways and car parks, in the Corbusian or Meisian styles. Either way, the kinds of building and street forms traditionally associated with higher densities were out of favour and under critical attack.

While his own country was rolling headlong into one of the all-time great love affairs with a piece of technology, the automobile, Schmitt made the heretical suggestion that there could be advantages in living without, or at least with far fewer of them. The pair, in their separate writings, also made the point that high-density forms were capable of making a small city footprint thus allowing for more land for farming and nature in closer proximity to city life. And looking ahead, Prescott was explicitly dubious of the relevance of suburban living to the likely needs and lifestyles of a vastly expanded and technologically more sophisticated twenty-first century population. Overall attention was drawn to the mutually reinforcing interplay between density, the 'diversity and depth of urban services' (meaning all public and commercial services, including transport) and the richness of urban life.

Yet, for all their discussion of (and partiality for) dense urbanism, they also appreciated that high densities could not, in themselves, guarantee dynamism in the city. Density required at least one companion in the form of good connections to bind the pile of parts (households, commercial and other enterprises, buildings, street blocks, districts, etc) into dynamic wholes. For Prescott at least, the best urbanism relied on the right mix of density *and* connection – where each part was 'integrated' into the district, and each district into the city. Both authors' discussions of physical form were circumscribed: they were less concerned with how the city looked than how it worked. However, both were emphatic that there were many positives to high-density living, and that Hong Kong had the potential to develop and exemplify these positives with its 'uniquely high-density environment'.

This is not to cast Schmitt and Prescott in the role of prophets but it is to recognize a certain foresight in their observations and analysis. Their words resonate strongly today, given the contemporary urban issues that we, humankind, need to address urgently. Four decades on, urbanization continues unabated with more people leaving the countryside and small towns for the largest cities. This is not only occurring within nations but between nations and continents. As part of this process, the number of automobiles in cities is likewise rocketing to generate more greenhouse gases and, in turn, global warming, amongst other problems. In addition there are, across much of the world, very significant demographic transformations, bringing with them changes in lifestyle and new demands for both location and dwelling types within the urban structure. All these points converge to suggest a re-evaluation of density and, therefore, Hong Kong.

## The Need for Compact Cities

Fingers are pointed frequently at cities as the villains behind our planet's critical environmental condition. They form an easy target for cities occupy little more than 2 per cent of the planet's surface but house more than half of humankind, and are highly visible. They also consume and produce disproportionately large amounts of resources and greenhouse gas emissions, respectively – the Clinton Climate Initiative claims some 75 per cent in both instances (C40 website, 2009): we know that their ecological footprints (that is, the land area required to support a city's construction and operation) are many times their built areas. But it is not the cities that should be targeted in isolation, rather our profligate consumption of resources: cities are merely the means by which we organize ourselves and our activities in space; and they exist in order to be efficient and effective in the processes of production and exchange – of ideas, information, goods and services. Cities' actual and ecological footprints vary enormously: American and Australian cities are generally more surface-consuming than their European and, in turn, Asian counterparts. And their ecological footprints accentuate these differences: the ecological footprint of the American city is typically 30 times that of the physical city while that of the average European city is multiplied by a factor of 10. In other words, cities may be a part of the problem but they also provide primary opportunities for solutions.

It is widely accepted that denser living and building conditions in compact cities have more intrinsic potentials to become less resource consuming than more sprawling cities with sparser living and building patterns. Jenks and Dempsey (2005) suggest that denser cities offer three major advantages, noted as 'environmental, economic and social':

◆   Denser urban living makes possible more effective public transport, more journeys on foot through proximity, and more benefits to buildings such as insulation and shared services from adjacency; all of which lead to significant savings in energy use.

◆   More homes can be serviced from less extensive infrastructure, which lowers the costs of constructing and managing services.

◆   And greater concentrations of people mean that a greater range of social, health, recreational and other services can be offered in closer proximity.

The dominant low-density urban condition is the suburb. Klug *et al.* (2007) have reviewed a range of European, Japanese and American studies that examine the social costs of suburbanization (that is, of low-density city extensions) through a period of thirty years from the 1970s. Their conclusion is emphatic: that lower densities increase the costs of service provision and that building density is the 'key parameter' influencing social costs. Further there was 'a clear correlation between population density and upkeep costs per capita' (upkeep refers to maintenance and operation): they find that both capital and operational costs are lowered from concentration (*Ibid.*).

In a rather more specific study of density and energy use, Hui concludes that Hong Kong's high-rise compact forms bring real benefits to the city – by virtue of a more compact distribution area and far less energy expended on movement. In particular, several authors have highlighted Hong Kong's low energy consumption for travel compared with almost every other big city in the world (see Kenworthy, 2001, 2008; Mahtab-uz-Zaman, 2003; Zaman *et al.*, 2000; Tong and Wong, 1997). However, Hui also points to some potential disadvantages of high-density living: it can, for instance, create road and micro-climatic conditions that result in more, not less, energy use – for instance, cars consume considerably more fuel in slow moving traffic and homes use more air-conditioning when contending a city of massive building forms that stifle the natural flow of air.

Density is clearly a key word here, with Hong Kong now more deserving of attention as a case study in dense urbanism than it was in Schmitt's day. There is an environmental crisis with the need to consume less energy and fewer resources per capita, and to effectively reduce urban ecological footprints. In the developed world, there is also huge demographic change: just as the extended family gave way to the nuclear family as the primary unit of living in the early to mid-twentieth century city, so the nuclear family now gives way to a predominant household size of only one or two people. With this demographic change, there are associated transformations in lifestyle, with changing personal relationships and work arrangements, including more flexible working hours, more home offices blurring the line between home and work, and a consequent demand for convenience and proximity to essential and leisure services, private and public: there is also more part-time work including for old people, to give yet more blurred boundaries – between part-time and full-time work, and between working life and retirement.

The environmental imperative strongly suggests denser 'small footprint' cities as one solution. The demographic change suggests a demand for even more dwelling units for the single and other small household units to occupy. The latter implies even more sprawling cities, if densities continue to slide as they have through the twentieth century. However, these twin changes (environmental and demographic) invite another interpretation, for which the evidence is already strong: that the structural changes in demography bring with them a counter-reaction to suburban living, or at least suburban sprawl. The demands from many of the smaller 'new lifestyle' households are for 'urban convenience', a condition that can only be met by higher urban densities offering a greater variety of activities and facilities in close proximity. In other words, the desire is for a more vital urbanity.

It is a trend well underway in even sprawling America, although detailed reports are surprisingly few. This is partly because of suburbia's sheer vastness, which tends to make the intensification of small existing and new areas seem relatively insignificant. An early report that made the trend amply clear appeared in the March 2008 issue of *The Atlantic Monthly*: entitled 'The Next Slum', it foreshadowed dramatic change for many if not most of the low-density suburbs around US cities (Leinberger, 2008). Christopher Leinberger, a visiting fellow to Washington's Brookings Institution, reviewed the consequences of America's changing demographic structure, focusing on associated housing preference and changes in the fabric of the nation's cities.

His message was that more people are living singly or as childless couples, including same sex couples. Where children are part of the household, these tend to have been born at a later stage in the parents' lives and be fewer in number than with the previous generation. At the same time, these people are seeking proximity to urban facilities, work and each other. If present trends continue, he refers to one US study that predicts a surplus of 22 million large lot dwellings (that is, dwellings standing on lots of over one-sixth of an acre, which is still large by international city standards) over the seventeen years to follow: this is about 40 per cent of all such lots that existed in America at the time of writing. Leinberger's point is that low-density, low-intensity suburbs are starting to head in the direction of 1960s inner cities – to be 'characterized by poverty, crime and decay', and he cites American suburbs that are already succumbing to violence, theft, rapid physical decline, and expensive municipal surveillance and upkeep.

In the third quarter of the twentieth century, the nuclear family of mother, father and children, made up approximately one-half of American households. By 2000, this was down to one-third, and by 2025, it will be more like one-quarter. With old people surviving longer and living more independently in their later years, they are also seeking urban conveniences. By 2025, the number of family households with children and single person households is expected to be more or less equal.

With these changes come different lifestyles. 'Most Americans now live in single-family suburban houses that are segregated from work, shopping, and entertainment; but it is urban life, almost exclusively, that is culturally associated with excitement, freedom, and diverse daily life' writes Leinberger: they are seeking places that have more convenient shopping and services, busier and safer sidewalks – places that are more enjoyable for walking. They are in effect seeking 'vitality'.

He refers to the inner areas that have regenerated in recent years but even more to new 'suburban cities', such as a centre of twenty small blocks at Belmar in Lakewood, Colorado, where there is 'a 60% premium per unit area over the single family homes in the neighborhood around it'. The abruptness of the change is underscored by the fact that the Belmar small urban blocks replaced a regional suburban shopping mall! Leinberger uses the terms 'lifestyle' and 'faux urban' to qualify the character of such centres, and so highlights their strengths and weaknesses. On the one hand, they are a consequence of the changing social structure and a desire for new, less car-dependent and probably healthier lifestyles at higher densities: on the other hand, many also perpetuate something of a sanitized 'Main Street' theme-park-like quality in the kind of urbanism that they provide. Nevertheless, they show changes, and demands for proximity to the kinds of urban services that come only with higher living densities.

If Japan is an indicator of urban things to come, more small stores within walking distance of home will open for all of the day. By 2002, convenience stores occupied more of Japan's surface area than all of the nation's department stores, and handled more business. Ninety-five per cent of Japanese 7–11 convenience stores or *combini* are open day and night. Further, at least 70 per cent of all *combini* customers travel less than 5 minutes for their purchases. *Combini* are in effect highly compact (typically around 100 m²) and highly organized multifunctional corner stores in which shopping as well as other transactions such as banking, travel and car-hire, and even microwave cooking can take place; and where goods can be purchased in very small quantities – single items at a time (Klauser, 2002).

## Complexity, Density and Intensity: Sources, Scope and Intent

While *density* has already received a good deal of discussion, we have so far rather assumed familiarity with the term, and given little explicit attention to the conditions it may embrace. The concept of density has its origins in the field of physics referring to a quantity of mass per unit of volume. The field of urbanism has adopted and adapted it to refer to the mass of people or building over a unit area of land. When referring to people, the most common figures indicate residential density: that is, the number of people dwelling on or over a unit area of land, the latter being measured most commonly in square kilometres or miles at a city scale, and hectares or acres at a local scale – for instance 15,000 persons per km² or 39,000 per square mile (150 per hectare or 60 per acre). If referring to building, the most usual expression of density is the floor-to-site ratio (abbreviated to 'FSR', or termed 'plot ratio' in many places) where the floor area is expressed as a quantity in relation to the site area: for instance, where a building covers the entire site with two and a half floors, then the FSR is said to be 2.5 or 250 per cent. Thus, with these most basic measures, the term 'high density' refers simply to the packing or stacking of more people for the purpose of sleeping and eating, or of building floor area over a given site area.

Following experience of living in Houston, London and Hong Kong, with average densities of 9.5, 42.3 and 300.5 respectively across their built-up areas, a person's ideas about what constitutes high, medium or low density will vary. For the Houstonian and Londoner anything more than 50 or 100 persons may be judged high, or even claustrophobic; while for the Hong Kong resident, who is commonly used to densities of 500 or more, these same densities may seem rather sparse, even lonely. Further, the Hong Kong judgment is more than immediate in that it is, as we shall discover, rooted in Chinese social practice and deeply cultural.

Density may refer also to more complex and sophisticated notions, such as all the people who occupy a site or area for the full range of activities that it offers, whether in residence, working, shopping or whatever they may be doing. In fact Hong Kong records some extraordinarily high working densities too, again probably the highest in the world: the city's central business district has over 1,700 jobs per hectare, which is over 70 per cent more than New York's central skyscraper district and over 300 per cent more than central London. At 775 jobs per hectare, the job density across the whole of inner Hong Kong is proportionately even further ahead than any other city (Bertaud, 1997). Further, density measures may take on dynamic aspects and involve change, for instance, the diurnal patterns of density fluctuate as activities open and close or come and go through the night and day: some areas are full at certain times but empty at others, some are consistently dense but with different occupants doing different things at different times: again Hong Kong is extraordinarily dense with different groups of people at different times through the 24 hours of the day – the inner city job density of 775 jobs per hectare is accompanied by a residential density of 804 people per hectare.

Also there should be no preconceptions about density and overcrowding for too often the two are equated with each other. It is possible, for instance, to live in a very tall building of spacious apartments that houses the same number of people as a squat structure of the same footprint. In other words, the densities of people will compare but those of building (floor area to land area) will contrast. Both people and land densities have been high over most of Hong Kong for most of its history, and it is hard to make judgements on what constitutes overcrowding as this is in part culturally determined. In the West, it has been common to associate density with crime and sickness, and the statistics have been convincing. But it should be noted that Hong Kong has experienced relatively low crime rates, is a place of longevity and very low infant mortality: in the latter areas it ranks among the fourth best places in the world alongside Andorra, Macau and Japan (for longevity) and Singapore, Sweden and Japan (for survival at birth).

In development circles, it often seems that the quantity of density is an end in itself, and 'high density' equates with or is somehow seen to ensure some greater quality of vitality. Concentrations of people and/or floor area, however, do not guarantee vitality. Here, it is necessary to consider something more than the number of residents or static quantity of building per unit area. Vitality infers dynamism, which in turn involves interaction between people in a range of activities and transactions: it infers something that is more than the sum of the parts. We shall refer to this condition as *intensity*, and again, turn for an indication of meaning to physics, where the term refers to the amount of some quality of force or energy, such as heat. In the city, intensity may be seen to refer to the presence of some kind of interplay between peoples' actions to produce positive synergies that become evident in the successful functioning and liveliness of a place. Thus we must distinguish intensity from *density*, and explore what it is that takes a place beyond mere density to exhibit intensity.

Over the last fifty years, several significant urban design texts have dealt with this question, directly or otherwise, and all have turned their attention in some major way (some almost exclusively) to issues of connection – to the quantity, qualities and ordering of spatial connection. All stress that many synergies between urban activities depend on movement, and that this is influenced substantially by the structure, patterns and form of connection. As Hillier and Hansen (1984, p. 2) have made clear in their spatial theory, 'the ordering of space is about the ordering of relations between people'. Nevertheless, the parade of urban design-related writers who have contributed to this position is much broader.

In 1961, Jane Jacobs challenged a primarily Modernist planning world by advocating more and shorter streets to give more choice, convenience and vitality to an area: it would give more route options, and more strategic crossing points and corners; induce more stopping, loitering and meeting points; and create more favourable location points for the generation of economic and other activities. It was a proposition based on her observations of how certain quarters of some older American cities actually worked.

Inspired by Jacobs's writing, Christopher Alexander (1966) gave further credibility to her notion of the city as 'organized complexity' with a more reasoned and theoretical base: he posited that 'the city is not a tree' in his landmark article of that name, using the Venn diagram to illustrate the nature of relationships between urban activities. The nub of his argument is simple: that urban services and facilities are symbiotic and cannot exist in isolation from each other. A sun-receiving building plinth of sitting height, a bakery selling coffee as a sideline, a newsagent, dry cleaner, and a tram stop will have little effect upon each other if situated far apart: but if more or less adjacent and connected, it is possible for a person to drop off the stained garment, buy a take-away latte, pick up the morning news, and take a seat to read it until the tram appears for the journey to work or wherever: together they make the process of living and travel more convenient, and a good deal more pleasant. Connection between these five elements means more frequent use for all: they interact by virtue of their proximity and the form of the spaces that join, and lead to them.

Hence, one set of such relationships generates a certain level of intensity. Cities are extremely complex accumulations of these kinds of sets, which can overlap almost infinitely. A mathematician, Alexander was quick to point out that given twenty such elements, if isolated by way of a tree network, there are only nineteen possible relationships or sub-sets but if all are connected with each other there are over 1 million possible subsets, underpinning Jacobs's notion of complexity. The nature of connection may also be conceived more literally as a network – the streets, paths and other spaces and systems that connect the city's parts – and illustrations in Alexander's original article show planners' simplistic creations of tree networks bringing relative isolation to each neighbourhood or similar part when compared with places that are more connected by way of a multidirectional lattice-like net.

These writers laid the foundations for a broad-range of later more applied work by others. Influenced by Jacobs and Alexander, the authors of *Responsive Environments* (Bentley *et al.*, 1985) made 'the quality of permeability' ('the number of alternative ways through an environment') as their first of seven basic principles for good urban design: further, as part of their kit of urban design tools, they offered a simple method for quantifying a street's level of connection to the wider district street system. But it is more recent theoretical work that leaves us in even less doubt about the validity of Jacobs's and Alexander's pioneering contributions on connection: in particular, that of Bill Hillier, Stephen Marshall and Nikos Salingaros.

Hillier (1996) sees the city as a 'movement economy' whose success, or otherwise, is related directly to its spatial configuration. It is the nature and visibility of spatial connection that determines movement, and it is the latter that generates economic and other activity. Small changes in spatial structure can trigger big changes in movement and hence a place's potential activity. Hillier and his team have developed sophisticated computer-based methods for measuring how well a particular space is integrated into the wider spatial systems of the locality and city, thus he is able to speak of levels of district (or 'local') and city-wide (or 'global') integration. In this context, Hillier points out that 'places do not make cities' but 'cities make places', the success and vitality of a particular place being much related to its degree of integration within the wider urban structure.

Stephen Marshall's *Streets and Patterns* (Marshall, 2005) complements Hillier's work in that he provides us with a simple but tangible classification of types of urban network at cross-city and local levels. He shows how different scales of tree and grid networks combine with each other (gradations of Hillier's 'global' to 'local' scales) to help or hinder movement.

Even more recent is the work of another scholar from mathematics and information science, Nikos Salingaros (2005): he has extended the discussion of city structure by way of analogy to the human brain. With the exception of Alexander, he is more abstract than those previously cited, and to that extent is less convincing in his own right: but if placed in the context of the others, he provides an enlightening addition. For him, the city 'mimics human thought processes', in that its vitality and creativity also depend on establishing multiple connections: the brain and the city are both networks made up of nodes and connections that, if allowed, to self-organize, will emerge into increasingly complex but ordered systems. Organization is graded hierarchically across scales – for instance, the paths and streets of the city range from short narrow alleys to roads of increasing dimensions. If the connections between scales are missing or disrupted, the system becomes dysfunctional. This correlates entirely with Hillier's notion of the city as a series of interfaces between scales of movement, with integration between the most local and global movement as the key to success.

Yet another contributor to this urban theme is Ayssar Arida (2002), who also enters the city by way of analogy, with quantum theory as his focus: particles cannot be understood in isolation but only through their interrelations and interconnections. The quantum world, in the words of W. Heisenberg, 'is a tissue of events in which connections of different kinds alternate or overlap or combine and therefore determine the texture of the whole' (Heisenberg, quoted in Capra, 1991). Likewise the city is a complex system of nodes of differing scale (from, for example, a newspaper stand to an national sports stadium), each with a radiating field: the interaction between the fields from two or more such objects or activities will depend on connections and may be positive or negative: if positive, there can be very powerful synergies. For instance, we have seen several successful interactions between bookshops, DVD shops, cafés and cinema lobbies.

With all of these writers, it is interaction that brings vitality and intensity to a place through multiple scales of connection from the very local to global. Thus if we return to the notion of 'density', we can appreciate this does not guarantee vitality or *intensity*: it is in the form and pattern of connections (physical configuration) that we find the hardware that determines the kind of movement that will generate these. Such patterns may be more or less *legible* or *intelligible* to Lynch (1960) or Hillier (1996), respectively: if more so, then activity is likely to thrive with more intensity. Activity consists primarily of interactions or transactions, whether it is buying or selling, a pensioner on the park bench watching children at play, or the commuter breaking his stride to catch the weather or stock market information on an electronic window display. It is to all of these kinds of phenomena that Salingaros is referring when using the term *exchange*, or the late Ashihara (1989) when referring to a city's *content*.

Thus, intensity is a product of much more than density, and to appreciate this, we have to turn to the connective networks. Networks and nodes allow and encourage the items of density (in cities, human beings and their activities) to connect and exchange in all sorts of economic, recreational, artistic, social and other transactions – legal or otherwise, noble or base, costly or free, etc. Here, the word 'allow' is crucial, for physical networks may allow but management, land-use control and by-laws may not. For instance, buskers may know precisely where the most effective performance places are in a city (these will be among the most connected of places with high densities of pedestrians) but city by-laws may prohibit such transaction between public and busker. Similarly, pedestrians are acutely responsive to street conditions: streets with long blank walls are less engaging than those with windows to see through and doors to enter, or equivalent 'information'. Basically, density is an asset only if the dense elements are well connected physically and visually, and government and management do not deter connection through restrictive policies and regulation. Density may then realize its potential or *emerge* as *intensity*, a condition characterized by multiple functions:

*Population Density + Connection across Multiple Scales = Intensity*

Most of the above writers make reference to design principles or concepts and planning-cum-management approaches that enhance or limit levels of intensity in urban places through spatial configuration or regulation. For instance, the design of bifurcating tree networks tends to separate and isolate a city's functional components (shops from medical facilities from cinemas from markets, etc) whereas grid or lattice networks should enable freer multi-directional, and therefore more convenient movements between points. Basically, good connective networks and density bring more people and functions into closer proximity to each other, with the potential for more exchange. Jane Jacobs and her successors also refer to the direct control of activity through such instruments as the zoning of uses or prohibition of activity through the law. Zoning control can have the same effect as a tree-like street network for it too keeps potentially synergetic activities and/or physical components apart. As a means of controlling city development, planning authorities have often exercised their authority over both in negative ways. Thus, strengthening intensity through complex connective networks must be a priority.

## Rethinking 'Ground'

None of the above writers deals at all well with three-dimensional connections in cities: in fact to say that they have tended towards 'flat earth' viewpoints of urbanism is probably no exaggeration. They have dealt essentially with conventional at-grade street networks, yet the movement networks in large dense cities accord increasingly to other configurations: the principles of connection and complexity that have been established for the ground plane must be revisited, adapted and applied to cities, which function effectively with multiple grounds. With its very high urban densities, high-rise buildings and steep topography, Hong Kong is inevitably one of these cities: there are, for instance, extensive areas of slender towers over interconnected multi-level podia; there are buildings that can be entered and left at very different levels but where you are still passing directly from building interior to *terra firma*; there are many streets of steps and even escalators; and there are vast multi-level markets, multi-storey stables for horses, triple-decker ferries, etc. (For examples of these and other multi-level components, see Chapter 7.) From the past, there are old walled villages and subdivided shop-houses with many volumetric qualities and quirks. Here, we explore these extremely three-dimensional places – their morphologies, densities, connections, and relationships. Hong Kong is an obvious case study for it evolved from the outset as a compact and intense city: it remains that way today, an intenCity, and shows few signs of changing course. It is therefore also an urban laboratory – encouraging further experimentation with density. Our line of thought is backed-up by Mike Jenks (2009) in an article subtitled '... another route to sustainable urban form': after outlining the advantages and disadvantages of several types of urban structure, Jenks concludes that Hong Kong is a very good example of a high-density city model that is working well, and therefore worthy of attention. He is influenced in turn by the work of Stephen Lau and his co-authors who, earlier, assembled much evidence to this end (Lau *et al.*, 2005).

In Hong Kong these various built forms and more have come together as three distinct but highly connected parts to make a unique urban system: the long lean linear city with its flat reclaimed and steeply stepped cross-section that is Victoria on Hong Kong Island; the sky-scraping small footprint new towns strung out as beads on railway strings across the New Territories; and the in-between, in time and place, more mixed conglomeration of the greatly widened Kowloon Peninsula and its east and west extensions, Kwun Tong and Tseun Wan. Kowloon, is now the most central place (more central than Central), being the hub between old Hong Kong, the new towns of the New Territories, and new China, and a site that invites the imagination and speculation. All three are investigated here, where our approach is broad. On the one hand, it has within it elements of W.G. Hoskins's idea of the 'making' of physical places as historical process, as demonstrated in his classic work, *The Making of the English Landscape*, published over half a century ago (Hoskins, 1955). On the other, it is concerned with the design ideas that have shaped Hong Kong and with the contemporary generation of ideas that might shape its future city. As such, our work spans past, present and future: it is both historical and speculative.

# 2 Precedents

In 1974, Ruth Sidel published the results of her extensive studies into the community life of Fengsheng neighbourhoods in Peking (as it was then called). Her research presented with clarity the crowded conditions she observed, made possible by the capacity of the Chinese population to deal with problems of congestion. Sidel had taken as her case study the city of Fengsheng because it was considered to be representative of Beijing with an average residential density of around 91,000 people per square mile (351 people per hectare) with the majority of buildings being one or two storey. The average square metre per person was frequently as low as two.

Similar statistics can be found in Li Choh-Ming's book from 1959, *Economic Development of Communist China*. Li's data are similarly dramatic and report on the average housing space per capita in 175 Chinese cities as 3.5 square metres per person, varying from 4.9 square metres in small cities to 2.2 in big cities. These statistics may be challenging to us today but they demonstrate that until very recently it was common in China to live in small spaces.

It is in this context that we consider the provision of residential space in Hong Kong. Public Housing has accounted for 40 per cent of housing in Hong Kong and is typically inhabited by immigrants from China, many of whom arrived as refugees with few or no possessions. The capacity of these residents to cope with what would be considered in other communities as extremely crowded conditions is closely linked to their previous experiences and has deep cultural underpinnings. Their arrival in Hong Kong offered the possibility of a better life for which the immediate limited personal space could be tolerated. Under such conditions, those living in public housing estates adjusted to living in conditions that most Westerners would find impossible. Such cultural responses to density have been noted as enabling higher densities in Chinese societies such as Hong Kong and Singapore (Yuen, 2005).

In the variety of conditions in Asia that have prevailed throughout history, the demand for accommodation has led to the development of several distinctive responses to the need both by the provision of space and its adaptation to intense use. We believe two precedents have special relevance to Hong Kong's morphological development: the walled village and the shop-house.

## Walled Settlements in China

Walled settlements appeared early in the development of Chinese civilization. Hays notes evidence of fortified towns with rammed earth walls before the middle of the third millennium BCE (Hays, 2008). Walled towns and houses have been a part of Chinese culture ever since. The traditional form of the dwelling in China is that of a courtyard house, an arrangement of enclosures ('rooms') arranged on two or four sides of a rectilinear courtyard and typically accessed on the south edge through an opening to the outside world. This courtyard house, with its enclosing walls and single opening, is itself a prototypical form of a walled village. Gathered together in clusters, houses form, for example, the *hutong* (or traditional Beijing neighbourhood) of long and largely anonymous walls punctured by periodic openings through which access is gained to family courtyards. In southern China the courtyard house was less common; the village house was often a single rectilinear structure with openings mainly on the south side. Arranged tightly in rows, these houses formed villages with defensive edges even if not surrounded by formal walls.

Walled villages are not a common form in China, limited to the south-eastern coastal regions, perhaps reflecting the prevalence of pirate activity. In other regions walled enclosures around collective habitation were limited to cities or territorial limits. The village and neighbourhood are important social units in Chinese society. In addition to being defensive structures, walled villages were also self-managed social units. The village elders and the *kaifong* (a term used in Hong Kong for the village

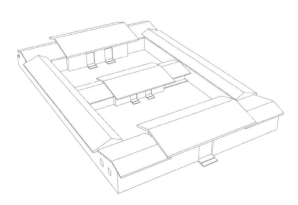

**2.1.** Chinese courtyard house.

committee) maintained customs, organized education, administered basic justice, regulated commerce and oversaw ritual duties.

A particular and distinctive form of a walled village that emerged in China is that of the Hakka in southern China. Immigrants to the region, the Hakka found themselves in conflict with the indigenous population and built defensive structures in which to live and store their goods. Rather than building a wall around individual dwellings, the Hakka created monolithic structures of three or more storeys in which the whole clan lived. More akin to the urban tenement, these earthen structures accommodated on the lowest levels the artefacts of subsistence: livestock, grain, tools, wells and workspaces. On upper levels, there were temples, armouries and dwellings. Comprising thick walls formed in circular or rectilinear plans with few openings on the outside, the inner courtyards were lined by balconies providing an open communal volume.

## Walled Settlements in Hong Kong

Walled villages were common in Hong Kong; it is estimated that twenty-three walled villages existed within the territories' boundaries prior to the Second World War (Hayes, 2001). The area that is Hong Kong today was first settled in the tenth century CE and by the sixteenth century CE was well settled (Carroll, 2007). In 1661, however, the Qing government evacuated coastal areas for security reasons. Residents were allowed back in to

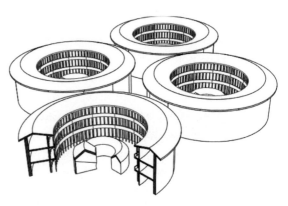

**2.2.** Hakka walled settlement. These are found in round and rectilinear forms: both show a mix of uses through their two or more levels and veranda-cum-balcony circulation on each.

these areas after 1669. At this time the Manchu forced the Hakka to migrate again, this time towards the coastal areas of Guangdong. Thus, Hong Kong became home to many Hakka who then erected their walled villages. As piracy diminished after the reign of Qianlong (1735–1795 AD), the massive walls became less common. In Hong Kong the practice of piracy continued through to the nineteenth (even late twentieth) century.

Smaller villages are typically clan settlements; everyone in the village is related through patrilineal heritage to common ancestors. Reflecting this, villages were sometimes named for the familial lineage of the occupants (often referred to as the *clan*). Thus, one of the extant walled villages in Hong Kong is known as Tsang Tai Uk (曾大屋) – the Large House of the Tsang, the name reflecting too the monolithic nature of these walled villages. It is thought that this name was used when the Tsang family took in many refugees after the Second World War. This instance, in Sha Tin, is a rectilinear inhabited wall built in 1864 enclosing three additional rows of dwellings within. In contrast to this single clan, the nearby Tai Wai, was occupied by sixteen family lineages. Built in 1574 during the Ming Dynasty, it was known earlier as Chik Chuen Wai (Chinese: 積存圍).

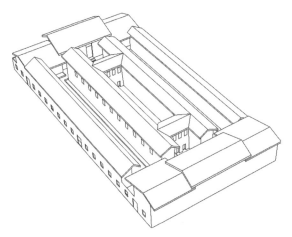

**2.3.** Walled village of Tsang Tai Uk, Hong Kong. This traditional structure of one and two storeys was a high-density settlement.

**2.4.** An interior living space within a Hong Kong walled village. It shows the spatial arrangement within: a mezzanine provides upper level space and the bed is a volume within (under the mezzanine). A basic 'ladder' stair connects the levels.

Villages might be occupied by a single lineage, where all inhabitants could trace their common ancestor, or multiple lineages, but seldom were they open to all. Membership of the villages was protected by custom; admission was given usually after extended acquaintance. Since a village depended on local resources for its existence, admission meant granting access to land, food and water, hence membership of the community was not extended lightly. This characteristic of protection and exclusion was a principle manifest in the infamous Kowloon Walled City, which is described below.

Chinese settlements were generally laid out according to cosmological and geomantic belief. As exemplified in Beijing, their plans were governed by a primary north–south axis (Boyd, 1962). Likewise, geomancy and other conventions guided also the walled villages of Hong Kong. However patterns varied as their makers married principle and convention to any special demands of circumstance and site (Wang, 1998). Where defence was primary, the wall was dominated by four corner towers, the thick walls housing animals, farming and defensive functions. The primary entrance is centred on the south edge. On occasion an ancestral temple is located at the northern end of the central axis. Internally the streets align east to west, allowing most dwellings to have their entrance on the south side in keeping with Chinese norms.

Wai (圍), the term used for a walled village in Hong Kong, means also 'defence' and 'surround' (Lung and Friedman, 1995). The term is used inconsistently in Hong Kong, applied to some, not all, walled villages and also to villages without walls. The etymological root for the character representing walled village may be observed in its two components, 囗 and 韋. The first shows a boundary element, used commonly in compound characters indicating bounded places – from gardens to prisons. The second shows feet walking about an object, possibly a building (Shirakawa, 1999). The full ideograph thus implies an enclosed area with buildings that is traversed by walking. (The character for walk has also a second meaning: 'leather'. This too has associations with walking since it is a material used in the making of footwear. However, the first meaning appears to be the more pertinent, and it is possible that the inclusion of 韋 in the compound character for walled settlement predated its use for leather.)

## Kowloon Walled City

When the British settled on Hong Kong Island in 1841, the Chinese had long maintained a walled fort on the other side of the harbour. Established as an Imperial outpost to oversee the salt trade in the Sung Dynasty (960–1297 CE), it was reputedly also home for a brief period to the Sung Emperor as he fled the Manchu invasion of south China in 1277. When the British settled, this fort became an important vantage point from which to monitor these interlopers. In 1847, the Chinese authorities expanded the small fort in recognition of its increasingly important role, accommodating 150 soldiers in addition to the senior officers and other inhabitants, creating an imposing walled edifice to state the Imperial claim to the land (Girard and Lambot, 1993; Welsh, 1994).

In 1860, the British expanded their presence to the north shore of the harbour, taking the Peninsula of Kowloon up to a line that became Boundary Street, just to the south of the fort. In August 1898, they negotiated the lease of the land north from Boundary Street, taking over the area now known as the New Territories, in order to provide for better defence of the harbour and the growing town on its shores. By this date, the Walled City was already notorious for it was associated with opium, gambling and prostitution, activities that gathered around its walls. In the course of the lease negotiations, the Chinese ensured that the fort remained Chinese territory, including access to the shore to supply the fort. By the time the British took over the newly leased territory, however, the defence implications of allowing the area to remain in Chinese hands became apparent so, in December 1899, the Walled City was taken over by the British. In doing so, the British ignored the problem of Chinese rule of the site, a problem not resolved until 1987.

An area of 2.6 hectares, 121 x 213 metres, the city had a population of approximately 200 civilians and 500 garrison members when the lease was concluded. When the British soldiers finally marched in to the Walled City, they found it was largely vacant, the last soldiers having disappeared in the final days before their attack, leaving 150 civilians and one magistrate.

When it was occupied by the British, the wall surrounded a typical defensive settlement, a number of single-storey courtyard buildings aligned east–west on axial streets; a photograph from 1865 shows that the area inside the wall was not fully occupied. In the following decades these structures were allowed to deteriorate and by 1940 the British decided to demolish everything inside the walls with the exception of the residence of the principal military officer, the school and one private house. By this point, reclamation along the eastern edge of Kowloon had isolated the Walled City from the bay and rendered its pier irrelevant. When the Japanese occupied Hong Kong during the Second World War, they demolished the walls and used the stones to extend the airport runway which had been established on land adjacent to the old fort.

With all its physical manifestations removed, the land continued to be perceived as outside British rule. Once refugees started to flee from China after the war, many decided to reside on the site of the Walled City. By 1947, over 2,000 squatters lived there. When the British tried to remove the squatters forcibly, riots broke out in Canton and Shanghai where the British Consulate was set alight. This violent reaction persuaded the British to cease the evictions, initiating a policy of essentially ignoring the area. Quickly, the former reputation for the area returned, with brothels, drug dens and criminal societies finding refuge, although this time they were inside the zone and not around its edges.

By the 1971 census, over 10,000 people were reported to be living in the 2,185 dwellings in the Walled City. In its condition as a location of illegal activities, it is likely that the number was significantly higher. In the mid 1980s the population was estimated at 35,000 and the structure had risen to twelve to fourteen storeys, qualifying as a high-rise even though it lay under the flight path in to Kai Tak airport, at a point just before the aircraft touched down.

The issue of governance of the site which had permitted the unfettered development of these few hectares was finally resolved and the decades of growth ended. The handover of Hong Kong had been negotiated in 1984 when the Sino-British Joint Declaration was signed. Knowing that the territory reverted to China in 1997, the British and the Chinese governments could agree that the special territorial position of the Walled City was no longer relevant. It was therefore possible for both governments to address the health and safety concerns about the area by agreeing to its demolition in January 1987.

In its later years, the intensity of built form could not accommodate all the necessary movement at the ground level. Also the ground level streets could not justify their existence with constant pressure on available space to live, work and survive. With ever diminishing space at the ground level and extruding structures above, circulation space had to be moved to the higher levels of the Kowloon Walled City. This had more than one advantage. Firstly Kowloon Walled City was built on a 1:9 slope which resulted in 15 metres level change along its length. Having an additional movement system at the third or fourth floor allowed for continuous horizontal circulation and relieved the pressure from the lower movement system. A network of three-dimensional branching streets was gradually created, allowing for multiple accesses at different levels; the boundaries between inside and outside, between one building and another, between private and public became gradually more and more blurred. Access lanes were often less than 1 metre in width which allowed inhabitants to jump across from one building to another. The roof tops offered the possibility for continuous movement across the whole structure and in and out of building circulation gaps. Postmen were specially trained to jump from one building to another to facilitate post delivery which would otherwise have been difficult.

Kowloon Walled City was not only a great example of three-dimensional movements but also of adaptability and intensive mixed use. The minimal spaces in the structure had to constantly transform. A dinner or tea shop would transform into bordello or mah-jong parlour and then into dormitory. The production table for noodle making would change for dinner and homework, and later on serve as bed for the whole family, while a plastic toy factory would double as an illegal den for opium users. No room in Kowloon Walled City could afford to satisfy just one function. The rooms varied in size but even the smallest room would have had to satisfy many functions during a 24 hour period.

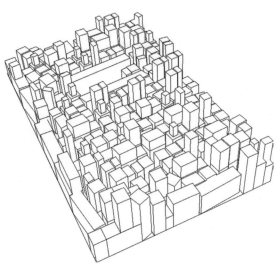

**2.5.** Kowloon Walled City housed 35,000 people on just 2.6 hectares. It provided a complete range of urban services (power, water, heath services, schools, religious, employment, shopping, etc) and had a truly 3D volumetric circulation.

Kowloon Walled City was in the peculiar position of being both inside (surrounded by) and outside (the jurisdiction) of its host city – separate from Hong Kong, yet joined with it and dependent. It was these inherent contradictions that gave the informal city its momentum, and underpinned its survival and growth. They fired its capacity for improvisation and adaptation, and ultimately its development into a large and comprehensive urban system of self-generating forms. The result was an impressive mega-structure that, as we shall later demonstrate, shared certain characteristics with its larger and formal 'partner'.

While walled villages in China have taken many forms, those in Hong Kong are of interest in this study primarily through their Hakka heritage. In Tsang Tai Uk, for example, we see a thick encompassing wall in which a variety of functions are contained, in a volume that creates a tall and substantial protective enclosure. The traditions of Hakka forms suggested that a variety of functions are contained in a volume that also affords other outcomes, most obviously defensive enclosure and support for particular forms of collective social relationships.

Although only 20 per cent if its population was Hakka (the substantial majority being Hoklo), Kowloon Walled City developed the volumetric village form to an extreme. This intense and dense structure is best known in recent years for its exuberant and unfettered structure, its height being limited to 45 metres only by proximity to Kai Tak airport. Had this not been the case, perhaps the volumetric nature of the space would have led to yet more innovation. However, this distinctive spatial development was both rapid and short lived, lasting less than twenty years.

**2.6.** A typical edge of the Kowloon Walled City: this was as much as most Hong Kong residents saw of this remarkable mega-structure.

Initial structures were extended so that a ten storey building might grow with two more levels added later. With no space between buildings, circulation was not restricted to the ground plane. Links were made between buildings at any level; floors in adjacent buildings did not align. Circulation was enabled by a labyrinth of corridors and internal streets as well as across roofs or through courtyards deep inside the conglomeration. Delivery of goods was by foot, up ten storeys or more.

Acting as one structural web, individual buildings were not constructed to an adequate specification. Shallow trench foundations were used for these tall buildings, not the piled foundations normal in Hong Kong. Standing on its own each building would have collapsed; being hemmed in on three of their four sides, they were held up by adjacent structures, themselves structurally inadequate. At the time of demolition, the area was estimated to have accommodated 8,800 apartments and 1,045 commercial establishments (Smart, 2006).

In addition to residential purposes, the Walled City was home to many activities. The manufacture of textiles, toys and food, especially fish balls, were all undertaken within the labyrinth, ensuring that inhabitants did not have to venture beyond its boundaries to lead productive lives. Infrastructure systems developed internally where possible or were drawn from the surrounding city. Seventy-seven wells supplied water which was pumped to the roof tops and gravity fed to residents who paid those who controlled the pipes. Electricity was initially taken illegally from the main city supply but after a fire in the 1970s this was regulated and metered, a tacit acknowledgement by both the government of Hong Kong and the inhabitants of the Walled City that not all aspects of urban development could remain unsupervised. Every horizontal surface area was at a premium, the ground was inhabited or used for circulation, so the roof was the only location available for the storage of inorganic waste, a resource then mined to produce whatever of value it hid.

As Popham (1993) notes, the Walled City materialized as an 'organic megastructure' without design or planning, constantly morphing to accommodate changes in population, opportunity and demand. In this, it is related to the walled villages of China, the *Dai Uk* (great house) and the Hakka clan dwellings.

## Chungking Mansions

The closest development to Kowloon Walled City that still exists in Hong Kong is Chungking Mansions. Built in 1962 as a chic estate at 36–44 Nathan Road in Tsim Sha Tsui district, today Chungking Mansions are best known for offering the cheapest visitor accommodation in urban Hong Kong.

Although originally built as residential development, today it accommodates a variety of low-budget hotels, shops, restaurants and other services. From chic residential building in 1960s Chungking Mansions have transformed over the years into a structure that some now call 'the scent of Kowloon Walled City'. There are an estimated 4,000 people living in the Chungking Mansions today. Most come from the ethnic minorities, particularly Indians, Pakistanis, Bangladeshis, Sri Lankans, Nigerians, as well as Europeans and Americans. It has been estimated that members of at least 120 different nationalities have lived in Chungking Mansions in the years since its construction. In a similar way to Kowloon Walled

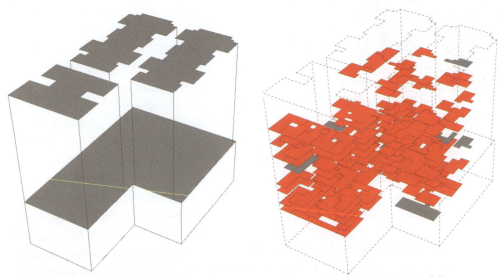

**2.7.** Chungking Mansions. The building has four main parts: podium and three indented blocks (left). It is home to many nationalities and a great variety of commercial uses, which permeate to the highest floors (right).

City, Chungking Mansions have been a centre for drugs and a refuge for petty criminals and illegal immigrants (Lau, 1997).

The difference between Kowloon Walled City and Chunking Mansions is, however, significant. Purpose-built as a city-block size monolith, Chungking Mansions were provided with necessary services in compliance with regulations. In the subsequent forty years of habitation the buildings have seen periodic purging of accretions and modifications such as ventilation shafts that have accommodated drying racks from hostels, production storage from a dyeing factory, and the descent and collection of garbage from a variety of businesses and restaurants.

In common with Kowloon Walled City, Chungking Mansions could be considered as a complete city within one structure. It managed over the span of forty years to transform from the original singular residential function to become a place of multiple programs that cater to a wide mix of cultures without manifesting the community tensions that so often emerge in cities of such cultural differences.

## The Hong Kong Shop-House

The mid 1950s photograph of Hong Kong (figure 2.8) shows a street lined by a colonnade, with the names of the business painted on the columns, advertisements

hanging from the façade, and washing from the residences above. Extra amenities are squeezed out of small spaces – a narrow wrought iron rack creates a garden, and some balconies are enclosed for additional rooms. These are the shop-houses of Hong Kong.

Few examples of its type remain in the centre of Hong Kong today. In Wanchai, a small block of such buildings has been rescued from demolition in the development of an adjacent tower and turned into a restaurant as a commercial caricature of the original form. In the centre of the city, the commercial Pedder Building (as it is now known) takes outwardly the form of a grand extruded shop-house. In common with its lesser cousin, this several storey building provides a colonnade over the pavement to give protection from rain and sun for pedestrians. After completion in 1924, it housed British trading offices but is now filled mainly with fashion outlets. (In this particular example, the ground floor

**2.8.** Hong Kong Street in the 1950s with the colonnaded footway visible along the street.

is raised up a few steps, permitting an unusual basement.) While this example is perhaps the tallest and most sophisticated version of the type, lower and simpler structures once lined most streets of Hong Kong and Kowloon. Further, these are related to a basic shop-house form that appeared across much of South East Asia.

A distinctive typology, the shop-house is a widespread building form that is found from Taiwan in the north-east, through Fujian province to Malaysia and Singapore in the south-west. Variants of this form can, of course, be found more widely, but in this swathe the form has developed particular characteristics. The narrow frontage, deep lot appears elsewhere in Asia and draws upon other cultural roots. It has been noted that the urban form of two-storey terrace houses lining the street was to be found in Spanish controlled Manila in 1573, and later in Dutch-controlled Malacca and Batavia, before the establishment of Singapore (Lim, 1993). Although the typology of a mixed-use, commercial and residential building can be found across the region, the term *shop-house* appears for the first time in Penang in 1884 (Tjoa-Bonatz, 1998).

Evolving from a common need to provide cost-effective housing and commercial trading space, the co-location of a shop with residential accommodation can be found throughout the world. Distinctive to the southern Chinese form, however, we find a two-

**2.9.** The Pedder Building of 1924 is a commercial building, bearing some characteristics of the shop-house form.

**2.10.** Street view of colonnaded shop-houses in Shiqi district, Zhongshan, *c*.1980. Zhongshan is close to Hong Kong.

(seldom three-) storey structure on relatively narrow and deep lots, sharing party walls with its neighbours and opening fully on the ground floor to the fronting street. This building form has been identified as early as the thirteenth century and appears in the Treaty Ports of China (*Ibid.*). Ideal for trade in a sub-tropical climate, it offers a generous exposure of trade to passing traffic. With multiple generations of the family providing continuous attention to the commercial purposes, and accommodation found in the shop or elsewhere for non-family members, the structure is a flexible residence, warehouse and trading zone.

The form of the shop-house that is found in Hong Kong appears to have taken a long path from its close neighbours in Guangdong and Fujian provinces. As it was constructed in the late nineteenth and early twentieth centuries on Hong Kong Island and parts of Kowloon (especially Yaumatei), it owes more to the expression of this typology articulated in Singapore and Malaysia than in Taiwan. While the latter is more similar to that in the provincial capital of Fujian, Xiamen (known in the West as Amoy), the Singapore model came to absorb imperial British notions of urban form and developed characteristics to accommodate the tropical conditions (Lim, 1993). That this built form returned to southern China by appearing in Hong Kong after gestation in the Malay Peninsula is not surprising. Penang was taken by the British in 1786 and Singapore was founded by the treaty of 1819, flourishing after the Anglo-Dutch Treaty signed in London in 1824 that provided the British with a firm and stable division of trade in the region, with the Dutch relinquishing claims over the Malay peninsula (including Singapore) in exchange for singular rights over Sumatra and Java. Even from the treaty of 1819, Sir Stamford Raffles had, on behalf of the East India Company, set out to establish a trading post with an appropriate infrastructure and urban order to support trade.

Raffles had determined in 1822 that the house was to have a veranda, which ensured that the public was provided with a covered way along the street edge. The Penang Assessment Regulation 1826 determined the width, stating that a 5 foot (1.5 m) wide pathway had to be left between the house and the drain, and allowed this to be built over so that the second and higher floors projected to the street (and

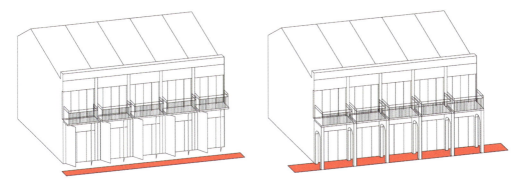

**2.11.** Penang shop-houses – earlier (left) and later (right) types. The later version followed Raffles's legislation, specifying a 5 feet (1.5 m) veranda-cum-footway between building and street/drain.

drain) edge. This continuous covered passageway was adopted widely in the region (*Ibid.*) and came to be a defining feature of the tropical shop-house, differentiating it from its Chinese origins and the typology as it evolved in Taiwan.

Once the British gained control over Singapore and Penang, the Chinese in the region saw opportunities for trade and employment. Growing from small initial settlements, the subsequent recruitment of more Chinese from southern China, especially Fujian and Guangdong provinces, ensured that the Chinese populations in both settlements became substantial (Lee, 2003).

Following the re-ordering of the town in the 1822 town plan, Raffles provided the Chinese community a chance to work from a clean slate to re-establish a densely inhabited trading district. Faced with the need and opportunity to establish their trading sector of Singapore, the Chinese community took references from their cultural source and erected shop-houses of the kind found in southern China. The buildings emerged with the basic narrow frontage, deep plan, and one or two storeys accommodating commerce, storage and residential needs. With the particular opportunity for land ownership and governed by town planning ordinances and building regulations derived from experience in London, in 1824 Raffles created a particular set of conditions in which the Chinese cultural form evolved into a distinctive regional typology (*Ibid.*).

Chinese land speculators developed larger plots of land by subdividing into long narrow lots to maximize the number of frontages created, resulting in deep lot proportions. Regulations permitted a maximum of three storeys, with lots between 15 and 20 feet (4.5–6.0 m, the length of commonly available timber joists). From this emerged the typology – a narrow building about two or three times as deep as it was wide, and two or three floors high. The deep and narrow form led to the introduction of a courtyard half way through the lot to provide both light into the middle but also to improve cross ventilation in the depth axis, since the closely packed houses offered no side ventilation. In the early twentieth century, a back lane was introduced to enable services and night soil collection away from the main entrance.

The Singapore shop-house therefore can be seen to have established its essential morphological parameters from a combination of cultural derivation and regulatory control. As it appears in Singapore and elsewhere, however, the particular and distinctive formal expression is clearly different from that of southern China, manifesting a European vocabulary on its façade. This is attributed to the influence of George Dromgold Coleman, the first architect to reside in Singapore and the Superintendent of Public Works from 1833. Coleman mastered the adaptation of European traditions of building form to the tropical climate and established Neo-Palladianism as a significant architectural language there. From these sources, the Singapore shop-house emerged by the middle of the nineteenth century as a pastel coloured, painted and plastered brick façade, typically of two storeys, with small windows lightly articulated with classical European ornamentation. As the typology developed in the latter part of that century, the buildings became

**2.12.** Singapore shop-houses.

wider, with three bays of windows where there had been two, and three storeys with more generous floor to floor heights. More affluent owners decorated the façades with columns and pilasters, installing windows with fanlights and glazing, and decorating the surfaces between with Chinese motifs.

In 1926, the Architects Ordinance was passed in Singapore that required all buildings to be designed by qualified architects. Coincident with the development of the Modern Movement in Europe, the architecture of the shop-house took on an expression and construction vocabulary of modern built form. The façade became less articulated and the building grew in height once the height limit was relaxed in the 1950s. As reinforced concrete became more prevalent, the façades emerged with strips of windows as wide as the lot with spandrel panels below. While the shop-house ceased to be a viable form in Singapore by the 1970s, it continues to flourish throughout the region. Current developments in Kuching, Sarawak, for example, extend the shop-house as an integrated development of up to five floors for mixed office, residential and commercial application.

Although introduced by the Chinese, the shop-house came to be a common form across Singapore as it was adopted by other communities, spread by British regulation to Burma and Hong Kong, returning from whence it derived in Manila and Xiamen, and into new territory, such as Thailand (Lim, 1993).

While we cannot identify the earliest example of such a building in Hong Kong, it appears soon after the British settled on the island although with some variation from the specific forms of Singapore or Penang, emerging from local exigencies as much as from an imported form. As described above, the shop-house was well established as an urban building type in the Malay peninsula by the time the British first arrived in Hong Kong. With the rapid growth of the population on Hong Kong Island, however, built form evolved quickly to accommodate the changes while addressing health and safety concerns. In May 1841, as the British settled on the island, there were some 7,400 Chinese residents there, including 2,000 boat people. By October the same year the recorded population had grown to 9,000 people and, by 1847, the population was around 23,900, excluding the troops of the garrison, increasing further to 39,000 in 1853 (Pryor, 1983, p. 2).

Initially, the majority of buildings in the Chinese districts were long and narrow, their frontage limited to the span of a readily available timber joist of Chinese pine, approximately 4 to 5 metres in length. The building plots were deep, reaching as much as 18 metres in length. If intended to house just one family, the severe shortage of housing demanded that these structures quickly had to cope with accommodating several families and individuals. Soon, the need for space was addressed by the addition of illegal extensions to the only available opportunity, the street façade. Typically these took the form of verandas constructed in wood, which were subsequently enclosed in whole or in part to provide additional habitable space.

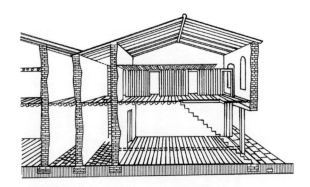

**2.13.** Early form of shop-house in Hong Kong – two storeys without colonnade. The upper floor is divided into cubicles or 'cabins' above the ground floor shop. There is a cockloft over the cubicle level and a space for cooking at the rear. See figure 3.5 for plan. (*Source*: Chadwick, 1882)

While attempts were made initially to use conditions in the Crown Lease to regulate development in the interest of public health and safety, these were ineffective. The first Building Ordinance was put in place in 1856, fourteen years after Hong Kong became a British colony, to set minimum standards in the construction of houses as well as ensuring that adequate and safe areas were provided for fires for cooking (Chadwick, 1882). Since the wooden verandas were considered fire hazards, the 1856 Building Ordinance prohibited enclosing them into inhabitable space. The Ordinance did not make any provision for rear access or rear yards or for adequate lighting and ventilation. To provide maximum accommodation, however, buildings were erected to the boundaries of the plots, and densely inhabited, unventilated spaces became the norm.

In 1878 another Building Ordinance was put in place in order to further ensure fire safety and structural stability. In this amendment, wooden verandas were declared illegal and henceforth all verandas had to be masonry, supported at the ground level by the colonnade along the pavement. The built volume could then be extended legally at all but the ground level to the edge of the street, establishing a definitive urban form that came to typify the city. In this way, the urban shop-house in Hong Kong emerged as a form very similar to that determined by Raffles in Penang, and for eighty years, the majority of buildings were of the colonnaded type.

The traditional shop-house was built to house one family. Arranged with the shop or workshop at the ground floor and residential activities on the upper floors, they functioned well, allowing domestic or commercial activities to spill out into other spaces as needed and often to the street outside. Typically, meals

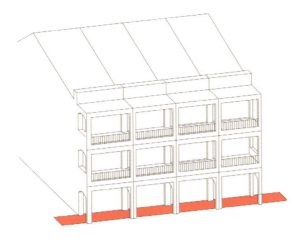

**2.14.** A later form of Hong Kong shop-house – of three storeys, and with colonnade, balconies and footway.

were had sitting around a table in the shop space or on the pavement outside. The sorting and storage of goods took place in the residential portion when stock levels were high. Raffles had addressed these issues in Singapore by legislating that commercial activities could not be extended to the covered way, ensuring free passage for the public along the whole of the street frontage. Inevitably, however, the demands of space and commerce were difficult to contain. As Lim (1993) noted, the covered five-foot way developed a notion of public space that, when regulated to ensure its use only for public access, confronted the regional notions of the ambiguity of urban space for concurrent private and public use.

The pressures of a rapidly increasing population and the topologically pre-scribed shortage of land on which to build meant that the problems of Hong Kong quickly diverged from those of Singapore and Penang, resulting in

**2.15.** Shop-house, Johnston Road, Wanchai. This four-storey shop-house projects into the street with a colonnade and balconies. Once a shop-house of cubicles, it is now a restaurant and bars. Though occupying only a short length of road, stripped of the many advertising signs it once bore, and dwarfed by neighbouring buildings, this building represents the kind of structure that once lined most of Wanchai's main roads and streets.

developments in the shop-house not manifested on the Malay peninsula. The orderly form of the two- or three-storey shop-house was soon modified to accommodate the extended families or other tenants. The high ceilinged shop area adjacent to the street, with its 5 metre clearance, soon developed a mezzanine floor which was used for storage or sleeping. Upper floors were subdivided by partitions into the rooms and each room housed at least one family. As the demand for accommodation continued, long airless corridors were lined with rented beds: this is probably the origin of the cage dwellings that are still to be found in Hong Kong.

While the shop-house has come to be glamorized in recent years, the real situation for the people who lived in these intensely inhabited buildings was difficult. In Chadwick's Report of 1882, we find several descriptions of the terrible conditions in which the inhabitants lived. Typically without rear lanes, these buildings were without ventilation and light except from the front façade, resulting in very poor conditions within. With the constraints placed by contiguous development on three of the four lot boundaries, and limits to possible expansion onto the streets, activities were elevated to the roofs. Unlike shop-houses of the Malay peninsula, roofs were not always black tiled and pitched but increasingly flat, and connected by the building's stairway to the floors below. Since most roofs were of similar height, these soon became a community space, providing continuity at this upper plane and accommodating some activities often found at street level.

After Chadwick's second report (Chadwick and Simpson, 1902), a Public Health and Building Ordinance was enacted in 1903 which specified the provision of open space at the rear of the building, ensuring ventilation to rooms at the back; it also reduced the permissible building height, which was now limited to the width of the street, down from one and a half times the width of the street. The implications of these changes reduced considerably the habitable space on a particular site. With no commensurate reduction in population, the demand for habitable space was no less, consequently

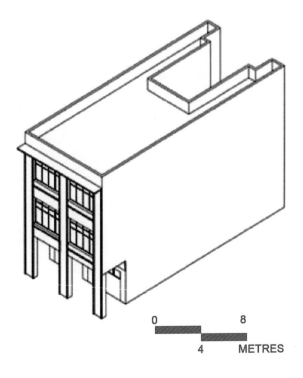

**2.16a** and **2.16b.** Shop-house, with colonnade, 1945.

**2.17.** A post World War II variation on the shop-house theme – without colonnade, Tsim Sha Tsui, 1950. (See also figure 3.28 for a drawing of this building.) Many post-war buildings were like this one, marking an end to the 'colonnade era'. As the 1950s progressed, it became increasingly common for upper floors to be cantilevered over the street pavement, giving 'a scent of the colonnade' – see figures 4.9 and 4.11.

illegal extensions began to appear on the roofs of buildings, and activities such as cooking and washing appeared in the streets and back alleys.

The shop-house form took another step towards the modern built form of Hong Kong in 1935 when the Public Health and Building Ordinance of 1903 was split into a Building Ordinance and a series of Public Health Ordinances in which the permissible depth of a building was further reduced to 10.7 metres, verandas were transformed into enclosed inhabitable space and, by 1956, the supporting arcades removed in order to provide better visibility for the road users, thus cantilevering the building over the pavement. With this reduction of the building footprint and an ever increasing population, the predilection to build higher gained momentum.

# 3 Long, Low and Intense
## From Possession Point to World War II

At the time Britain took possession of Hong Kong Island, the British Foreign Secretary, Lord Palmerston, referred to it as 'a barren rock with hardly a house upon it', and with some justification. This lump of igneous 'rock' was just 12 kilometres long from east to west and 6 kilometres across at its middle – about 70 square kilometres in all: along its spinal range there were no fewer than nine sharp peaks rising to between 430 and 552 m, below which the land fell steeply to the sea almost everywhere. It was a rugged and formidable landform, devoid of natural resources, much stripped of vegetation, and inhabited by only few people. When Captain Charles Elliot raised the British flag at Possession Point in January 1841 to mark the beginnings of a new colony, there were about 5,650 on the island distributed through some twenty villages, most of which were in the south (Owen and Shaw, 2007): these were according to other sources mostly farmers, stonecutters and fishermen.

The particular site chosen for settlement was a sliver of shoreline in the shadow of Victoria Peak, Mount Gough and Mount Cameron whose summits reach 552 m, 479 m and 439 m, respectively. At its closest point to

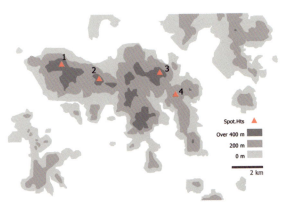

**3.1.** Hong Kong Island's rugged relief: steep slopes, coastline and little else. The numbered peaks are: 1. Victoria Peak 552 m; 2. Mt. Cameron 439 m; 3. Mt Parker 531 m; and 4. Mt. Collison 347 m.

**3.2.** Hong Kong's urban beginnings. Following Captain Charles Elliot establishing the British colony in 1841, the town grew quickly as a long thin band of building, steeply terraced beneath a ridge of peaks.

**3.3.** Possession Point today. This once waterfront promontory and point of colonial possession is today marked by a sign-cluttered junction at the bottom end of the short (106 m) steep Possession Street and the long flat east–west Queens Road, from which neither water nor mountain is in view.

water before reclamation, Victoria Peak stood approximately 1,200 m inland rising through nearly half as many metres to give an average slope of approaching 1 in 2, or more accurately about 46 per cent. (At the same point, the Island's edge has since been pushed out a further 400 m into the harbour.) It is an understatement to say that it was a most difficult site squeezed between mountain and sea. But as a point for trade, it had two magnificent advantages: proximity and protection. It was on China's doorstep for trade, and it had well-sheltered deep water immediately adjacent. Shelter was necessary for the ships that would have to defend the colonial outpost and ply the China trade in seas swelled unexpectedly by typhoons.

Since that time, millions, the vast majority Chinese, have flocked to Hong Kong Island, which has been extended through reclamation by one-fifth of its natural area to accommodate them. Nevertheless, the site of the city has remained extremely constrained, with building channelled west and east to snake its way along the north shore in a sinuous band. The town on this north coast (known initially as Queenstown, and later as the City of Victoria) may be fairly described as the world's longest, skinniest, densest and tallest – if the four terms are used collectively to qualify each other. In the years following settlement, the town, dwarfed beneath the peaks, would extend as a thin strip along the shore of Victoria

Harbour: the latter was part of a 2 kilometres wide strategic shipping channel that separated Hong Kong Island from a small promontory on the Chinese mainland known as Kowloon Peninsula.

In 1861, two decades after settlement of the Island, Britain acquired about 9 square kilometres of the Peninsula plus near-by Stonecutter Island. Much later, in 1897, it extended its jurisdiction to a larger and less regular projecting land mass to the south of the Sham Chun River – to be known as 'the New Territories'. From the tip of the Peninsula grew the City of Kowloon, shorter and broader than Victoria but with time no less dense. Its name was derived from the Chinese *Kau Lung*, meaning 'Nine Dragons', which referred to the peaks rising immediately beyond Britain's 1861 acquisition. Beyond Kowloon and its immediate extensions, a series of tall, small footprint 'new towns' was planned that today reach for the skies from mostly rail-side sites in the New Territories. Individually and collectively, Victoria, Kowloon and the new towns constitute forms of urbanism unlike any other places on earth with specific consequences for living, working, travel and relationships with nature. This chapter (and the next two) will explore these forms, their components, dominant typologies and relationships.

The main British settlement consolidated around where the prestigious commercial and administrative 'Central' district stands today. Within six months of settlement the government had sold land to merchant houses for *godowns* (or warehouses) and offices in Central itself, in Sheung Wan to the west, and in Wanchai to the east, thus foreshadowing a long thin harbour edge city. Sheung Wan was the place where the more numerous Chinese were allowed to build their first district. This rose quickly as an intense area of both work and living, dominated by a particular building typology: the Chinese shop-house. It set a model that was to spread, street after street, both westwards towards today's Kennedy Town and eastwards towards Causeway Bay beyond the central colonial administrative and military area.

It was this string of districts that formed the beginnings of the City of Victoria, which expanded only slightly across its north–south girth but became extremely elongated from west to east, and remarkably intense. In the process, there was significant reclamation to transform strips of water into city ground. Consequently, two types of roads and streets emerged. There were long east–west roads that paralleled the shoreline, with straight roads on reclaimed land close to the water, and more curvaceous ones on the contoured lower slopes above. Contrasting with these, the north–south streets between sea and foothill slopes were short and irregular. Several of the long streets started life as foreshore promenades or wharves (or *praya* in the local parlance, as borrowed from Macau) but were later transformed into conventional streets with buildings on both sides, following successive bands of reclamation – most notably, Queens and Des Voeux Roads. These constitute Victoria's central nervous system and provide, in Hillier's term, the 'global' connections – from end to end of the long settlement. The short north–south streets are less ordered and 'local', of walkable lengths and often

**3.4.** The beginnings of Victoria's urban structure of 'global' roads and local streets. During the early years of settlement, the pattern of movement in the City of Victoria was established quickly: Queens Road took a flat contour-determined 'line of least resistance' close to the coastline, offering 'global' west–east connection between city districts; while short steep and often stepped or 'ladder' streets ascended the slope southwards and perpendicular to the water. This established the city's basic structure, which we experience today in a slightly widened and greatly elongated form.

extremely steep. In fact many are more stairs than streets, although only a few have names that are true to their form, such as Ladder Street in Sheung Wan.

The institutional centre developed by the British authorities (around today's Central district) was a slightly more spacious district, and with a greater, though not exclusively, European flavour. Government House, the Anglican cathedral and other establishment buildings were built on the ridge below today's zoological and botanical gardens with the major banks, hotels, commercial and retail buildings close-by to the north and west. Further west, mostly up-slope, and to some extent mixed in, were the houses of Europeans; and to the east was the military void, a scatter of barracks, stores and spaces.

However, the main body of this sinuous city was made-up increasingly of narrow streets flanked by shop-houses as the dominant building typology. The Chinese community demonstrated immediately its preferred housing type, and the British responded with designated Chinese areas as well as Chinese law for the Chinese. There was a corresponding European district where British law prevailed. And along the foreshore, within and beyond the main built-up area, were the *godowns* or warehouses whose activities and contents were central to the Colony's prosperity. Above the line of dense urbanism was an extending scatter of spacious villas and gardens, which were the exclusive domain of both Europeans (*taipan*) and Chinese business chiefs, providing the latter adopted European building styles.

On a cold foggy morning in January 1885, the Australian priest cum scientist, Julian Tenison Woods approached Victoria from the water. He held in his mind's eye a powerful impression of what he saw and noted the scene by way of recollection:

> It may be defined as thick rows of masts: then handsome terraces of houses rising tier above tier
> upon such a steep incline that they looked as if each higher range were founded on the chimney
> pots of the other. About half-way up the houses ceased, and then diagonal and zig-zag roadways,
> with scattered villas rapidly ascended into the clouds. (Woods, quoted in O'Brien, 1984)

While memory of oodles of chimney pots may be exaggerated, the image of masts, tiers of row housing on stepped terraces, and large villas scattered sparingly above by zig-zag paths is powerful and well founded.

## The First Dominant Building Typology: The Chinese Shop-House

Throughout the nineteenth century, neither building height nor street width was controlled in Hong Kong. Nevertheless, the usual height for these shop-houses was two to four storeys, with variable depths of between 9 and 18 metres, and 4 and 6 metre widths determined by the typical lengths of the Chinese fir poles used to support the floors. Inside, floors were designed as free space, which allowed for cubicles to be erected in lines along each floor: cubicles were rented for occupation by singles, families or other groups. Usually, only the front cubicle enjoyed direct light. The building width was right for a line of cubicles, each measuring very approximately 3 m x 3 m plus another metre or so for circulation, including a staircase, each section of which would flank one of the side walls. All or part of the ground floor would house one or more shops, although small commercial and workshop activities would commonly permeate deeper and higher into the building, and also operate from cubicles. At the rear of each floor was a 2 or 3 metre space for cooking, although this activity was commonly performed on the street, roof or balcony, all offering better conditions – more space, better air, greater hygiene and more convenience.

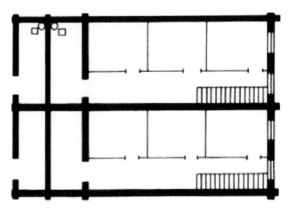

**3.5.** Early shop-house plan showing the first floor divided into cabins or cubicles (5): cookhouses with smoke-holes can be seen at the back (left). See also: section, figure 2.13. (Adapted from Chadwick, 1882)

These cramped conditions quickly established the high densities and multi-level living, which became hallmarks of Hong Kong. With ultra-squeezed conditions, space was the city's challenge for both domestic and commercial endeavour, fostering physical ingenuity and improvisation, and social tolerance. Frames and platforms are to be seen standing astride the roof pitch in some old photographs – presumably for clothes drying, recreational escape from the frenzy of life below, and possibly to keep watch.

At the front, especially on the flatter and wider streets, it was common for colonnades of at least 1.5 m width to run along the street edge. The shop-houses would stand right beside each other along the street, and in many cases, they would occur in immediate back-to-back formation, to make each street block, more or less, a solid mass. Exceptions tended to be on the more sloping sites, where a space of one or two metres might form a cleft between the building rows. Normally built of plastered brick and topped by pitched tiled roofs (although flat roofs also appeared quite quickly), this building typology dominated the townscape to give form to streets and blocks. And within the street space, verandas or, later, colonnades would offer shade and shelter, much-needed in the summer months. Climatically Hong Kong lies at the interface between tropical and temperate regions and its seasons reflect this. Summers are under the influence of the tropical south with southerly air bringing high humidity (81 per cent) and mean minimum and maximum temperatures of 27°C to 31°C in July: on average, rainfall is experienced on twenty-five July days and can be heavy. The region is certainly typhoon-prone. By contrast, winters are a time in which northerly continental winds blow to bring much cooler and drier conditions: January minimums and maximums average 15°C and 18°C respectively. Above the urban areas, which occur mostly below the 200 m contour, the peaks experience frosts and even heavier rains.

Most writing refers to the old Hong Kong shop-houses as 'tenements' but this name can be misleading for those familiar with British notions of nineteenth-century tenement living. For instance, Glasgow tenements of the same period were purpose-built flats, each unit an integral part of the initial design, though extremely small and sharing yard and lavatories. In the notoriously crowded Dublin tenements, families would occupy single rooms in a house that had been built for and previously occupied by one family and their domestic servants. In Hong Kong the outside would appear as a standard shop-house but the inside would offer free space for subdivision into cubicles – cage-like spaces devoid of services. As outlined in the previous chapter, it was a model and lifestyle that can be traced to Chinese precedents in cities such as Guangzhou (Canton) and Shanghai, to Chinese-influenced British colonial models in Singapore and the Malay States, as well as to Chinese walled villages in the immediate region, including parts of Hong Kong's New Territories.

Such building was largely unregulated through the nineteenth century, although some fifteen years after settlement, the government made some attempt to address the acute absence of services and lack of

**3.6.** The colonnaded street edge was the common sight along the flatter streets by the early twentieth century.

maintenance. In 1856, it brought in a Building Ordinance driven by issues of health and safety – for instance, new dwellings were to include privies and ash-pits. It also covered some aspects of construction, cleansing and repairs. Part of the legislation was directed against the enclosure of balconies and extension through temporary add-ons – an early indication of overcrowding in the city. These were rudimentary moves and did not address other basic issues of lighting or ventilation, and did little if anything to 'shape' the city beyond set and familiar patterns: as indicated previously, building height and road widths were not dimensions of concern.

In 1878, there was further legislation intended to ensure greater structural stability and safety from fire: the building of timber verandas was to cease in favour of masonry colonnades. At this stage there were shop-houses, without and with verandas: they also existed with cantilevered balconies from the upper floors. Where verandas did exist, they were usually of timber or cast iron and would commonly run through the full height of the building (or at least through all but the top floor) to form upper floor balconies: moreover, these were frequently enclosed to gain extra accommodation. Thus a street profile including a covered walkway with enclosed building above – a prototypical colonnade – was established long before 1878. At the same time, there were 'real' masonry colonnades supporting balconies over the street (sometimes of generous

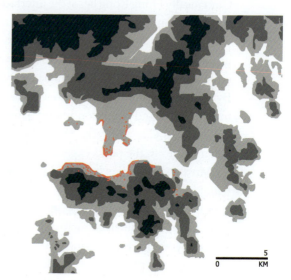

**3.7.** Urban settlement on Hong Kong Island, 1887. The string of almost continuous settlement is between today's Shek Tong Tsui (then Belchers Point, which is now slightly inland) and the vicinity of North Point.

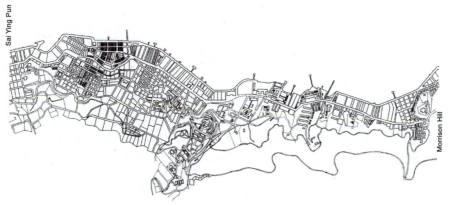

**3.8.** Area of densest settlement on Hong Kong Island 1887 – from Sai Ying Pun to Morrison Hill, a distance of about 4 km.

width) in both public and private buildings. Hence, although the street with covered walkways was not new, the masonry colonnade was now mandated to become effectively the Colony's dominant urban typology: it was no longer a lightweight lean-to and optional extra but a standard and integral part of the building and street; and, as we shall see, it remained that way for almost eighty years.

By the early 1880s, shop-houses stretched with varying intensities between Belchers Point (the end point of Queens Road West today) and Causeway Bay in the east, a distance of a little over 6 kilometres, although this was interrupted towards its middle by a semi-void of military land (Wong, 1978b). However, the width of the city lay in sharp contrast: it remained narrow, although the dimension varied considerably narrowing and bulging between perhaps 100 m and 500 m, rather like a snake after swallowing uneven sized courses in close succession. On foot, it was typically a five minutes dawdle across and a brisk one hour's walk in length! Altogether, the built-up area, including the generously spaced military area, was no more than three square kilometres. With a population of approximately 140,000, a conservative estimation of gross density is 500 persons per hectare.

By this time, many Hong Kong people would already have been living, working or both on reclaimed ground. Between 1851 and the 1880s, several significant reclamation projects of up to 10 hectares took place from about Kennedy Town in the west to Causeway Bay in the east. But 1889 saw the biggest reclamation proposal put up so far: for a thin strip of new land along the western half of the city's shore, traversing Central, Sheung Wan and Sai Ying Pun, stretching over 3 km (half the length of the city) with an average width of 84 m. When completed in 1904, it had added over 26 new hectares to the most intensively developed part of Hong Kong: these included over 13 hectares for building and more than 12 extra hectares for urban space, mostly roads, including a new *praya* in the form of Des Voeux Road. It laid the ground for a new face to the water, and condemned the old waterfront roads to roles of 'corridor' streets – that is, streets flanked by buildings on both sides.

By 1901 the city on Hong Kong Island had added yet another 100,000 people to reach about 240,000, and an average gross density of at least 700 people per hectare, though this was not evenly spread. For the vast majority of city dwellers, there were limited means of getting around town on *terra firma*: generally, one either walked or hired a rickshaw (*jinriksha* when first brought in from Japan) or sedan chair. There were over 700 registered rickshaws in the city, and close to 600 registered sedan chairs, with numbers rising. The advantage of the sedan chair in hilly Hong Kong is evidenced by thirty registrations (1901) in the high and rugged district of the Peak (Leeds, 1998). Circa 1900, there is much truth in describing the main land-based public transport system as a complementary mix of long free-wheeling rickshaw drives along the city's contours, and shorter (in distance if not time) wheelless sedan rides across them – an east–west and north–south multi-modal but albeit human-powered movement system.

**3.9a** and **3.9b**. Des Voeux as *Praya* (left photograph and section). **3.9c** and **3.9d**. Des Voeux as 'street' (right photograph and section). Des Voeux Road is one of very few long flat 'global' roads to have duplicated Queens Road on reclaimed land. The left images depict Des Voeux Road 'reconstructed' as an open waterfront space (or *Praya*, which it once was) – as it might have been had further reclamation not taken place. The right image shows it as a formed street in the 1950s. Reclamation for the *Praya* was completed in the early years of the twentieth century, when the tram was established: today it retains the tramline along its centre but passengers ride without water views.

As for horse-drawn vehicles in Hong Kong, Leeds dismisses them as insignificant 'as the climate was unkind' to them: so too were the contours. Certainly, in the many old paintings and photographs we have seen of Hong Kong, any beast of burden is a rarity, and then usually without carriage and associated with pleasure or the military. Were there ever hansom cabs that travelled Hong Kong's streets and the same question may be asked of horse-drawn buses? If so, we can only assume that they were few and far between, and that Leeds is correct in his conclusion. Further the writings of the previously cited Australian cleric, Julian Tenison Woods, would tend to confirm this: he thought Hong Kong 'peculiar' because of its 'crowded by-streets and lanes … absence of horse-carriages (and) presence of chairs and jinrikshas' (Woods, quoted in O'Brien, 1984).

There was at least one exception to human-powered land vehicles: the single land-based mechanically driven piece of public transport was the funicular Peak Tram, which opened in 1888. It travelled a track distance of only 1.4 km but over ground with an average slope of 1:3.7 turning a previously arduous climb into an easy ride. But it was an extremely expensive ride by the standards of the time, and served only a small band of well-heeled residents, trippers and tourists. Consistent with the city's wider structure, this north–south route was short and its angle of ascent sharp, to provide a vertical transit mode. Its builder was in fact the owner of

**3.10.** Passenger vehicles for across and along the contour. The picture shows a Japanese *jinrikisha* (right) and sedan chair (left). The rickshaw (shortened from *jinriksha*) was imported to Hong Kong from Japan in 1874. By that stage, the sedan chair, used in China from early times, had already been used as a vehicle for mounting the colony's steep slopes. Thus rickshaws plied the relatively flat and smooth streets while sedan chairs crossed the contours to provide complementary modes of movement. In old photographs of Hong Kong rickshaws can be seen standing on the long global roads while sedan chairs wait on 'ladder streets' for custom. (*Source:* Hitchcock, 1917)

the Peak Hotel, which attracted many Europeans seeking a breezy and relatively cool refuge from Hong Kong's debilitating summer heat and humidity. This mechanical piece of tracked infrastructure was also supplemented by the sedan chair at higher levels. The funicular survives to this day.

Of necessity, there were also boats. Victoria was long and thin and flanked by water, and sibling Kowloon was across the harbour. Wharves were a regular feature from Kennedy Town to North Point. Boats were a part of the movement system, along Victoria City and across her namesake harbour, with ferries commencing regular cross-harbour services in 1880.

## Dense, Skinny and Steep: Victoria

In summary, at the beginning of the twentieth century, Victoria was long, thin and dense, and made-up largely of narrow bands of flat reclaimed and steep foothill land with an extremely tight street network. This consisted of a handful of slightly wider 'global' east–west routes, which held together a mesh of countless, short, narrow and mostly north–south streets that were the heartland of the many local districts strung west and east from Central. Many of the short streets and alleys were so steep as to incorporate or be built entirely of steps, including the aptly named, Ladder Street – another feature of the city's verticality. Flat or steep, hawkers would jostle for the precious space to peddle their wares and services (barbers, fortune-tellers, food-sellers, in fact all manner of vendors); while a great variety of goods-for-sale would spill out from the open-fronted shop-houses. Most streets were narrow, just a few metres wide, with their built edges rising mostly through to two, three and four storeys – in other words, they were usually taller than they were wide, to give a tight sense of enclosure. In fact, many were alleys more than streets of only 2 or 3 metres width; and where the streets were wider and flatter, colonnades, verandas or overhanging balconies would effectively compress the section profile.

**3.11.** One of the many stepped or 'ladder' streets that climb the foothills (taken in the 1950s).

In this sinuous but labyrinthine structure of bustling enclosure and shop-houses, few people would have had the experience of actually living on the ground: the vast majority, at least 80 per cent, would have returned 'home' to an upper floor space, most likely a cubicle, in a city that was already organized on vertical principles. Landlords would let single floors to what we might term 'floor-lords', each of whom would divide and sublet their particular floor by cubicle and cockloft. Accommodation on top-floors would sometimes be set back with its own 'ground' in the manner of a penthouse. And like barnacles on the backs of a host

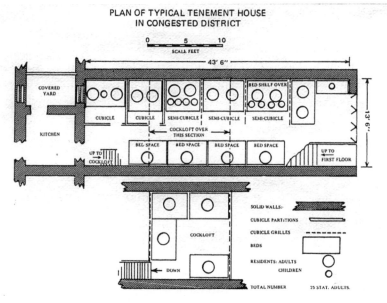

**3.12.** Shop-house occupancy. The plan shows cubicles, semi-cubicles and bed spaces and the number of adults and children in each, within the volume of a shop-house (in this case, ground) floor: it includes a cockloft over the centre. While this case is taken from a 1935 report, it describes a condition to which Chinese people had long been accustomed – from first settlement and beforehand in other cities and walled settlements. From such examples, it is not difficult to understand the extraordinary densities of some Hong Kong districts: if this building maintained similar densities over just three floors even without further cock-lofts, the net and gross densities would be in excess of 9,000 and 6,500 per hectare respectively. (*Source*: Housing Commission, 1939)

creature, decks, sheds, cages, drying poles and other add-ons would cling to roofs and walls for clothes drying, recreation, or simply more accommodation.

Add these stratified and symbiotic existences in and around individual buildings to the steeply angled disposition of most of the city on its cramped site, and we have a linear urban form that offers anything but a horizontal experience. Life within this snaking volume would have been intensely local with shops and services immediately to hand and on several levels – both within buildings and up the slopes. Movement demanded a pair of strong legs, with stairs and steps ubiquitous, an accepted part of life, inside buildings and on the streets. Further, almost the entire population occupied a place within a few minutes walk of both mountain and sea, though these would not have been visible to most from their miniscule 'interiors', or even from the tight street spaces outside. Where there were views, the mountain could loom ominously close and dark, losing all depth, in a southerly direction, while the harbour could sparkle magically silver to the north.

In this set-up, while most individual buildings may have had only three or four full floor levels, there were more if cocklofts are included within the generous ceiling heights and roof structures. Also, some buildings could be entered at more than one level because of the slopes, which were steep. The main grid of Sai Ying Pun (at the west end of Victoria) measured just 300 metres square but the cross-streets rose through a slope of at least 1 in 4. Parts of Sheung Wan and even Central were similar, and life within some sections was astoundingly dense (up to 4,000 persons per hectare) with an intensity of street activity to match. It was a

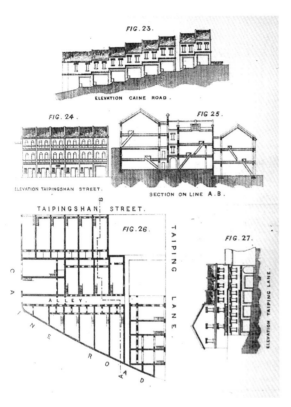

**3.13.** Shop-houses on a sloping and irregular site – between Caine Road and Taipingshan Street, Sheung Wan. This set of drawings, from *Report on the Sanitary Conditions of Hong Kong* of 1882, shows well how the configuration of shop-houses was adapted to topography and irregularly shaped sites in both plan and section. The shop-houses are orientated in four directions, have entrances from six 'fronts', stand at many different levels, and display volumetric connection across much of the site. (The report is one of two prepared by sanitary engineer, Mr Osbert Chadwick for the British Government in 1882 and 1902: they are key sources of information on Hong Kong's early crowded and insanitary conditions and were influential in bringing limited change to regulations and development of shop-houses and public sanitation in Hong Kong. The second report, co-authored with Professor Simpson, addresses housing design and construction in greater detail.) (*Source*: Chadwick, 1882)

concentrated and compact district with unusual vertical dimensions. Further, these districts foreshadowed characteristics of pattern and form that were increasingly to characterize Victoria until after World War II. The collective number of levels in the city was great, and the three-dimensional structure truly complex.

Above these densely packed districts, six boundary stones were placed on the foothills in 1901 to mark the edge of the City of Victoria; and all but one can still be seen today in their original locations.

## New Century, New Regulations, New Transport

Soon after the turn of the new (twentieth) century, two changes occurred to influence city building. There was a revision of the building regulations, prompted by rapidly deteriorating sanitary conditions. And a tramline was laid on the flat reclaimed land at or close to the harbour.

The tramway, first mooted in 1881, formed a long public transport spine that offered cheap and regular connection along some 13 km of shoreline. Construction commenced in 1903, with the first double track sections opening in July of the following year from Kennedy Town to Causeway Bay. Soon afterwards, following Causeway Bay reclamation, a single

**3.14.** and **3.15.** Street intensity. The density of occupation of the buildings was matched if not exceeded by the intensity of activity on the streets, which served as kitchen, workshop, market, playground and more. These photographs, dating from the 1950s, show the continuation of old practices.

track was extended eastwards to Shau Ki Wan, although this was quickly converted to double track after World War I. The system also included a 3 km branch-circuit into and around the only piece of adjacent flat land, 'the Happy Valley' of horse racing fame.

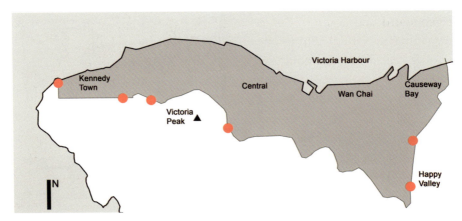

**3.16.** The City of Victoria boundary stones were set in place in 1903: a visitor to the city may still see five of the six in their original positions. But even today, after extensive foreshore reclamation, the land bounded by the stones, while some 7.6 km long, is typically little more than a kilometre wide, except in the vicinity of the relatively flat Happy Valley district where it extends to more than 2 km. Soon after the stones were set, a tramline was built through Victoria and beyond to Shau Ki Wan to the east: this greatly extended an already linear city.

Though the line began with single deck cars, it was only eight years after the first trams went into operation that they were replaced by double deckers, in 1912. Today Hong Kong's tramcars are the world's narrowest – just 1.98 m wide. Also, it is the only all double-decker tram system in the world. Hong Kong trams are slim-line vehicles for a slim-line city designed to move the most people on the minimum mobile footprint. And, like many other components of the city, they started life as a waterfront feature but became one of 'inland' streets without shifting their tracks – thanks to subsequent reclamation.

The new building regulations came by way of the Public Health and Building Act of 1902. The title is indicative of the circumstances out of which it was born: from 1894 plague visited Hong Kong regularly, and over the following eight years, some 8,600 people died. It was recognized that insanitary conditions were a

**3.17.** Hong Kong's slim bodied trams, which ply a 13 km track between Kennedy Town in the west and Shau Kei Wan in the east, were a vital force in generating the city's linear form: the system has been all-double deck since 1912 (see also Chapter 7).

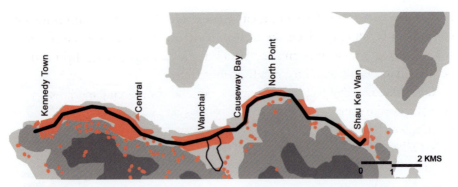

**3.18.** Kennedy Town to Shau Kei Wan tram route through the urban area at the time of World War II. The Kennedy Town to Causeway Bay section opened in 1904 but was quickly extended to Shau Kei Wan. There are fifty-seven stops at approximately 225 m intervals.

major cause, hence the new Act embracing two parallel building standards: one for land leased before the legislation and one for that leased afterwards, the latter being more stringent. The major concerns were with deep building plans, excessive building heights in relation to street widths, and too little space per inhabitant. Under the new ordinances building heights could range from 7.6 m to 23.2 m, but with height tied to street width: maximum height on new leases was equal to the street width but 1.5 times the width on old leases. Maximum building depth was 12.2 m except where additional windows could ensure extra light and ventilation. Open space was required at the rear equal to not less than one-half and one-third the roof area on new and old leases respectively, ensuring rear lanes, small yards and/or light wells. There were also minimum space standards, although these were impossible to administer, and were routinely flouted: an area of 4.65 m² and a volume of 15.56 m³ per person were required in a cubicled building, and 3.25 m² and 9.34 m³ for one without cubicles. Clearly, the new rules would bring

PLAN Nº 2

## CHINESE TENEMENT HOUSE
### OLD STANDARD TYPE
BUILT AFTER 1903
SCALE 1 IN. = 8 FT

**3.19.** Typical shop-house plans that followed 1902 legislation as illustrated in the *Report of the Housing Commission 1935*, in which they were referred to as 'Chinese Tenement Houses, Type A'. Each includes a yard, a ground-level latrine, and a kitchen on each floor. (Compare this with the much earlier plan shown in figure 3.5.)

little change to the basic form of the city. In other words, the city's most common component building typology, the mixed activity shop-house, was the accepted form. The regulations were an attempt to bring a little more space, light and air circulation to a familiar and seemingly inviolate form.

It was the tram that had greater impact upon the city's overall morphology by encouraging the shop-house to spread its territory and intensity further along the coast, especially to the east. Thus those areas of Victoria east of the central military zone (Wanchai and Causeway Bay, North Point and Shaukiwan) were to intensify between the two World Wars and accentuate Victoria's already dense and linear form.

A 1924 visitors' guidebook drew attention to the fact that only very small areas had a European flavour, and that 'the Hong Kong experience' (to use a contemporary phrase) was mostly Chinese. From Central, 'both Queens Road and Des Voeux Road, going west, soon lose their European appearance, apart from their width, the trams (in Des Voeux Road) and other modern touches. Nearer the central district, the shops conform more with Western standards, but further along they are typically Chinese with their open fronts, their teeming life and their countless signboards'. Similarly, 'Along the Praya itself, leaving behind the big shipping offices in Connaught Road ... the visitor will find all the usual Chinese street life'. And on the eastern side it was no different: having passed through the naval and military area, the wanderer could 'choose the waterfront or the road through Wan Chai. The former will show him the usual busy Praya, the street lined with curio shops; mostly Japanese; the waterfront crowded with small craft. The road through Wanchai is the typical Chinese street, with signboards, if anything more numerous' (Kelly and Walch Ltd, 1924).

Victoria and Kowloon continued to expand with no concession to density. In 1931, many of the twenty-five major statistical districts supported more than 1,500 persons per hectare with one reaching well over double that figure (Schmitt, 1963). Though the city continued to extend, with the aid of public transport, it remained intense: by World War II, the urban strip that had extended from Victoria was some 18 km long – thirty times longer than it was generally wide.

In the 1930s, came yet another round of review to building regulations, with a new Building Ordinance in 1935 taking effect in the following year. The nature of the change was similar to that of 1903: tinkering with the dimensions of a known typology, resulting from the twin concerns of health and hazard. We can see the common dimensions of the previously existing shop-houses that lead to the 1935 legislation in H.R. Butter's report of 1939 on *Labour and Labour Conditions in Hong Kong* (cited in Leeming, 1977): three to four storeys in height, including a ground-floor shop; 13.3 m deep; 4.1 m wide; with 4 metres between floors; a front colonnade; and a small back kitchen next to a covered yard. With the new law, standard building heights were limited to three storeys unless built of fire-resistant materials, in which case they could rise to five: higher buildings were possible but required special permission. There was a further reduction in the standard building depth (down from 12.2 m to 10.7 m) and stricter latrine standards. But the minimum space standard per inhabitant was effectively reduced to the 1903 figure for the non-cubicled house for all domestic dwellings, with or without cubicles. Thus, within the overall package, densities were permitted to rise slightly but in marginally healthier and less fire-vulnerable units. In short, there was again no typological change resulting from the Ordinance, and hence no basic morphological change to the wider city.

In a city of such unusual density, shape and topography, one may well be wondering about the place of the motorcar in Hong Kong? The tram catered well for journeys along the city's flat spine while most other journeys were short and steep through streets thronged with dense activity and people. It was not a very useful vehicle and it should not be a surprise that it was slow to make its appearance. In 1910, there were just twenty cars in the Colony, 500 ten years later, and barely 5,000 as World War II approached (Leeds, 1998, p. 15). This is extraordinary when compared with London where by 1910 there were over 6,000 licensed cabs alone (Inwood, 2006). Nevertheless, though motor vehicles were few in number, movement between Victoria and Kowloon was sufficient to justify a cross-harbour vehicle ferry by 1933.

## New City, Old Forms: Kowloon

So far, we have dealt only with 'the barren rock': but as already noted, Britain made a second acquisition of territory twenty years after acquiring Hong Kong Island. In 1861, it extended its jurisdiction across the harbour onto the facing Kowloon Peninsula and nearby Stonecutter Island. The motivation was primarily military as it would be easier to defend the harbour (the Colony's jewel and *raison d'être*) with

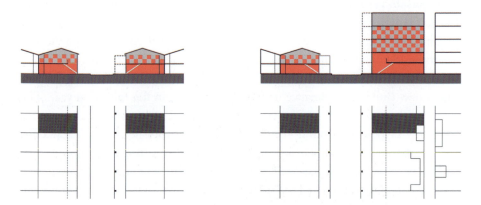

**3.20.** Street sections and plans showing the changing form of the city – from the original shop-houses of two storeys without colonnade, to four storeys (five with ground floor mezzanine) or higher, with colonnade. It also shows a progression from street blocks without a rear service lane to those with such provision, and the adoption of the flat roof. While red indicates commercial activities on the ground level, this was very variable with the ground floor sometimes used for residential purposes and upper floors for commercial or cottage industries, commonly both.

attacking positions on both sides. The new territory was tiny: roughly 9 square kilometres in area, and measuring just 5 kilometres from north to south and half as wide: it was barely one-tenth the size of Hong Kong Island which was itself small. Today's Boundary Road is a remnant from Kowloon's settlement and a reminder of its earliest northern limit. To the south, less than 2 kilometres (about 1.25 miles) of water separated the new terrain from the relatively established but still infant Victoria.

Kowloon was a mix of low hills and rice paddies, with a shoreline that was part sandy and part muddy inlets between low promontories. However, while the peninsula's contours were less demanding than Hong Kong Island's, initial development was comparatively slow. When acquired by Britain from China in 1866, the inherited population, mostly rice farmers and fishermen, was about 3,000: it rose to 15,000 by 1887, and to 25,000 ten years later. It was not until Britain made further territorial expansion into the adjacent 'New Territories' in 1898 and was partner to the linking of Kowloon with the Chinese city of Canton by railway in 1911 that urban development started to accelerate. The single track steam railway not only connected with China but also made a small crack in the rugged hill barrier, whose peaks known officially as the Lion Rock Ridge were dubbed locally 'the Nine Dragons of Kowloon', to connect the new city of Kowloon with the newly acquired territory beyond. This gave the region at least shades of a hinterland status. The new land may have been close in distance but it seemed remote to any would-be traveller. Rugged and inhabited by robbers and tigers, crossing the granite 'dragons' was a task for the brave-hearted. Tigers roamed the hills until after World War II, the last one being shot in 1947. Before this tenuous track, the main links between urban Hong Kong and the territories were by boat, or via the vulnerable Tai Po Pass towards the west end of the range.

In 1898, the first year of Britain's lease of the New Territories the Lockhart Report (1899) estimated the population to be approximately 100,000 in 423 scattered villages. Most were closely settled and many were walled. While various forms of agriculture were the most common activities, fishing, salt-making, oyster farming, lime-burning, brick-making, the manufacture of joss-powder and even limited ship-building added to the range of economic pursuits. In particular, the walled villages displayed characteristics that had carried over into the design and occupation of Hong Kong's city buildings: rectilinear plans, dense building, multiple levels, mezzanine floors, tight external spaces; and intense occupation.

When compared with Hong Kong Island, development on the Peninsula during the early decades of settlement was slow but soon spurted. At the end of the first twenty-six years, in 1887, inhabitants numbered just 15,000, and over the next ten years (1897), rose to just 25,000. But after Britain's acquisition of the adjacent New Territories in 1898, and especially after establishment of the rail link to Canton in 1911, Victoria's across-the-harbour offspring city really began to 'take-off'. The railway not only tunnelled through the intimidating dragon hills to distant China but also provided a rapid and safe connection through to at least part of the hitherto neglected lands of the New Territories between. At the time of the opening of the railway, Kowloon's population had topped 56,000 (69,000 if 'New Kowloon' extensions are included). After two decades of railway operations, it had jumped to half a million, and more than this figure if extensions are included. By 1941, it was closing in on Hong Kong Island with 580,000 people (compared with the Island's 709,000), although by this time the more restricted city area of Victoria and that of Kowloon were probably not dissimilar.

From the outset, the Kowloon urban landscape took on many of the characteristics already familiar in the buildings and spaces of Victoria. The established practice of flattening and extending the land by razing hills, filling bays and swamps, and extending foreshores was extended to the Peninsula, though the landform was far less extreme. But with more extensive flat ground and a more indented and reclamation-friendly shoreline than Hong Kong Island's, plus by this time a government more experienced in reclamation and leasehold development, some things were different. Reclamation was more in patches than strips. Grids tended to be more extensive and regular. And in terms of economic activity, more space-gobbling industries, such as shipbuilding, engineering, power plants and cement works, although not absent from the Island, found it easier to find suitable land north of the harbour. Further, almost all the reclamation was done by the private sector on leasehold marine lots that were laid out to government specifications: similarly, much of the road building came from leaseholders building half the width of the roads adjacent to their properties. In this process, the once curvaceous coastline succumbed quickly to the surveyor's straight edge to take sharp angular forms.

Yet again, it was familiar but marginally more capacious, street-aligned shop-houses that filled the new and slightly more generous grid blocks to form somewhat more spacious and generally more regular streets – following from government survey and its 1902 Public Health and Buildings Act. The common street experience was of three- and four-storey shoulder-to-shoulder shop-houses (occasionally lower and higher) incorporating colonnades that flanked streets more or less continuously. While 40 m or thereabouts seems to be a typical width for a street block, length varies enormously from 40 m to almost 200 m, although blocks usually included service lanes. However, while external space standards were greater than in old Victoria, the cubicle remained the common internal living condition with occupancy rates remaining much the same. In other words, Kowloon's districts were only marginally more spacious variations on Victorian themes. Also, the internal uses of the shop-houses were no less mixed with buildings packed with commercial activities, family industry and domestic living (which, for many, amounted to little more than sleeping and storage).

By World War I, Tsim Sha Tsui and particularly Yau Ma Tei had begun to take shape, with a military district, Whitfield Barracks, separating the two. The inter-war years saw these areas consolidate. The earlier cited 1924 visitors' guidebook notes that buses had started to run to what were regarded as 'outlying centres – Hunghom, Old Kowloon City, Yaumati and Shamshuipo' and observes that these districts were 'rapidly merging into one big centre' with further prognostication that 'soon the whole peninsula will have become a vast, well-laid out city' (Kelly and Walch Ltd, 1924). These districts lay between just 2 to 4 kilometres from Tsim Sha Tsui. In fact Tsim Sha Tsui, Yau Ma Tei, Mong Kok, Tai Kok Tsui and Sham Shui Po were soon to make a more or less contiguous band of densely built-up shop-house districts, strung together by the famous Nathan Road. The road was in place within four years of Kowloon's settlement and quickly evolved into a tree-lined boulevard. It was extended after the New Territories were acquired to become the Peninsula's structural spine and central movement. However, in early life it was not appreciated as a piece of insightful infrastructure, earning the nickname of 'Nathan's Folly': but with its Cheung Sha Wan Road extension, it came to connect all the above-named and other lesser districts over a distance of more than 4 kilometres. These east side districts dominated the Peninsula: they were closest in travel time to the densest and administratively and commercially important centres of Victoria. From there, ferry crossings were at their shortest and significantly within sight of the 'mother' city: while reclamation presented few problems.

Thus, Kowloon's structure also tended to be linear, but shorter and fatter than its Victoria counterpart, as reclamation advanced westward towards Stonecutters Island. Today, it is hard to appreciate just how much Kowloon was a series of elongated waterside grid block districts when the Japanese invaded in 1941, given the amount of reclamation that has taken place since. The main built-up area ranged at that time between 300 m and 600 m in girth and about 4.5 km in length, or between five and ten short blocks wide but over thirty long blocks long, although slightly uneven in their continuity.

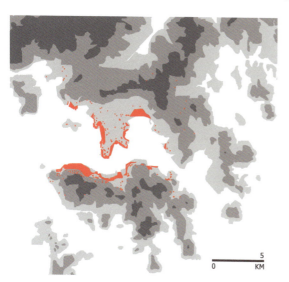

**3.21.** Urban settlement on Hong Kong Island and Kowloon Peninsula, 1924. From Victoria, urban development extended and consolidated in the new century eastwards and northwards beyond military-occupied 'voids' on the Island and Peninsula respectively: at this stage, both extensions are linear (along the coastline) and of similar size.

## Cross-Harbour City: Victoria-Kowloon

For the combined city of Victoria-Kowloon, the life blood was the harbour and its thousands of boats that ferried things and people between the two halves. While boats had crossed the harbour since before the British moved into Kowloon, the first regular cross-harbour ferry (the Star Ferry) started in 1880. Licensing of ferries commenced in 1918, with the first franchise awarded to the Hong Kong-Yaumati Ferry Company (later Hong Kong Ferries) in 1923. For the ferry companies, the 1920s and 1930s were decades of rapid expansion with key terminals at Sheung Wan, Central, Wan Chai and North Point on Hong Kong Island, and at Tsim Sha Tsui, Yua Ma Tei and Sham Tsui Po on the Peninsula, plus lesser ones elsewhere. Like the trams, they quickly became double (and later triple) decked people movers across what was probably the world's busiest harbour.

On land, rickshaws remained strong until World War II, although the 1920s saw the appearance of buses. These became more significant in the 1930s particularly in and beyond Kowloon, where there were no trams and more space for them to move, and longer distances between ferries and settled areas. On Hong Kong Island, they also played an increasing role within and particularly beyond Victoria. The first services started in the early 1920s, and were regularized through a tender system in 1933 when there were fifty-nine buses on Hong Kong Island and 115 in Kowloon and the New Territories. Through the depressed 1930s, growth was not significant, and stagnated completely when most vehicles were seized for military use during the Japanese occupation. The long haul single-track Kowloon-Canton railway served in a limited way also as a local line, stimulating some settlement in the New Territories, especially around the stations at Sha Tin, Tai Po Market and Fanling from 1910 and Sheung Shui from 1930. Thus, while ferries and trains carried people to and from Kowloon, rickshaws and buses supplemented these to provide transport within the city itself: unlike on Hong Kong Island, there was little place for the sedan chair on this relatively flat and further flattened surface.

World War II and the years following saw dramatic changes in population. For the first time since British colonialization, Hong Kong's population plummeted following the Japanese invasion in 1941. There was also massive destruction and neglect of its building stock and

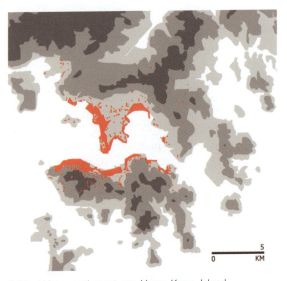

**3.22.** Urban settlement on Hong Kong Island and Kowloon Peninsula, 1945. The most notable expansions (compare with the 1924 map) are to the west of Causeway Bay at North Point and Quarry Bay on the Island and to the north and west of Yau Ma Tei (at Mong Kok and Sham Shui Po) on the Peninsula. Kowloon was growing fast. In the period before the Japanese invasion (1941), Kowloon's population was more than half a million and closing in on that of the Island's urban areas. With the invasion, Hong Kong's total population plummeted by over a million but within two years of the War's end, the increase exceeded loss.

urban infrastructure. But after the restoration of British rule, it rose again – even faster than it had fallen, reinforced by a massive influx of refugees fleeing a China experiencing revolutionary unrest. In the two years between 1941 and 1943, the exodus involved over one million people with the population dropping by over two-thirds from 1.64 million to just half a million. But after the Japanese surrender in 1945, it jumped by 1.3 million in a similar two-year period to 1.8 million in 1947.

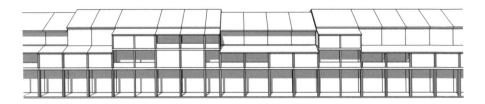

**3.23.** Shop-house street edge. This shows the basic form of an older street edge – with colonnade and balconies, many of which were 'reclaimed' as indoor living, working or storage space. By the time of the Japanese occupation (1941), most streets, especially those on reclaimed land, were lined with three- and four-storey (sometimes higher) shop-houses. However, their demise was rapid in the years following 1950.

In the same year, according to figures either given by or calculated from Hopkins (1972), Hong Kong's 'primarily domestic' buildings numbered 22,716, and averaged 3.2 storeys in height, with 'Chinese tenement type' buildings (Chinese shop-houses or very similar buildings) comprising 93 per cent of the total. Two years later, this had risen to 24,621, with an average of 3.4 floors, and 90 per cent shop-houses. Thus around 1950, shop-houses were still growing in absolute numbers but slipping slightly as a proportion of all domestic buildings. Nevertheless, Hong Kong-Kowloon remained a city of shop-houses that rose typically to three and four storeys.

For the fifteen years after 1951, each five-year period brought an average increase of half-a-million inhabitants. Altogether, the staggering post-war increases were of a scale to which no government could have responded with adequate new housing and infrastructure. In the circumstances, squatter settlements mushroomed mostly on the city's margins on higher slopes. However, while tending to occupy higher levels, squatter structures (rather than dwellings for there were also industrial and agricultural squatters) were themselves 'squat' – that is, mostly single and occasionally two storeys. By 1949, there were already 300,000 squatters in Hong Kong, a number that would rise in most years through the 1950s with large settlements on the immediate fringes of Victoria and, especially, Kowloon. It was not only on hillsides that squatter buildings appeared in high places: tens of thousands of Hong Kong people lived in illegal dwellings on the roofs of city buildings, mostly shop-houses. While some were more in the form of extensions, most were more like new buildings on new ground. In other words, roofs had joined filled sea and swamp as a widespread form of artificial ground: in some cases, entire street blocks would serve more or less as a 'second ground': it was reclamation from air rather than sea.

For more than a century a single multi-level typology housing mixed uses had constituted the city's most prevalent building component – the shop-house. Though generally built up to only four storeys, because of Victoria's steep site and the way most buildings were subdivided volumetrically (including cocklofts) and extended with roof dwellings, existence in the city was more of a multi-level experience than most other urban places. The shop-house typology together with grander commercial and institutional buildings, *godowns* and factories came to cluster in a string of dense urban districts traversed by a handful of global roads paralleling two totally artificial shorelines. The Island's slim-line city stretched east–west along the 13 km tram route, and the Peninsula's city ran north–south, along the shorter Nathan Road: one was extremely linear in form, the other more moderately so. The two were connected from points along

**3.24.** Shop-house, 1940. The shop-house can still be seen, singly and in groups, on Hong Kong Island and Kowloon Peninsula but they are quite rare. This four-storey 1940 building, complete with colonnade and open balconies, stands in Hong Kong's Central district – a reminder of the century-long period through which the typology came to dominate the city's urban fabric.

their lengths by a mesh of cross-harbour ferry routes. In the city's congested spaces, most movement was of necessity either pedestrian or pedal-powered. (The latter refers to the trishaw, a tricycle-and-rickshaw hybrid, which had been added to the list of vehicle types.) The engine-powered vehicles of the public transport system were, like the city itself, squeezed and multi-deck whether tram, ferry or part of the emerging bus system. And immediately beyond the official city were the unofficial fringe squatter towns, which were more often than not on elevated ground with good views, a paucity of infrastructure services and with densities measured in thousands per hectare. Just as roof dwellings had a symbiotic relationship with their host buildings, so squatter settlements bore a similar relationship to the city.

**3.25**. The tallest commercial building in Hong Kong at the time of World War II was the Hong Kong and Shanghai Bank built in 1934. At thirteen storeys and 70 m, it stood literally head and shoulders (given its form) above the mostly classically styled nearby buildings of four to eight storeys. This photograph was taken in the 1950s and, on the right of the picture, the Bank of China can also be glimpsed: the latter was completed sixteen years later in 1950 to include seventeen floors and stand 76 m high. It too remained Hong Kong's highest building for another sixteen years, during which time the city 'massed' considerably.

To describe Victoria-Kowloon at any stage through the first half of the twentieth century as a 'compact city' would be an understatement. It was much more: ultra-concentrated urbanism where gross densities of 500 persons per hectare were considered to be moderate, 2,000 common-place, and 4,000 no freak incident. To describe it (especially Victoria) as a 'linear city' is also no exaggeration. And given the nature of the subdivided shop-houses on steeply rising sites, it was to an extent a 'volumetric' city. It was against this background that Hong Kong was to experience even greater population pressures in the decades following World War II with huge influxes of refugees from China. This prompted, for the first time, substantial changes to building regulations and an urban and housing policy, which in turn brought fundamental changes to Hong Kong's building typologies and overall urban morphology – different but even denser. Further, this included expansion into new areas, especially to the east and west of Kowloon and even beyond the once intimidating dragon peaks.

◆ ◆ ◆ ◆

POSTSCRIPT: The Owen Appendage

Thus far, the humble shop-house has featured prominently as a key typology in Hong Kong's urban development, appearing in both this chapter and in Chapter 2. If the various references to it are pieced together, there is a consistent story of minor changes in form, each following from government legislation driven mostly by health and safety fears. The more noteworthy legislative contributions to this incremental process of change occurred in 1856, 1878, 1902 and 1935 (see pp. 46, 53 and 55). This final year also saw the establishment of a wide-ranging enquiry on the Colony's housing conditions, with a particular focus on overcrowding and tuberculosis, from a Commission appointed by the Governor, Sir William Peel. In the resulting Report of the Housing Commission, delivered in 1938, one part is of particular interest here: an appended technical memorandum by Mr W.H. Owen, ARIBA. In this, he indicated, with plans and sections, how the Hong Kong 'tenement building' (alias shop-house) had evolved over the Colony's eight decades of existence. While never departing from its basic form and the standard fir pole width (16 feet or 4.9 m), the shop-house had progressively become shallower in depth and made small gains in the provision of plumbing and cooking facilities, and of yards or light wells, the latter being means to improve light and ventilation. In addition, the '5 foot' passageway as a colonnade along the street beneath balconies had become almost standard, at least on the city's flat streets.

The Owen appendage was however not simply a retrospective study, for the past was merely the pathway to understanding Hong Kong's condition of the time. The document moved from past through contemporary examples of shop-houses to proposals for the future. In fact, drawings from the Owen appendage have already been used in this chapter to illustrate the kind of shop-house that followed from the 1902 legislation (see figure 3.19). In figure 3.26 there is an illustration of the type of shop-house that was being built at the time of his writing.

In this 'latest development', labelled 'Type A' in Owen's document, the ground floor shows a colonnade (the 5 foot way), a shop, cockloft towards the rear with its own staircase, and a staircase springing from the front of the shop leading to the first floor: a store and kitchen and separate latrine are divided from the main building by a small yard, which is almost one-third of the area of the lot. Each of the three upper floors shows a balcony, a large room divided into four cubicles (although the front cubicle is termed 'room' in the plan), and a kitchen and latrine detached from the main house and accessed by a bridge. The removal of the kitchen from the main living block and the provision of upper floor latrines is the incremental improvement over the early twentieth-century model in figure 3.27. In

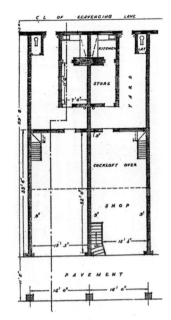

GROUND FLOOR PLANS

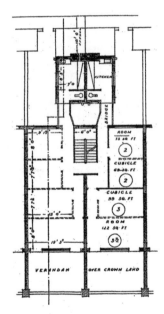

UPPER FLOOR PLANS

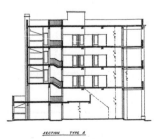

SECTION TYPE A

3.26. Typical shop-house design at the time of Owen's writing: ground floor plans (*top*), upper floor plans (*middle*), and section (*bottom*).

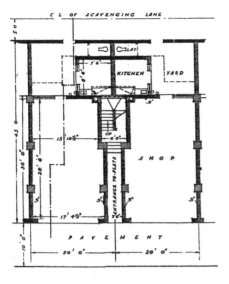

GROUND  FLOOR  PLAN.

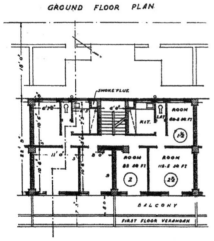

UPPER  FLOOR  PLANS

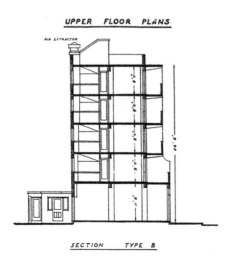

SECTION  TYPE  B

addition, the stairs to the upper floors are not above those leading to the first floor but form a compact stack of return stairs at the rear of the building.

These drawings show that the upper floors are different in kind from the ground floor, implying a stronger (conceptual) differentiation between ground and above, with commercial activity at ground level beneath layers of residential occupancy. The ground floor is clearly marked 'shop' and each of the upper floors as accommodating $10\frac{1}{2}$ people per floor (presumably half representing a child), giving a total lot residential population of $31\frac{1}{2}$ (assuming the 'cockloft' or mezzanine within the ground level volume is commercial). Owen also indicates that a bathroom might occasionally be included, that a shower might be more efficient with water than a bath and could be collocated with a squat toilet in a small room, and that Hong Kong had eight public bath-houses. There were also private bath-houses in the city although these are not mentioned.

Owen's most significant contribution is, however, his model for the future, which is a distinct departure from the traditional shop-house plan, while arising very much out of the shop-house experience. Consistent with this tradition, the plan shows two shops at the ground floor: but these are separated from each other by a central corridor leading to a rear staircase, which in turn leads to four residential upper floors. To the rear at ground level, there are two kitchens and latrines as an extension to the main building but accessed via the rear yards. At the upper levels, the rear staircase gives access to a corridor, which is parallel to the street and leads to six separate rooms – flats rather than cubicles with shared facilities. On each side of the staircase is a kitchen and latrine. Also, there

**3.27.** Owen's proposed model: ground floor plan (*top*), upper floor plan (*middle*) and section (*bottom*).

is access to the flat roof. This model is premised on a widened building footprint (two building lots, each 20 feet wide, which is slightly wider than two old lots) and concrete construction (with some floor spans exceeding the dimension of the old fir pole joist). Nevertheless, he keeps the same building height and manages to squeeze in one shop and four residential levels above the shop, within a height that previously contained one shop including rear cockloft, and three residential levels above.

While noting that his proposal did not conform to the prevailing by-laws, he asserted several potential advantages over previous types: lower construction costs; lower rental costs per residential unit; increased shop area; better serviced accommodation; improved lighting and ventilation; and higher overall income from the building. The building would also have offered greater privacy. The estimated occupancy rate across the six rooms per floor was twelve people: thus with four residential floors the total population would have been forty-eight.

The configuration of the upper floors and the use of the central stair suggest that this design draws on Owen's knowledge of house design in England. In separating shop from dwellings, and in making each floor independent of one another and accessible by way of a central staircase, he represents the first official step in transforming the shop-house into a flat or apartment building. The deep and narrow plans between party walls of previous models prevented an internal division of space into anything other than cubicles: these also favoured open stairs at right angles to the street – altogether a more volumetric spatial composition. At the same time, the provision of the open-fronted shop at the ground level is a direct continuation of the shop-house.

The appendage and model captured the attention of Patrick Abercrombie who referred to the 'outstanding value' of Mr Owen's lengthy technical Memorandum in his post World War II report on the Colony's planning: the Hong Kong Preliminary Planning Report 1948. In other words, Abercrombie validated and reinforced Owen's proposal and it would seem that many post-war buildings, both pre- and post-1956 legislation, and the 1956 legislation itself were at least influenced by the proposal and Abercrombie's stamp of support, even though most buildings included only some of the proposed components and principles. For instance the building shown in figure 3.18, c.1950, has a centralized staircase accessed from the street and kitchen/toilet facilities

**3.28.** A flat-fronted variation on the shop-house theme, c.1950. (See also figure 2.18 for photograph of this building.)

0    8

4    METRES

projecting from the back but maintains an arrangement more akin to cubicles within.

Although Owen's proposed new housing appeared only as a technical memorandum appended to a commissioned report, in our view it represents a significant moment in the evolution of Hong Kong's built form. First, it demonstrates official recognition of the significance of the shop-house in Hong Kong. As Abercrombie wrote 'It would be pedantic for the planner to condemn the practice which obtains in Hong Kong (and is indeed common in the East) of giving up the entire ground floor of the residential area to shops, workshops, warehouses, stores, etc. There appears to be a demand for this continuous bazaar on the groundfloor...' (Abercrombie, 1948). More important, it 'roots' the next chapter's 'massing' phase of development in the shop-house tradition, while sowing the seeds of more vertical arrangements in which separated and layered functions emerge. It thus heralds the precedence of a more layered and compartmentalized vertical arrangement of space and activity over a more volumetric and mixed one.

# 4 Massing and Rising

## The Post-War Decades

### Refugees and Tumbling Trade

In the late 1930s Japanese occupation of China advanced closer to Hong Kong. By 1939, it had reached neighbouring Guangzhou, which triggered hundreds of thousands to flee the province and other areas into Hong Kong. From 1936 to 1941, the Colony's population rose steeply from less than a million to over 1.6 million. In the latter year, Japan invaded and occupied Hong Kong, and people fled the place in even greater numbers than they had arrived over the previous years: there were also deportations and deaths, and the population plummeted to around a half-million by 1943. Following the surrender of the Japanese in 1945, British rule was restored to the Colony and many former Chinese residents returned plus more refugees. By 1947, the population had more than tripled, to 1.8 million, but Hong

Kong's infrastructure and building stock was hopelessly depleted (see Cuthbert, 1998 and Leeds, 1998). In the years following the Chinese Revolution (1949), Hong Kong was again inundated with refugees, and the inflow continued for many years. From 1951 to 1966, each five-year period brought an average increase of half-a-million inhabitants. Altogether, these are staggering numbers, and it is hard to imagine any government coping with the demands for housing and infrastructure.

The result was a mushrooming of squatter settlements mostly on the city's margins between sea level and 300 m, but with concentrations on steeper land towards 200 m (Wong, 1978a). However, while squatter buildings tended to occupy the higher ground, they were themselves 'squat' – that is, mostly single storey. By 1950, there were probably 300,000 squatters, possibly 330,000, in Hong Kong (Rooney, 2003), a number that would rise in most years through the 1950s with substantial settlements, including squatter industries and services, on the fringes of Victoria but mostly Kowloon. At times, it was estimated that some 25 per cent of Hong Kong's population was living in such informal settlements. But it was not only on high hills that squatter buildings appeared in high places: in 1961, some 55–60,000 Hong Kong people were believed to be living in illegal dwellings on the roofs of city buildings (Leeming, 1977), mostly above shop-houses. While some structures may have been more in the form of building extensions, many were more like new buildings on new ground. In effect, the roof level became an informal reclamation project, and in some cases, entire street blocks would serve more or less as 'second ground'. Under the immense population pressures, Hong Kong people were effectively reclaiming ground from the air, or at least roofs, while the government reclaimed the sea.

However, while the years of maximum refugee arrivals and squatter numbers show some correlation, it should not be assumed that most squatters were directly from the ranks of newly arrived refugees. The dynamics of squatter residency were much more complex. While the sheer number of refugees clearly stretched Hong Kong's limited resources, the squatters were all sorts: homeless from natural disasters; the victims of demolition of dangerous structures, usually old shop-houses; tenants evicted by landowners embarking on rebuilding projects; people leaving congested tenements by choice; and more. Further, squatters were not necessarily in the category of extreme poverty, with the squatter towns often places of enterprise and industry. In short, squatter settlements formed a parallel and variant form of urbanism.

The rapid population influx affected the formal as well as squatter cities and occupation of many legal buildings reached saturation point. In 1957, the University of Hong Kong conducted an extensive survey which found that half of Hong Kong's inhabitants were living in cubicles. It showed that some 118,000 tenement floors were shared by 1.265 million people: each floor supported an average of 2.26 households, and each household averaged 4.7 people. There was an occupancy rate of eleven people per floor. Further, 70 per cent of all households lived in less than 11.15 m² of floor space (Maunder and Szczepanik, 1958; see also Maunder, 1969 and Pryor, 1972). These were certainly crowded conditions by any measure but the question remains of how overcrowded, as the concept of overcrowding is a relative one and related to context, especially the culture.

The influx of refugees was not the only effect of China's political transformation. The latter had twin effects on the tiny colony's economy: one devastating, the other invigorating. Hong Kong became more isolated, with its traditional role as a trading base between China and the rest of the world much reduced, as China shifted its trading preferences towards Russia and Eastern Europe. Further, the Korean War brought a further reduction in trade as the United Nations imposed embargoes on Chinese trade covering a great range of items considered to be of strategic importance. Since Hong Kong's *raison d'être* was trade, this seriously undermined the economy: the Colony had to manufacture a new role; and it was to manufacturing that it turned. The exodus from China brought into Hong Kong many businessmen experienced in industry, and within a relatively short time, the city-state became, with little exaggeration, a miracle of manufacturing. While pre-war Hong Kong is always remembered as the great *entrepôt*, the post-war city will be remembered as the great factory city.

As early as 1846 the first Governor, Sir John Davies, wrote: 'A large number of Chinese are employed in their respective shops and houses in the exercise of industrial trades and manufactures' (quoted in Leeming, 1977). Industry had not been very visible in the city as it was mainly in the form of 'cottage industry', except that the host buildings were not cottages but very often shop-house cubicles. Over a century later, in the 1950s, this old style industry expanded and was joined also by substantial factory production, which brought new building types to the city. These were most conspicuous on Kowloon Peninsula and to its north-east/east and north-west/west (New Kowloon), and towards each end of Victoria. However, through the 1950s, most industrial production remained in small factories within and at the edges of the city's established mixed-use districts, and often in shop-houses themselves – in Kowloon, this meant particularly from Yau Ma Tei towards the newly reclaimed land of Cheung Sha Wan. Classed, in the language of the times, as a *Newly Industrializing Country* or *NIC,* Hong Kong built up its export-oriented manufacturing.

Urban development in this period of instability tended towards four 'natural' courses:

◆   rapid redevelopment and intensification of places already built-up;

◆   development that extended existing areas – this occurred on both sides of the harbour but was particularly prevalent on the Kowloon Peninsula and beyond, and at the east and west ends of the linear city centred on Victoria;

◆   proliferation of squatter settlements on vacant city ground but mostly on the hill slopes immediately beyond the existing cities; and

 • informal additions (roof huts, etc) to existing city structures, whose collective population equated numerically with a substantial provincial town.

The first two constituted the 'regulated' or 'official' city and the last two the 'informal' city. All were dense. All were mixed use, usually including some manufacturing. And all lay within the broad sweep of land and water between the range of peaks that forms the backdrop to Victoria in the south and the Lion Rock Ridge behind Kowloon to the north. The main exception to this generalized description was the limited manufacturing that was jumping the city's edges to settle in the nearest outlying villages – mostly in the towns we now know as Kwun Tong and Tsuen Wan, although these became significant urban areas only in the 1960s.

**4.1.** Looking over Wanchai to Causeway Bay from 'the Peak' in the late 1950s. In Wanchai, rows of dense residential and commercial buildings occupy regular blocks on reclaimed land between hill and harbour. Around Causeway Bay are more massive buildings. Well-spaced villas can be seen on the lower part of the foreground hill: this contrasts with the distant hill, beyond Causeway Bay, which is packed with squatter dwellings.

Government responses to this rather complex and unstable situation were mainly as follows:

 • a massive resettlement scheme for squatters;

 • public housing programmes for the poorer segments of society; and

 • new building codes to encourage even more intensive redevelopment and, in turn, greater living densities.

These initiatives had some spectacular and sometimes notorious results. Squatter resettlement introduced radical new urban and building typologies to the Colony – but in structures that supported densities equal to the squatter huts that they replaced, mostly at the cities' fringes. Squatter densities usually resulted in little more than 2 square metres of land per person and the early replacement housing maintained such densities. The code changes brought a quantum leap in the height and mass of buildings – and an increase in the density of building and people on existing city blocks. And the public housing schemes of the period also contributed to the high density tradition. It was this period that brought about the widespread hyper-densities (measured in thousands per hectare) that prompted the writings of the earlier discussed Schmidt and Prescott (see pp. 8–11).

## Rising from the Ashes: H-Blocks and a Culture of Congestion

Apart from several scattered areas of squatters on the Kowloon Peninsula and across the south coast of Hong Kong Island (especially in the vicinity of Aberdeen), the main groups of squatter settlements sprouted in two places: across the foothills of the Lion Rock Ridge to the north of Kowloon (including the earlier mentioned Kowloon Walled City) and on the hills behind that narrow belt of urban settlement that follows the western half of Victoria's tram line from Causeway Bay to Shau Kei Wan. Their one- and two-storey buildings were assembled from a wide variety of salvaged materials to step, cheek-by-jowl, up the hillsides in *ad hoc* group forms. In their many thousands, they were initially mostly devoid of infrastructure, including sanitary services. There followed, through government provision, minimal facilities: for instance, one standpipe per 500 people, from which the community would collect their water, and latrines and bathing facilities at one per 100. Although low in profile, they were remarkably dense and extremely hazard-prone, particularly to fire and land slides. Disasters were frequent, but one is remembered more than all others – both for its size and effect on government policy. It occurred at Shep Kip Mei on Christmas Eve in 1953, when 53,000 people lost their homes in a single night. A human tragedy of immense proportion, it was imperative that accommodation be provided – as much and as soon as possible. The extent of the influence of this particular fire on resettlement and housing policy is a complex subject and may have been overestimated, which is a view expressed in Smart's searching investigation, *The Shek Kip Mei Myth: Squatters, Fires and Colonial Rule 1950–63* (Smart, 2006).

While the Hong Kong government had previously given some legitimacy and services to some squatter settlements, the government's first step into resettlement housing was a pilot scheme of eight six-storey buildings on the site of the fire that raged through the Shek Kip Mei township. Squatter densities had been high – up to 4,900 persons per hectare in mostly single-storey huts, giving barely 2 square metres of ground per person. The authorities were intent on redeveloping 'only squatter occupied land and Crown Land within the urban area' (Will, 1978) and in the new development, the space standard was set at 2.2 $m^2$ per person. Thus, for instance, eight six-storey blocks with sixty units per floor housing at least five persons per room would support a population of approximately 15,000. This

**4.2.** Squatter settlements such as this housed both refugees and Hong Kong residents.

is significant for at least two reasons: it was the Hong Kong government's first major step into public housing; and it employed building types that continued the practice of high-density living in structures of modest (six storeys) height. Further, the new building occurred within the landscape bounded by the hills that gave visible containment to Victoria and Kowloon.

The earliest building type is a fascinating and memorable form. It was a block with an H-shaped plan and rose through six or seven storeys. It had continuous perimeter balconies giving access to strings of back-to-back single-room dwellings that shared communal toilets and washing facilities on the connecting cross of the H. The individual units were in many respects similar to the former shop-house cubicles but with direct access onto a balcony corridor allowing for public access. The first 'Mark I' type blocks were completed in 1954. Mark II types followed between 1961 and 1964 but offered only minor variations: they were extended upwards to include an extra level (making seven storeys) and the gaps at the two ends of the H-blocks were in-filled with stairways.

Early blocks were intended to be residential on all levels. But it was realized quickly that the ground level would better serve as shops, and that some home-based light or cottage industry would need to be tolerated at higher levels. An example would have been the assembly of plastic goods such as imitation flowers. In addition, much-needed schools were sited on the roofs of blocks, although with some reluctance on the part of the authorities: thus, the schools and play spaces shared the roof at the seventh or eighth levels. Some of the industries in the residential units proved either too noisy or noxious and had to be controlled: the government's response was to build similarly shaped but more spacious five-storey blocks for small-scale industrial activities, with access by stairs and ramps, and space that could be rented by one or more small modules. The first of these flatted factories appeared in Cheung Sha Wan, a Kowloon extension, in 1957 – just three years after their residential cousins. Although the ground floors of the residential H-blocks were given over to shops, itinerant hawkers swelled the trader ranks in all available space around the blocks, which also brought an accommodating government response: in 1958, it constructed extensive market shelters beneath which hawking could occur.

Through the later 1950s and early 1960s, scores of these blocks were built. Twelve re-settlement estates were completed by 1959, the biggest being at Wong Tai Sin below Sz Tsz Shan (Temple Hill) in North Kowloon with twenty-nine blocks, equating to 67,000 residents. They rose on many other hill slopes below the Lion Rock Ridge and elsewhere, transforming landscapes from contour-following squatter settlements to contour-dominating resettlement H-blocks, on land which was harshly re-shaped into stepped platforms, and with forms designed without reference to relief.

The government's actions were cautious, mostly reacting to pressures rather than anticipating and innovating with foresight. First, it built within the existing built-up area and perpetuated the familiar cubicle-like spaces. Then it reluctantly allowed, and even facilitated, the shopping and industrial activities to occupy the places to which these naturally gravitated, and allowed the schools onto the vacant highest levels.

Yet in conceding pragmatically to the pressures of the day, it created a radical new form of urbanism. In the Mark I and II residential and first-generation factory blocks, there was a unique meeting of the cubicled Chinese shop-house with the Modernist structure-in-space. There were also shades of Le Corbusier's community facilities at ground and roof levels with the latter as a second ground. Further access to each unit was external and

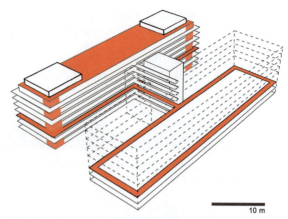

**4.3.** Re-settlement residential H-block showing circulation. Note: the diagram shows typical perimeter circulation for one floor only though this was repeated on all floors.

**4.4.** A street lined with resettlement Mark 1 H-blocks. It shows seven levels of perimeter access, including ground, and 'sky schools' just visible on the roof.

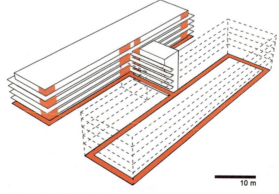

**4.5.** Industrial H-blocks: these were modelled on the residential blocks but were larger and with fewer levels.

visible: each H-block was actually a pair of parallel slab blocks with perimeter deck-access but joined at their centres by a service bridge: altogether, there were four points of access. Thus for multi-storey structures, they were well connected within themselves and to the wider district.

With little or no theory and a great deal of pragmatism, the shop-house had been transformed (a kind of inversion) from a traditional to Modernist form. The traditional street had evaporated according to the Corbusian gospel, but the congestion associated with the street replaced Corbusian verdure in the space between buildings. The result was dense living incorporating shopping, industry, markets, schools and play areas in new building types through seven or eight levels, with open public access. For all its limitations it was a city of multiple grounds, multiple uses and enormous vitality. It was intense urbanism of a kind that Modernist visions had never quite anticipated – with some irony, a Modernist 'culture of congestion', to borrow a Koolhaas term.

**4.6.** H-blocks: commercial activity occupies ground level and percolates to higher levels.

**4.7.** Between the H-blocks: spaces filled with hawkers' stalls.

Further, small single-space homes demanded initiatives from their occupants to use the volume as efficiently as possible. Tables and chairs were, for example, often of the fold-up variety, and folding or sliding doors would substitute for the more space consuming hinged swing type. Bunks would be built three decks high and each level provided with a reading light, a projecting storage shelf and curtains, effectively turning a sleeping platform into a micro living space. Bird cages, drying racks and other paraphernalia would be suspended from the ceiling and slim-line cabinets would stand tall against the walls. These and other volumetric strategies in space use migrated from the cubicles of the old shop-houses: they were also much in evidence in the Kowloon Walled City and remain a part of Hong Kong life. Many examples are presented sympathetically in Rooney's (2003) documentation of the use of small spaces by occupants of Hong Kong's government housing units: though published in 2003, her studies commenced in 1992 and involved spaces dating from the early years of public housing.

## Public Housing Reforms: Slab Blocks

Mark III buildings, introduced in 1961 (alongside the Mark II type H-block) were completely different from the earlier resettlement typologies. These were slab blocks with parallel rows of dwelling units accessed from a central internal corridor, with each unit having its own balcony: these stood at eight storeys and usually in L-shaped blocks. In 1965, this configuration was doubled in height to sixteen stories, given lift-access and extended into E-shaped blocks, as the Mark IV model. Two more Marks followed but with only slight variations: more varied room sizes and more space per inhabitant (Marks V and VI respectively). However, some basic features characterized all these later Mark types: they were composed essentially of slab blocks joined at right angles or staggered linearly to result in forms that were markedly more conventional, and with essentially private access. They were more conspicuous figures in a landscape, sitting on stepped hillsides with plans that conform to Maki's 'compositional' form whereby individual buildings are 'composed' on a two-dimensional surface as in a Mondrian painting (Maki, 1964). Officially, at least, they were no longer mixed use, and their central internal corridor access and absence of commercial facilities at ground level would have deterred, if not eliminated, non-residential uses.

Before the Shep Kip Mei disaster, the Hong Kong government had shown scant interest in public housing. But as the first resettlement schemes were being planned, it took on a broader role as a housing provider by establishing the semi-independent Hong Kong Housing Authority to provide low-income housing. In the programmes that followed, the early building and estate forms, and their locations are of interest here, for they bring a substantial new form to Hong

**4.8.** Phase 2 resettlement housing took a very different form. Flats in each slab were accessed from a central corridor. This internalized circulation, increased the management's control of space and reduced opportunities for other than residential occupation. This, together with the estates' 'compositional' plan form, introduced a more sanitized atmosphere.

Kong's urban landscape; and this appears to influence later resettlement housing types (Mark III and later). They consisted generally of slab blocks, rising up to twenty storeys, placed in angular, often rectilinear, formations. Blocks would have elevators, central corridor access, and were intended as single-use residential buildings. Facilities were more extensive and space standards more generous than in resettlement housing: for instance, they included, kitchen, bathroom and balcony and the space allocation was almost double with 3.9 m² per person. However, they were essentially single use, and with more restricted access than their Mark I and II resettlement counterparts. They were a more conventional product of international Modernism. The earliest example of direct public building was North Point Estate on Hong Kong Island, completed in 1958: those that followed included the So Uk, Choi Hung and Wah Fu estates of 30,000, 40,000 and 60,000 inhabitants respectively.

## New Regulations: More Mass and Cantilevers

Given the enormity of the housing need, another response was to change the regulatory framework to allow for far greater floor area and building mass on any given site. Private developers were then able to provide more accommodation on existing and new lots. A consequence of the new Building Ordinance of 1956 was a marked jump in building height with the limit doubling from the previous 70–80 ft (21.3–24.4 m): in certain circumstances, plot ratios of between 18:1 and 20:1 were possible, almost certainly the highest in the world (Cuthbert, 1998, p. 42). Buildings were allowed to rise through nine storeys devoid of lifts. There were some restrictions that required upper floors to step back according to the width of the adjacent street in order to ensure some measure of light at street level, and for some indentation of walls or provision of light-wells to ensure that rooms gained a minimum level of access to natural light and outside air. But whatever the site, the new ordinances allowed the height and mass of city buildings to expand enormously. The rationale was that new building materials (particularly reinforced concrete for flooring rather than timber) were safer, lifts were becoming more affordable in high-rise construction, and (most of all) the increasingly temporary metropolis was desperate for more permanent accommodation.

As was previously the case, permit arrangements in a leasehold land system could allow buildings to project over the street: this continued although the cantilevered floor now replaced the former colonnade. Since the late 1950s and early 1960s were years of tremendously vigorous construction, buildings from this era would dominate the character of most street blocks and streets for several decades.

From this new regulation came three dominant walk-up typologies:

1.  By far the most common was a variation on the *shop-house* – a simple vertically extruded version of the traditional typology, minus the colonnaded front, with a

flat roof, and extending often across two or more blocks. This was ubiquitous, west and east of Central, and in Old and New Kowloon.

2.    *Stepped-back blocks of flats*, usually occupying two or more amalgamated standard lots along the street, and stepping away from the street at the upper levels, the start and inclination of the step-back being determined by the width of the street.

3.    *Blocks of flats with streamlined curved balconies* rose on many street corner sites.

All three types took advantage of the nine-storey height limit that did not require a lift, although types 2 and 3 would sometimes rise higher and include an elevator: but the lift was both an expensive piece of building infrastructure to install and maintain, and also a space-consuming item on small sites.

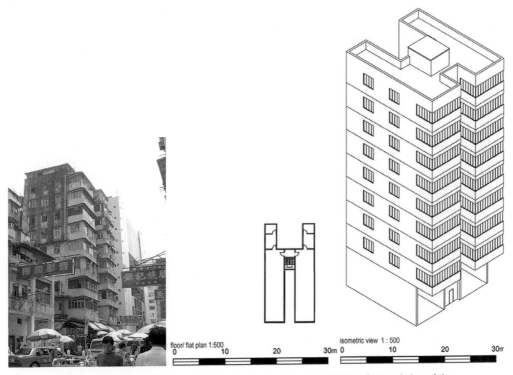

floor/ flat plan 1:500

isometric view 1 : 500

**4.9.** Cantilevered and indented. Built in 1960, this is effectively an extruded two-bay variation of the shop-house with cantilevered projections over part of the street: it is also deeply indented to satisfy light requirements and rises to the maximum allowed lift-less level of nine floors, under the 1956 regulations. Note the clear space, on a typical upper floor, facilitating division into cubicles, as in the shop-house. The photograph shows also a squatter roof-level building.

Fourthly, there was the *Massive Block* – a type that could rise well above nine storeys and therefore includes lifts: to do this, it would usually depend on a corner site, or at least a frontage onto one of the wider streets. Though some incorporated step-backs, and all had indentations of some kind (usually at the rear) to admit light and air, most put a vast flat face to two or even three street frontages to

**4.10.** A stepped-back variation on the shop-house theme (1957). The sloping façade is to allow sunlight into the street. Built on a double lot, one central entrance serves the equivalent of two six-storey shop-houses: the recess between the cantilevered projections is regulated to give light to the stairwell.

**4.11.** Cantilevered and curved. Corner buildings during the earlier part of this period were commonly curved. While the curve may have been a product of fashion, indentations and cantilevers were functional – attempts to meet light and ventilation requirements while maximizing floor area.. This building rises through three commercial and six purportedly residential to a total of nine storeys.

exert a 'massive' presence when viewed from the street, hence the nomenclature. Inside, circulation on each floor could be quite convoluted. All four types remain a common sight in the older established districts of Hong Kong and Kowloon. One feature shared by most buildings in all categories was the cantilevered floor over part of the street pavement: this offered weather protection over at least part of the sidewalk, and gave valuable additional floor area to the building above: such projections were agreed as part of the development approval process and required an additional payment.

Collectively, these building types transformed most Hong Kong streets in the building boom that followed introduction of the new codes. A major consequence of their appearance was the erosion of the colonnades that had previously given a distinctive character and rhythm to Hong Kong and Kowloon streets. These subspaces, flanked by gaping shop fronts and regular thick columns had given a very special spatial experience to the sidewalk. At the same time, higher buildings gave a more canyon-like feel to the street space. The street edge, with step-backs and indentations for light, was often less regular; and the skyline not only rose but showed greater variation. A city that had developed in the main at a modest three- and four-storey level suddenly doubled or tripled in height with higher variations on the shop-house theme, and with the step-backed and curved

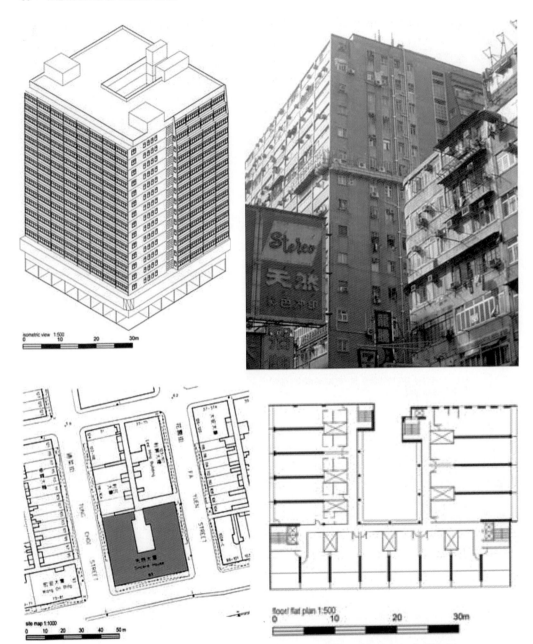

**4.12.** Massive Block (with typical upper floor plan, site plan and axonometric drawing). This large rectilinear building was amassed in 1964: it is a typical *Massive Block* of the period, built in a thick U-shape around a key-hole like light well: this one occupies an area equivalent of at least sixteen traditional shop-house sites at the end of a street block: the location is characteristic of the type.

corner building typologies to heights of six to nine storeys (plus an often quickly acquired squatter layer). And at many points, large masses protruded considerably higher – usually fifteen and twenty storeys – where the massive block took root.

At the same time, some things did not change. Most streets were not generally widened – although the absence of the colonnades could sometimes give the impression that they might have been. At street level, the flanking shops were just as teeming with activity, if not more so; for inside the higher buildings, occupants per floor area did not diminish, with the cubicle continuing as the home base for most Chinese residents. Developers would even include dotted lines on the floor plans of the new building types to make explicit to buyers and lessees their potential for subdividing into cubicles. Hence, more floors meant more people, which was the intent.

With a great intensity of building over the few years either side of 1960, the consequences of the new typologies were quickly apparent. Increased densities placed excessive pressure on the city's streets and other infrastructure (water, sewerage, power, rubbish collection, etc), as well as schools and health facilities. Further, the higher buildings were so cheek-by-jowl that problems of light and ventilation were hardly diminished. By the early 1960s, the regulations were under review.

**4.13**. Hong Kong massing: view over Yau Ma Tei towards the typhoon shelter.

## Regulation Review: More Height than Mass

In 1962, tighter regulations were mooted although these were not introduced officially for another three years. The twilight time of the relatively short-lived 1956 Ordinances saw an avalanche of building proposals for projects in established city areas, as developers rushed to take advantage of their more generous development provisions. With the new regulations, plot ratios fell substantially, and the development potential of some sites fell by over half, the plot ratio reducing in an extreme case from 18:1 to 8:1 (which was still very high). The new 1966 regulations had more variables, these responding to particular situations: there was a sliding relationship between plot ratio, building height and ground cover: with increased height and plot ratio, but reduced site cover. Open space controls varied according to the type of site, depending on whether it had one or two frontages, or was an 'island' site. Further, height continued to be related to street width, and building envelope was related to an angled calculation from the street's centre line.

Under the new regulations, one could build reasonably massively or stand tall and slim on a site but not both, and this had new effects on Hong Kong's streetscapes and skylines. However, by the then recent Hong Kong standards, their effects were slow to be experienced, as there was a slump in private building following the hasty building during the last years of the old regulations and a simultaneous banking crisis. The 31,000 domestic units that were completed in 1966 (approved mainly under the previous legislation) plummeted to about one quarter in 1968 – to less than 8,000. Thus the new ordinances had limited impact on the established urban area of the city during the 1960s.

They did, however, herald a new era, in which the podium-and-tower form, combining a large footprint at ground level, and a smaller tower 'footprint' at podium level, became the significant new typology. Initially, a podium was likely to be modest in size with a slim tower above, sometimes of pencil-like thinness, comprising just two small units per floor. While these continued, podia have expanded in mass and towers extended in height from the 1970s to this day. The larger forms are not absent from established areas but are most likely to be seen at their extreme in new towns, on newly reclaimed land with the podium adjacent to or including a railway station. The form now dominates urban development and is a *sine qua non* of Hong Kong urban life. Much more detailed coverage of this building type will follow in Chapter 6, including the introduction of the tower-and-

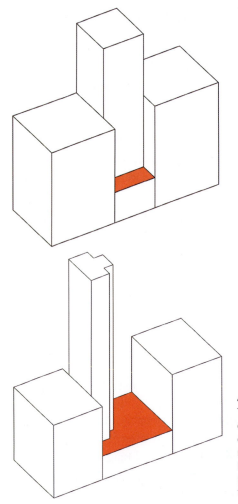

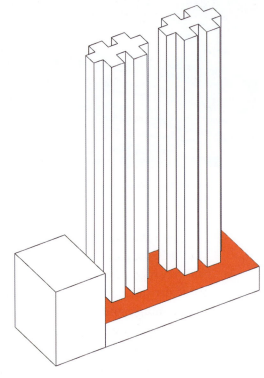

**4.14**. Small block podium + tower typologies. These appeared on amalgamated lots (2–4) within established street blocks. Squeezed between existing street-aligned buildings, the towers could rise as a stepped-back element between neighbouring buildings (upper left) or to one side of the podium (lower left) or as a free-standing element towards the podium centre (right).

**4.15.** Neighbouring small podium + tower types. To the right is a simple step-backed tower while the left-hand tower stands to one side of the podium. The building as a whole shows distinct layers of activity: towers form a distinct realm intended for residential above commercial podia, which in turn have street level shop-front and upper level office layers. However, the practice of dividing some tower flats into cubicles and using them for commercial/residential and industrial/residential purposes prevailed in early privately built towers.

podium structure to Hong Kong, which appears to have occurred in 1962, with a private sector building designed by architect, Andrew Lee King Fun.

## Change and Continuity

In Hong Kong in 1950, there stood nearly 25,000 'primarily domestic' buildings averaging three-and-a-half storeys in height. Ninety per cent of these were Chinese shop-houses, dating mostly from before World War II. A few years later came the start of the government resettlement and housing programmes and the 1956 building regulations, which were catalysts to new building forms. To give some idea of the tremendous transformation that the city underwent at this time, let us focus for a moment on 'primarily residential' buildings. In the eleven years following the new regulations (1957 to 1968), over half (52 per cent) of pre-war residential buildings was cleared to make way for new buildings. Just two years later, in 1970, 95 per cent of primarily residential buildings had resulted from post-war construction. New higher, and particularly more massive, buildings were now the dominant visual components of Hong Kong's urban landscapes. Through the late 1950s and early 1960s, higher buildings mushroomed: by 1967, some 835 primarily residential private buildings were over eight storeys and two years later (1969), there were 400 public ones as well (Hopkins, 1972, quoting A.L.C. Lu). However, it should be remembered that most of the new higher buildings had footprints that were of a far greater area than their shop-house predecessors. The impact of private housing was mainly in existing city areas, while that of public housing was more likely on the fringes.

Between the two new Building Codes, of 1956 and 1966, many two-, three- and four- storey buildings were demolished and replaced with new ones that were significantly higher. However, more significant than height was the increase in mass. Although the new buildings were higher, and some individually slender, they were not generally experienced in isolation: they were more likely to stand cheek-by-jowl across city blocks to create substantial street block mass. Within such configurations, the protruding typology of the 'massive block' may have

been distinguishable by its greater height but its profile was also dumpy: it was a case of mass by mass. The same applied whether it was a factory or dwellings, and most new factory buildings were barely distinguishable from those that were primarily residential. Further, factory units often shared space alongside dwelling units in the same buildings. At the micro-level the colonnades were disappearing from the street front to be replaced by the cantilever which was itself reminiscent of the earlier colonnade. Open fronts at ground level in both factory and residential buildings continued the traditions of the old shop-houses. Further, all of this occurred within the context of a familiar rectilinear street structure. And at the city's margins, while squatter huts were blighting the hillsides, they were not a new sight to Hong Kong: it was merely their spread that was new.

Another layer of complexity in Hong Kong's physical development was the informal additions to the 'official' or regulated city. It was common to expand living space through illegal *ad hoc* extensions in the form of enclosed balconies, protruding cages over the streets, floors inserted into light wells and roofs to cover them. As noted before, on flat roofs whole buildings rose, as if on the ground. And within buildings, holes would be cut in walls from one to the next to rid one or other of the need for its own

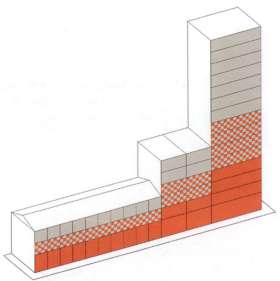

**4.16.** A one-block section of Shanghai Street (west side), Mong Kok. It consists of a row of shop-houses (1935), walk-up extruded shop-houses (1958 and 1960) and a smaller version of a massive block (1964). The red colour represents commercial (shops, commercial and professional services, and workshops) and the grey is residential: the colours are merely indicative of the mix of activities that occurred throughout the buildings with commercial dominating at lower and residential at higher levels.

The 1974 uses (based on Leeming, 1977) contained in these buildings were:

*Shop-houses*
Ground floor: Chinese and Western chemist, men's clothing and bedding, textiles, jeweller, tools and machinery, men's clothing, wedding costumes and bedding, and Chinese chemist
Upper floor uses included: Chinese doctor, workers' organization office, small factories and stores but mostly in residential cubicles.

*Extruded shop-houses*
Ground floor: Wedding costumes and bedding, brassiers, Chinese and Western chemist
Upper floors: photographer, bath-house, wig-making and knitting factories, Chinese doctor, acupuncturist, small warehouses, and residential cubicles

*Massive block*
Ground floor: two jewellers, Chinese doctor, and wines and groceries
Upper floor: offices, doctors, apartments, family residences and cubicled flats.

In total this gives at least twenty activities, which range through retailing, manufacturing, wholesale, professional and other services, plus several forms of residential living over a ground area of less than 1,400 m². This was quite typical of such street-aligned typologies at the time. The group shows the sequential increase in height and mass over three decades. The sites, which made up half a street block between a main and service street, have since been amalgamated to make way for part of the Langham Place complex discussed on pp. 105 and 128.

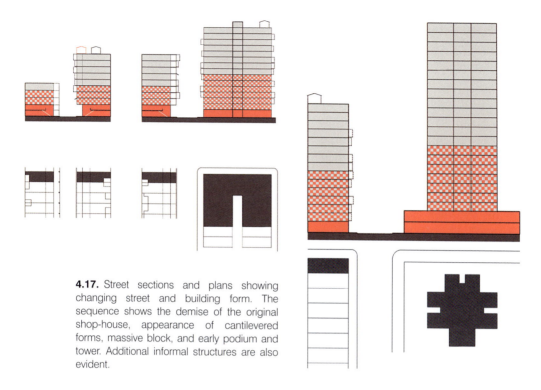

**4.17.** Street sections and plans showing changing street and building form. The sequence shows the demise of the original shop-house, appearance of cantilevered forms, massive block, and early podium and tower. Additional informal structures are also evident.

staircase, and so provide even more accommodation or storage space through the up to nine walk-up storeys. Thus movement was not only from the streets or alleys into individual buildings but between roofs and internal floors. The result was something of a three-dimensional labyrinth: such building groups showed more than shades of the earlier described Kowloon Walled City. Within the mass of a city block, there was volumetric movement.

In other words, much that was new was also familiar – variations on familiar themes. Despite rapid rebuilding, there were also strong continuities. Perhaps, the biggest change in appearance was at the margins with the government-built H-blocks and slab blocks. Yet in the former at least, there too was a strong element of continuity, for the resettlement H-block has to be admired for the way in which it cleverly married an innovative form with old living habits at maximum density and minimum cost. By the early 1960s in urban areas beyond the built-up districts of the old cities, H-blocks and slab blocks were the dominant forms. And these two official cities, traditional and Modernist, were juxtaposed with the informal spread of squatter structures that continued to spring up in any available interstitial space where tolerated.

## City between Ridges

There was a second layer to this familiarity. Victoria-Kowloon's districts (old and new, regulated and informal) lay largely within the confines of a geographically prescribed and visible landform – that is, within the grand sweep of land and water between the Hong Kong Island and Lion Rock ridge lines whose peaks gazed uninterruptedly at each other, across a space of little more than 8 km. Their strings of peaks rise to 552 m (Victoria Peak) in the south and 602 m (Fei Ngo Shan) in the north. This, it must be remembered, was at a time when most buildings were less than 40 m high and even those in the 'tall' category would not have exceeded 70 m. In other words, the ridges provided dramatic backcloths to a visibly and functionally 'contained' city.

Travel in the Hong Kong urban area was still all above ground and it was the heavily used ferries that offered the best appreciation of the whole sweep of the city from within. The ride across open water (the shortest being just 8 minutes) was between the two comparatively low but dense cities set between the ridges. Harbour and ferries were a defining characteristic of Hong Kong and this has been highlighted in a wide range of travel and fictional literature that has celebrated 'crossing the harbour' throughout Hong Kong's 112 year life as a 'twin city'. We have yet to find a travel guide that does not describe the wonder of this grand landscape as viewed from the Star Ferry as anything short of 'spectacular', 'breathtaking' or 'exhilarating': for instance Frommer's offers 'Riding the Star Ferry' as an 'unforgettable travel experience' of the highest order. The ferries and their landscape are to Hong Kong what rather more static symbols such as Sydney Opera House and Eiffel Tower are to other cities.

**4.18.** This 'extruded shop-house' rises through the maximum number of nine levels permitted without a lift: the roof carries additional illegal structures.

While more recently, fiction writer, Nuri Vittachi captures something of the spiritual dimension of the ferries, the harbour and wider landform through his *Fengshui Detective*, C.F. Wong, professional geomancer and unofficial super sleuth. Three people are leaning on the rail of the Star Ferry as it crosses an animated Victoria Harbour: the *Feng Shui* master himself, Wong; his client, who is seeking typical pre-purchase advice on the relative *ch'i* attributes of apartments in a new-town tower block; and Wong's inquisitive and forthright schoolgirl assistant, Joyce.

While absorbing the sweep of the landscape, Wong's client asks reflectively:

> Why does everyone love the Star Ferry? Why do I love the Star Ferry? It's old grimy, slow, crowded, out-of-date, and the terminus buildings are cramped and unappealing. Yet there's something – almost miraculously – refreshing about it. Even in this city where everyone is rushing-rushing-rushing … people will make a special effort to put the Star Ferry into their schedule. Why do we do this? (Vittachi, 2002)

Joyce uses the word 'magical' in her reply but she is contradicted by the

**4.19, 4.20 and 4.21.** Informal structures remain a common sight, despite authorities' best efforts to curb them. (*top*) Informal structures cover most of these roofs to form effectively a second ground; (*middle*) informal structures above market buildings in Yau Ma Tei; (*bottom*) informal constructions encrust parts of the upper half of this building in Jordan.

master who denies magic as the vital ingredient: for him, it is just 'Good Feng Shui'. Curiosity aroused, the assistant requests elaboration:

> The harbour and the Star Ferry are the feng shui centre of Hong Kong. It is not the map centre. It is not the geography centre. But it is the true centre. Hong Kong Island on this side, 10 times smaller than the Kowloon Peninsula on that side. But Hong Kong Island has very great ch'i energy. This balances the ch'i energy of Kowloon, also very strong. Look at the mountain. The mountain, the stars, the water – all combine to make ch'i energy flow into a pool on north side of the island. (*Ibid.*)

The geomancer goes on to refer to the five *ch'i* elements that surround the small party as they stand on the boat: the surrounding water, the extensive use of wood and metal on the boat itself, the fire to move it and the sun that shines on it, and the great earth mounds, which are the ridges, on both sides. He concludes that this is what makes so many people feel strong when they ride the Star Ferry.

In short, the harbour is the exhilarating life-generating 'good *ch'i*' heart of the place, assisted by the ridges to the south and north that were also the physical, functional and psychological edges. And it was one of the busiest: with a remarkable crisscrossing of ferry services, it held Victoria-Kowloon together. At the time of the new building regulations (1956), there were over 750 round trip cross-harbour services each day accounting for over 10 per cent of all round trip services offered by public transport in urban Hong Kong (and that includes services to the previously mentioned expansion towns of Kwun Ton and Tsuen Wan). But given the size and capacity of the ferries, these accounted for a much higher proportion of all public transport boardings: some 20 per cent in all. A decade later, each day there were some 345 plus 939 cross-harbour return trips by the Star plus Hongkong & Yaumatei ferryboats respectively (Leung, 1983, pp. 316, 319). For the entire two decades, from 1951 to 1971, the yearly percentage of cross-harbour trips fluctuated between 16 per cent and 23 per cent of all public transport passenger journeys in the city's life. It was a vital part of the Hong Kong urban system and psyche.

**4.22.** Hong Kong ferries on the harbour between the ridges: places of 'great *ch'i* energy'.

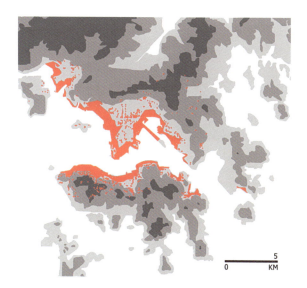

**4.23.** 1967 Victoria-Kowloon: a harbour-centred city between the ridges.

At this point it is worth noting two milestones that are significant in the process of change under investigation here. The first occurred around 1950, when the population of Kowloon and its extension, New Kowloon, became as populous as the Victoria-centred urban strip on Hong Kong Island. As the decade advanced Kowloon grew rapidly to overtake its parent city: by 1961, old Kowloon and its extensions in New Kowloon had a population of 1.5 million while the whole of Hong Kong Island had just two-thirds that number. Although the centre of political and corporate power remained firmly in Victoria's Central district, the geographical centre of gravity of the combined Victoria-Kowloon city was shifting across the Harbour, and with momentum.

The second follows just over a decade later, in 1963, and reflects the process of industrialization that followed Hong Kong's dwindling *entrepôt* trade. In that year, Hong Kong's exports returned to and exceeded the 1951 level for the first time, with industrial exports as the significant new contributor (Lo, 1992). The post-war years are often quoted loosely as Hong Kong's time of industrialization. In fact, the 1950s were very much the kindergarten years for the Colony's factories, with more substantial expansion and greater maturity coming only in the 1960s and 1970s. In 1963, there were approximately 7,500 industrial establishments in Hong Kong and they involved about 275,000 people: at the end of the 1970s (1979), the number of establishments had grown over fivefold and the number of people had risen almost exactly threefold (*Ibid.*). Most of the manufactured products were exported. Urban Hong Kong's resilience through these difficult years (which included a banking crisis and two instances of social unrest) was very much linked to this industrial expansion. Morphologically, the impact of a fivefold factory increase was large.

## Kowloon Ascends: On Industrial Wings

Given the pressures for factory land, the first directions for 'spillover' were along the lines of least resistance east and west of Kowloon, around and *in* the (reclaimed) bays on each side of the Peninsula. What had started on the west side of Kowloon in Yau Ma Tei and Tai Kok Tsui and pushed out to Cheung Sha Wan, was to now jump to the more distant Tsuen Wan, though still a mere 10 km away. On the other side, San Po Kong (ex-airport land) was an early 1960s growth area for factories,

**4.24.** Looking from the Island ridge across Victoria-Kowloon To Lion Rock. In the distance, there are signs of expansion (squatters and industrial settlement) on both sides of the Peninsula.

with more development beyond – in Kwun Tong, although still no more than 8 km or so from Kowloon. These were the Peninsula's industrial wings spreading east and west although still contained by the ridge of which the Lion Rock peak was a part.

While squatters and industry had been spilling out towards Kwun Tong by the early 1950s, a decision was taken in 1953 by the government to 'plan' the area as an 'industrial satellite': reclamation and development continued for two decades. In its early years, it served effectively as a 'guinea pig' for later new town development.

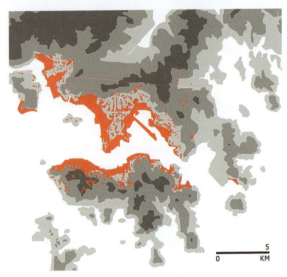

**4.25.** Urban and industrial growth beyond New Kowloon: west to Tsuen Wan and east to Kwun Tong, but still within extended ridgelines.

Similarly, some industry had spread westwards towards and into the old village of Tsuen Wan: this was also designated as an industrial satellite but converted to new town status in 1960. It was in these places that the large-scale creation of land specifically for general industrial purposes first occurred, and the districts grew at staggering paces to become the Colony's industrial heartlands – in fact, Hong Kong's workshop to the world.

Kwun Tong's emergence and form deserve some closer attention, as they are indicative of the Colony's wider industrial growth. In 1957, the first factory arrived following three years and 21 hectares of reclamation. By 1963, the year in which exports returned to earlier levels, there was just over a square kilometre of reclaimed land with 170 factories and 22,000 workers, and a residential population of about 110,000. Five years later, the number of factories had more than tripled and the workforce very nearly so. By 1971, there were almost 90,000 workers in over 1,300 factories. While reclamation in the local Kwun Tong district ceased in 1965, it continued elsewhere in Kowloon Bay and further afield.

From the outset, Kwun Tong's development pattern foreshadowed one that would repeat itself along waterfronts throughout the Colony's process of industrialization. This consisted of an old main road running more or less along the old shoreline (Ngau Tau Kok Road) and a new and straighter road (Kwun Tong Road) less than 100 m away but built mostly on fill. On the seaward side of the road, the flat canopy of reclamation was broad and occupied mostly by factories, including some of the earlier mentioned resettlement factories; while on the landward side, the hill slopes were dominated by flatted homes. On these slopes, there had been some pre-existing villages and small-scale terracing of the land for agriculture and village buildings. There had also been limited post-war hill-cutting and sea-filling, the building of an oil depot, and refuse dumping in the area. Post-war, squatters had extended their domain up the hillsides, which after 1953, prompted government clearances and the reshaping of hills to extensive terraces fit for its large residential typologies. Between the two 'zones' of factories and dwellings came the commercial facilities – around Ngau Tau Kok Road but north of Kwun Tong Road. However, although such separation might have been the wish and intent of the authorities, it was not quite as 'clean' as that.

The first buildings by government were resettlement H-blocks, which took over the lower slopes about a former inlet: this was the Tsui Ping Road Estate, completed in 1958 and therefore one of the earliest resettlement estates in Hong Kong. Close-by, there followed some private thirteen-storey tower clusters on the upper slopes of a ridge rising between two former inlets: these were relatively slow to take off as the private flat development in Kwun Tong moved more slowly than either private factory or public flat building. Between the Tsui Ping Road Estate and the private housing, long public housing slab blocks were inserted – these effectively blocked sightlines between the private and H-block housing, perhaps intentionally so. And in the early 1960s on higher slopes to the west (Sau Mau Ping) rose more long slabs of government housing. In most instances the land had been shaped to accommodate their right-angled formations, but in a few, their straight lines were angled in linear formation along the cut shelf that ran along the contour. Between the flat ground of the factories, which became increasingly flatted, and the rising ground of the estates were the shops, markets, commercial and community services occupying a central place at a natural meeting point of the old coastal strip, the industry on the flat, and two small natural valleys, with Kwun Tong Road and other roads that ran approximately along the 30 m contour, as intended boundary lines to a conceptual centre.

The authorities had zoning desires but the results fell short of intent, or at least hopes. The densities at which they continued to build were extremely high. People's lives, given their meagre resources and long working hours, were inevitably local. The new public housing and private estates were commonly planned as super-blocks with loop roads and culs-de-sac, although pedestrians could usually move across the space without reference to formal service roads: sharp contours in the way of retaining walls and hawkers' stalls were probably the biggest barriers to free movement. Some buildings in the commercial centre were not dissimilar to those in the old centres in that shops and services continued at ground and in some cases higher levels, with living above – some of which continued in rented bunks or cubicles. In the densely inhabited H-blocks, all ground level and scattered upper level units were used as shops and workshops. The design of the government's slab blocks, with internal corridor access, made them easier to control than the H-blocks and separation of uses was more successful. The private flat estates had some services at ground floor but businesses other than professional services were not obvious elsewhere. Nevertheless, the in-between spaces towards the

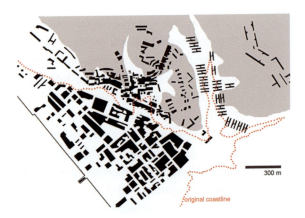

**4.26.** Kwun Tong in the early 1970s. The map shows the original coastline (red) and higher land (above 50 m in grey). Large footprint factories occupy the reclaimed land. The earliest buildings and commercial core rise on valley land and lower hillsides by the old coast (centre). Resettlement H-blocks occupy the valley beyond and slab blocks are on the hill in the upper right. Between the old core and the H-blocks, a string of private apartment blocks occupy a spur of higher ground that offers both views and convenience. (Adapted from Leeming, 1977)

central district and in and around the resettlement estates were often teeming with itinerants and hawkers stalls. Given the background of Hong Kong's street traditions, the plying of local services in interstitial spaces was inevitable. As for signs, Leeming (1977) noted that these were far fewer in Kwun Tong than Old Kowloon so giving the place a relatively drab appearance. In other words, the mix of uses and the external 'content' (people, goods, signs, etc) although still profuse, was rather less and patchier than in older areas. Thus life in these new industrial extensions continued to be lived at not dissimilar densities to older districts but with rather less variety and colour, and within a limited variety of mainly new mixed-use, residential and factory typologies, some of which were novel, others more conventionally modern.

Leeming notes also the extremely local nature of life in 1960s Kwun Tong. From his enquiries and observations, he surmised that most people in the local estates, particularly those west of Kwun Tong centre, would have experienced Kowloon rarely – perhaps only at holiday time, if then. In fact, almost everywhere in Hong Kong, post-war life was intensely local. Most movement was local and on foot: home and work were commonly in the same district, sometimes in the same building, or even within the same small unit of rented space. This was, of course, high density's *raison d'être*: to minimize travel. Life in Hong Kong was clearly circumscribed at three scales. First, by the edge ridges embodied in Victoria and Lion Rock Peaks, a crow-flying distance of 10 km. Second, by the 2 kilometre stretch of water that separates Victoria and Kowloon and accentuates their identities. And third within the districts, which are more in the form of a chain in Victoria and patchwork in Kowloon.

The local nature of 1950s living in Hong Kong and the subsequent expansion of travel and experience within the city are reflected in public transport passenger figures. In the eight years from 1951 to 1959 numbers were modest, hovering between about 225 and 240 trips per capita each year: and this in a city where the average service route (not passenger trip) length was less than 6 km. But the decade following 1959 saw a sharp upward spurt to about 400 trips per capita in 1969: there was only one year (1967) in which patronage dipped but that was in a year of political unrest and rioting.

The unrest of 1967 proved a testing time for the Colony and an interesting one for public transport – because of the unrest, Hong Kong added another facet to its multi-modal public transport system. Transportation workers went on strike and most people were rendered immobile since they relied on public transport, particularly buses, for their travel. Immediately, the general public took to stopping vehicles with space for passengers to seek rides. The goods vehicle with an open flat bed was the most common type called into service for this purpose, with passengers paying the sum previously paid on the bus or higher, depending on demand. Soon, vans equipped with seats were secured and an informal alternative 'bus' system established, mostly controlled by Hong Kong's triads. Since demand for transportation exceeded capacity, vans were overloaded and driven at speed to maximize the daily load and the number of trips. Safety was compromised and accidents occurred. Nevertheless, an unusual event had occurred: a spontaneous and informal public transport system had sprung up in place of a formal and ordered one.

Once the standard bus system was brought back into operation after several weeks of strike action, the government found it difficult to remove the 'illegal' network. As a consequence, it took action to co-opt the mini-bus network as part of the transport infrastructure and bring it under control. Regulations were enacted in 1969 to legitimize the service, specify the types of vehicle used, regulate their carrying capacity and their routes to ensure safety and reduce congestion. The vehicles came to be called 'Public Light Buses' and painted with a red band for identification as a 'bus'. Later, distinction was made between two types of licence: a red band was the signifier of one type, and a green band for the other. Red vehicles were permitted to operate largely, as had emerged during the transport stoppage, on routes established by demand, and operated when sufficient passengers were ready to depart, with fares fluctuating through the day. Green vehicles were required to operate according to a schedule, on regular routes and with set fares. The red vehicles encapsulated the idea of an organic public transport system that responds quickly to market need and they continue as a vital part of Hong Kong's movement system.

Public transport use, measured in trips per capita, continued to climb through the 1970s, excepting two years of economic depression. Thus the industrializing years were also ones of increased local movement. And, consistent with the earlier cited population change, the 1950s was the decade in which public transport use in Kowloon overtook that of Hong Kong Island (Leung, 1983).

In the years around 1960, public transport use took a significant rise both on Hong Kong Island and in Kowloon. A similar spurt in cross-harbour ferry use followed some years later, circa 1970; and the first significant jump in public transport use in the New Territories came later still, at the end of the 1970s. These increases show an

**4.27.** Public Light Buses, or mini-buses, in a Mong Kok street. Just over forty years old, they are a ubiquitous sight in Hong Kong and an essential part of the SAR's multi-modal public transport system.

extending pattern of movement that reflects both the spread of the city and, per-haps more important, the individuals' experience of the city and widening geographic horizons – extending these from the districts, to the 'twin cities' (one linear, one peninsular patchwork), to a singular 'twin city', and later to an extended metropolitan network of urban settlement.

By the 1960s Kowloon Peninsula ridge to Lion Rock ridge was filled to capacity, with official and squatter buildings. It had also become clear that its wings, the last of the areas with any further capacity south of the ridge, would rapidly follow. These areas (extending to Kwun Tong and Tsuen Wan, industrial satellite and new town respectively) were acquiring developments with new typological forms at 'old centre' density levels. It was also the decade in which the harbour (the busiest in the world and the only means of connecting Victoria and Kowloon) was becoming dangerously busy. In short, use of space and infrastructure was intensifying within a confined physical setting to crisis point. If Hong Kong was to grow, urban development had to take a quantum leap into new territory (literally the New Territories) and the congested harbour had to be crossed by more than ferries. The ridges were as much psychological as physical barriers, and the busy harbour a sacred watery heartland. The urban future involved more than extension and construction but dealing also with preconceptions about the physical dimensions and nature of urban Hong Kong.

## Breaching the Dragon Hills: New Infrastructure to New Towns

With this pressure for urban space, something had to give and that was the Lion Rock ridge, for there was not only potential space beyond this line of peaks but space that was en route to somewhere of importance: China. Immediately beyond the ridge, the area about Sha Tin had been considered periodically for reclamation since the 1920s but this had come to nothing. Sha Tin was one of three New Territories stations dating back to 1910 on the cumbersome Kowloon and Canton single-track diesel-hauled railway, and it emerged in 1965 as a designated new town, along with Castle Peak (later called Tuen Mun), five years after the first such designation of Tsuen Wan.

With the approval of Tsuen Wan's plan in 1963, the general parameters for Hong Kong's new towns were set. Tsuen Wan was to be 'developed into a self-contained community with a balanced land-use pattern designed to allow people to live within reasonable distance of their place of work, with adequate public services, communications and community facilities for the well-being of a population of 1.2 million to be attained by 1978' and 'a high-rise, high-density, and compact form' (Leung, 1983). Among the ambitious programme's priorities were size, speed of development, density and self-containment. The early new towns were specifically to be led by public housing and industry. In fact, Tseun Wan started with a 'found population' of 80,000 and grew to more than 0.5 million and 0.75 million over twenty and thirty year periods respectively – less than planned but highly impressive. Following its official designation as a new town, Sha Tin had an existing population of 25,000 before construction started as a new town in 1970: within fifteen years it was home to 0.33 million people and 0.5 million after twenty years.

Sha Tin is of special interest both for its built form typologies and the infrastructure it triggered; for the latter effectively cracked the Lion Rock range as a barrier to movement between the inner known world of urban Victoria-Kowloon and the largely 'out of sight and mind' territories beyond. Prior to the 1960s the only break 'through' the ridge had come in 1910 with the single track line of the Kowloon-Canton Railway (British Section) joining Tsim Sha Tsui and Lo Wu at the border with China; prior to World War II, there were just four country stations, Sha Tin, Tai Po, Fanling and Sheung Shui, and the line played a minor role in the internal life of the Colony. A second tunnel was driven through the ridge to transform the KCR line into double track in 1973 – as far as Sha Tin; within another decade the entire line through to China was double track and had undergone electrification. Meantime, two years after Sha Tin's designated new town status, a road tunnel was also completed (1967) under the Lion Rock Ridge and this became a twin tunnel eleven years later. It is of interest that the first road tunnel was conceived initially as a water tunnel and only later recognized as having value for road traffic as well: this primacy of pipe over road serves to emphasize just how long it was before the road was perceived seriously as a strategy for breaching the ridge divide.

Between the building of the first road and second rail tunnels to Sha Tin, a third was added to Hong Kong's wider movement network: the cross-harbour tunnel, from Central to Hung Hom on the east side of Kowloon Peninsula, which took its first traffic in 1972. Within eleven years of opening it had become the world's busiest four-lane highway carrying over 110,000 vehicles per day, to add yet another 'density' record to Hong Kong's impressive and expanding list. And yet another tunnel was to be added a few years later: this was part of the new underground Mass Transit Rail (MTR) line and also connected Central and Kowloon. In 1967, four lines had been recommended with a total length of 64 km. Initially, the government built part of the system as a Y-shaped (tree) system that ran from Central, Victoria, to Tsim Sha Tsui, Mong Kok and then branched west and east to the spillover areas of Tsuen Wan and Kwun Tong respectively. The latter opened progressively from October 1979 to February 1980, and Tsuen Wan three years later. When completed these lines were, respectively, 16.9 and 15 km in length and with sixteen and fifteen stations, giving the relatively short 1 km interval between stations – thus adding another dimension of intensity to Hong Kong urbanism.

Today, MTR is taken for granted and its initial effect is probably hard to appreciate. It certainly made more convenient the lives of many Hong Kong residents who were already used to moving about the city. For the large low-income sections of the population, it probably provided more an occasion for a novelty trip than a regular service for it was beyond their financial means. This point is made very clear by Hong Kong author, Xu Xi (2005), in her short story, *The Yellow Line*, the title referring to the line across which the traveller must not step while waiting for a train. Soon after the MTR's opening, a six year old resident of the Lok Fu government housing estate 'badgered his mother' to take him on the city's new transit wonder, the *underground iron*. Living at the far reaches of Old Kowloon, he had never ventured across the harbour to Victoria, only a few kilometres away. The mother submits to her son's demand and they duly depart for a one segment return trip to the neighbouring station, Kowloon Tong, without even surfacing. He is sworn to secrecy, as his father would consider it wasted money. While almost certainly reaching a speed he had not previously experienced, it was an anonymous subterranean outing: nonetheless it whetted his appetite for travel and introduced him to the simple procedures of underground train travel. He was quick to repeat the journey alone, and exit to a salubrious world that he was unable to place geographically visually or socially. For our six year old, 'underground iron' was both mysterious and liberating.

Finally, in 1983, there was one more tunnel which completed the 'breaking' of the ridges surrounding Victoria-Kowloon. While the Lion Rock and harbour tunnels were clearly the most important, piercing the backbone ridge of Hong Kong Island was also significant. Though little has been said about the south side of Hong Kong Island, there had been settlements there since before British rule and these had grown modestly, to be reinforced by post-war squatters and significant public housing in the 1970s, but in a state of relative isolation. The opening of the Aberdeen Tunnel in 1983 changed all that, replacing the steep and circuitous mountain and coastal routes between Victoria and Aberdeen with a few minutes of subterranean travel.

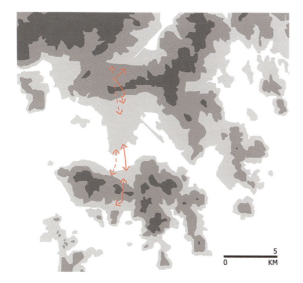

**4.28.** First-wave Tunnels. Between 1965 and 1979, new rail and road tunnels breached the Lion Rock ridge and passed under Victoria Harbour to give road access and rail commuter services between Victoria, Kowloon and Sha Tin new town. Harbour and mountains 'disappeared' from the travel experience. Like the proverbial frog in the well, many Hong Kong residents emerged from their harbour and between-the-ridges existence to find new horizons. Three years later, a road tunnel was completed beneath the Hong Kong Island ridge from Victoria to Aberdeen to complete the change.

Within a space of fifteen years, it was possible to cross by public or private vehicle between Victoria and Sha Tin new town without the immediate experience of ridge pass or harbour. The infrastructure changes that occurred during Sha Tin's infancy were very significant indeed. No matter how strong a place's formal qualities may be (and Hong Kong's are exceptional), tunnels negate topography: they tend to reduce a city to lines, nodes and abstractions. Travelling becomes a protected rather than exposed experience; it becomes less one of a series of places, and more point to point. As such, this array of tunnels altered the experience of Hong Kong's landform and cityscape, reconfigured mental maps, and changed the sense of timing in negotiating it.

Sha Tin's rise coincides with these changes and, in large measure, owes its growth to them. Further, the new town's morphology, with its extensive use of connected podia and tower forms, is also significant; for it translates into an extensive volumetric system with multi-level movement and broad areas of second ground, as well as widespread verticality

Table 4.1. First-wave tunnels that transformed the spatial experience of Hong Kong.

| Date | Connection | Type | Barrier |
|------|-----------|------|---------|
| 1965 | Kowloon to Sha Tin | Road – single tunnel★ | Lion Rock ridge – route beneath Pat Ka Shan (Beacon Hill) |
| 1972 | Victoria to Kowloon Cross Harbour Tunnel | Road | Victoria Harbour |
| 1973 | Kowloon to Sha Tin Lion Rock Tunnel | Rail (KCR) Double track tunnel replaces single track | Lion Rock ridge – route beneath Sz Tsz Shan (Lion Rock Peak) |
| 1978 | Kowloon to Sha Tin | Road – ★now twin tunnel | Lion Rock ridge |
| 1979 | Victoria to Kowloon | Rail (MTR) | Victoria Harbour |
| 1982 | Aberdeen Tunnel | Road | HK Island ridge |

in the form of clustered high-rise slabs and point blocks – in principle, similar to Hilbersheimer's 1924 vision of a vertical city, albeit with mostly towers instead of slabs. Sha Tin is rather different from Kwun Tong or Tsuen Wan, which were pressure-release sites along lines of least resistance within an extended but known physical container. Also, Kwun Tong and Tsuen Wan were more tarnished with older typologies and squatters. For these reasons Sha Tin has a double symbolism: it represents Hong Kong's extended urbanization beyond an earlier proscribed geography – breaking out of confinement; similarly it represents an urban configuration that became a ubiquitous Hong Kong and new town phenomenon – dense vertical living over volumetric services and infrastructure. In this way, it foreshadowed Hong Kong's future.

**4.29.** Massing at the 'periphery': Fok Cheong Building, King's Road, Quarry Bay. The building consists of several conjoined slab blocks, giving the whole a truly massive appearance from certain viewpoints.

If the population centre of gravity had jumped the harbour in the 1950s, the centre of the transportation system did likewise in the 1970s – with Kowloon increasingly the 'natural hub' between Victoria, and Kwun Tong and Tsuen Wan, and even an ambitious new piece of quasi-urbanity beyond the dragon peaks. This reinforces the Peninsula's potential as the centre of intensity, with the Nathan Road corridor, between Tsim Sha Tsui and Mong Kok as the most central place of all.

# 5 Vertical and Volumetric
## Post 1980

Through the 1960s and 1970s, manufacturing had dominated Hong Kong's economy. In the latter decade, the goods emerging from the factories became more diverse and sophisticated to include electrical, electronic and optical items, watches, and chemical products. But while Hong Kong's manufacturing was changing, so was its larger economy: just as 1963 was a marker in the emergence of an industrial Hong Kong, 1980 provided another significant marker, again heralding an important new phase in the city's economic development. In this year financial services nosed ahead of manufacturing in the value of exports, accounting for 26 per cent of exports: that was 1 per cent more than manufacturing (Lo, 1992, p. 15). Following the introduction of more open Chinese trading and foreign investment policies, Hong Kong was also regaining its *entrepôt* and service role. With these changes, and accompanying developments in banking, communications and transportation, Hong Kong was on the verge of true world city status. And it was during this phase that the city emerged quite literally as the skyscraper capital of the world.

## A World City Rises

Tall buildings were made possible over the last five decades of the nineteenth century through a series of technical innovations. First was the invention of the elevator by Elisha Graves Otis in New York in 1852, allowing people to move rapidly skywards within buildings without personal exertion. This was put to practical use five years later in Haughwout's department store, at 488 Broadway in Manhattan. Second was the use of the iron and, in turn, steel structural frame, which enabled a building to rise without the necessity for thick load-bearing walls and with a repetitive stack of identical floor plates. These inventions allowed for the slender tower, thin slab, or dumpier tall building around a light court. The third invention that allowed buildings to be both high and expand their girths was mechanical ventilation and Willis H. Courier's air conditioning of 1902.

Chicago, assisted by its great fire of 1871 and the need to redevelop quickly, was the most significant early player in vertical urbanism – starting with the ten-storey Home Insurance Building in 1885. However, New York was quick to overtake as the tall building capital, reaching seventy-seven storeys in 1929 with the Chrysler Building at 241 m, surpassed by the Empire State at 381 m and 102 floors two years later. Since that time buildings have reached greater heights in New York and elsewhere, including Hong Kong. However, the latter, though always dense, remained surprisingly low-rise for many decades. For instance, top hotels (such as the Hong Kong and Gloucester) would employ generous floor-to-ceiling heights, wide shady verandas, cross-ventilation, fans and lifts, but rise to six or, at most, eight storeys. Prior to World War II the Hong Kong and Shanghai Bank (1935), at thirteen floors and 70 m, stood significantly higher than any other building in the city: it was not eclipsed for fifteen years and then only marginally by its rival, the Bank of China which rose to 76 m. The rise in the relative heights of tall buildings did not proceed smoothly but advanced in quantum jumps. Over the seven years from 1966 to 1973, Hong Kong's tallest buildings shifted through a modest six storeys: from twenty-eight through thirty-one to thirty-four floors, to top the memorable 100 m mark. In the latter year, the Connaught Centre (easily identified by its colloquial nomenclature, which approximated to 'the tower of a 1000 arseholes') leapt to the fifty-plus storeys mark at 178 m from which Hong Kong's tallest buildings then rose steadily but very consistently over exactly thirty years to reach 415 m in 2003. The next quantum shift came with the rise of the International Commerce Centre and thirty additional storeys: this has another significance for it is in Kowloon, and is indicative of the centrality and potential of the Peninsula, now freed from the tyranny of the flight paths into old Kai Tak Airport (closed 1998).

Thus, with its expanded role as an international financial services centre, Hong Kong joined New York to embrace the skyscraper. But unlike New York, which has taken the building type as an instrument for concentration in and towards a centre, Hong Kong has taken it as an instrument for dispersal – both *concentration* and *scattered dispersal*. What this seemingly contradictory phrase means is that clusters of very tall towers are to be seen at the centre and periphery of the continuous built-up area, and almost everywhere between; and they are also to be found in scattered new towns beyond. Further, as indicated above, skyscrapers would be even more extensively distributed, had not the old Kai Tak airport been attached to the Kowloon Peninsula, where aircraft movements limited building heights across a substantial area until the last decade.

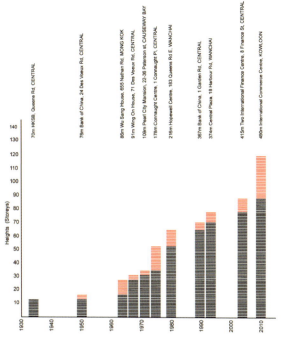

**5.1.** Hong Kong building heights – the sequence of tallest buildings

The hill barriers may have been slow to penetrate, but once breached, reluctance on the part of the authorities to extend city building into the New Territories evaporated quickly. Tunnels and train lines were, in a short time, commonplace. Since the completion of the 'first set' described in the previous chapter, two additional road tunnels have been driven through the Lion Rock ridge; and several other tunnels facilitating roads or rails have been drilled through more distant ranges effectively bringing New Territories new towns 'closer' together. Further there are plans to take the railway through the Hong Kong Island ridge to Aberdeen. In addition, two more roads and three more rail lines have crossed the harbour.

The result is that the New Territories have witnessed rapid growth, and taken an increasingly large proportion of Hong Kong's expanded population. New towns have continued to grow in number and in size: thus in addition to earlier generation developments, the 1980s and subsequent years have seen Tseung Kwan O (further east), Tin Shui Wai (far north-west), Tsing Yi and Tung Chun (both further west) added to the rail-connected list of new towns. To accommodate them, reclamation has continued at a rapid pace.

Nevertheless, while land and urban areas have been extended, there have been few fundamental changes in the approach to new settlement development. In the main, new towns continue to be in public transport-orientated small footprint high-rise forms, with rail playing a crucial role in linking them all together. Hong Kong's new towns, especially Sha Tin, are perhaps the most extensive, faithful and longest running production of built forms anywhere to employ CIAM and variant Modernist principles and forms in such high concentrations but with a strong rail overlay.

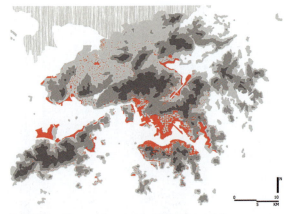

**5.2.** Hong Kong urban area 1994; the establishment of new towns beyond the hill barriers is apparent.

The stations in new towns and on newly reclaimed land next to old established districts are invariably parts of mega-structures or groups of mega-structures that are much more than mere stations and commerce. Each is a city within a city – of dense dwellings, an extensive range of urban services and, to varying degrees, employment. The form is usually a massive volume (or series of connected volumes) of shops, commercial and professional services, car parks, and recreational facilities such as gymnasia and cinemas – topped by forests of very large towers that contain homes, offices and/or hotels and associated leisure and business facilities. There will invariably be bus stations (for double decker and small 'light' buses), which may also be located at an upper level within the multi-level structure, and reached by ramp or from an adjacent elevated highway.

Within this generic frame, there can be significant variations of use and/or configuration. Some may be essentially commercial with towers of offices and

hotels. The majority, however, are dominated by residential towers. The commonest configuration includes the station at an underground level with embarking passengers moving outwards or ascending to the shops and other facilities, but some are elevated, in which case passengers will descend to the main shopping levels.

Above and/or around such developments are veritable forests of towers with four-figure (per hectare) densities, and 'multiple grounds'. Some of the towers are in effect clusters of joined towers that take

**5.3.** Sha Tin new town. The volumes of the podia are full of shops and services. Above, the podia decks serve as ground for the towers above. Outside, extensive systems of bridges and ramps connect the multiple 'grounds'.

**5.4.** Tseun Wan new town. The four level podium shows a volume of services, shops and restaurants: establishments at both ground and balcony levels have conventional doors and openings to the 'streets'. Above landscape and towers are visible on 'podium ground'.

advantage of common lift and stair shafts, and other space saving devices such as the scissor stair, which although not a modern invention, may have been used first in Hong Kong in modern times. (For more details of scissor stairs, see p. 137)

It is, however, the volumetric qualities of Hong Kong (multi-level activity, deck or bridge connection between buildings, or from building to sloping ground) that make it the world's No. 1 per capita escalator state. In 1998, with a population of less than seven million it had 5,325 escalators – ranking it between France and the United Kingdom, whose populations were almost ten times that of Hong Kong (The Elevator World Source 1999–2000, data quoted in Chung et al., 2001). If there were figures that incorporated escalator length as well, they would almost certainly raise Hong Kong's relative ranking even further, given the length of some of the city's installations.

These kinds of mega-structures are not only new town phenomena, nor are they just station-related. In smaller but no less tall developments, towers may sit over a podium or encircle a shopping centre – the latter giving a donut-type formation with a low centre, probably of multi-level shopping and services, surrounded by high towers: in addition, there will be at least a partial network of pedestrian bridges connecting the high-rise homes to the centre.

It is quite typical of Hong Kong that something which has been resisted for so long and arises out of necessity, once seen to work, is embraced in a matter-of-fact way to emerge as a kind of big scale city-state vernacular. Tall buildings, tunnels and trains are all in this category, and these have become the dominant formal and functional features of the new towns, reclaimed areas as well as more modest sized renewal projects on old town blocks. Thus the train station podium is another form of reclamation – in creating ground for tower living.

## Shifting Centre of Gravity

A very significant consequence of this extension of the movement networks and the associated building of high-density 'tower new towns' far beyond the ridges is that the Kowloon Peninsula became increasingly the best-connected place in the entire SAR (or Special Administrative Region) urban system. Thus the Peninsula of *relatively* low building heights is ironically now the most central – sitting at the cross roads between the south (Victoria/Hong Kong Island), north (Sha Tin, other new towns and China), west (Chep Lak Kok International Airport, Tsuen Wan and Tuen Mun) and east (Kwun Tong and Tseung Kwan O).

If we consider the Kowloon Peninsula alone, its central and western areas dominate and its spine remains along the legendary Nathan Road. The most central

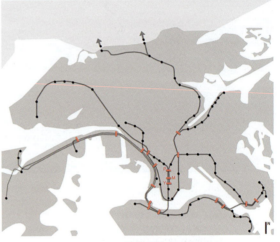

**5.5.** Hong Kong's rail network and stations, including exchange stations (diagrammatic and not to scale). The map shows Prince Edward (P), Mong Kok (M) and Yau Ma Tei Stations (Y) at the centre of Kowloon Peninsula and of the network.

places are the old vibrant and partly seedy districts of Mong Kok, Yau Ma Tei, Tai Kok Tsui and even Sham Shui Po, Cheung Sha Wan, Shek Kip Mei and the more salubrious Kowloon Tong. In this general area of approximately 2 kilometres by 4 kilometres there are no fewer than fifteen stations serving six rail lines that either pass through or start here: these are aligned north–south within the area but splay out in all directions once clear of the Peninsula. This means that all but one of the seven main rail lines are to be found here, with connections to the seventh (the Island Line) and to a few branch lines, such as that to Disneyland, all very easy. When it is considered that 70 per cent of Hong Kong residents live within seven minutes of a railway station, the extraordinary centrality of the Kowloon Peninsula, and in particular the Yau Ma Tei-Mong Kok-Prince Edward strip and its environs, becomes very clear indeed.

Further, the new Chep Lak Kok international airport brought huge change to those areas west of New Kowloon: along the new rail tracks associated with the airport's development, are Tsing Yi and Tung Chung new towns, which stand strikingly tall. It is also bringing

**5.6.** Tsai Kok Tsui vista: looking down an 'industrial street' flanked by flatted factories to a cluster of residential towers above a podium.

**5.7.** Looking across to Nelson Street from Langham Place's Portland Street entrance.

**5.8.** Portland Street entrance: the form gives an impression of 'sucking' people from the street.

**5.9.** Langham Place edge: while the interiors can be extremely active, much of their street edges can be 'quiet' – which is uncharacteristic of the general bustle of the Mong Kok district.

much change to the Peninsula's established built-up areas, especially the old industrial areas: for instance, while Tai Kok Tsui's landscape still retains many multi-storey factories of up to fifteen usually flatted floors and dirty streets packed with delivery lorries, fork-lifts and other industrial accessories, these are increasingly interspersed with housing towers above podia of parked cars or commerce.

With the removal of aircraft-related building heights, most of the Kowloon Peninsula can now reach for the heights that typify the rest of urban Hong Kong, with Mong Kok's multi-purpose fifty-nine storey Langham Place being indicative of this potential. With some fifteen levels of shopping, this complex is placed strategically close to the Mong Kok MTR station, and has a direct connection to it at lower basement level. As with the outdoor elevator system in Central's Shelley Street, the shopper or *flâneur* can enjoy an escalator-assisted ascent but return to the ground or underground as a pedestrian via a shop-flanked path – in effect, it is a spiralling hill-street of mostly small shops, although in this case, internal. West of the shops, across Shanghai Street, is the rest of the development, occupying much but not all of the next block, and also consisting of a podium, hotel tower and roof garden. The two blocks are connected at two upper levels across Shanghai Street. It is a spatial configuration that raises important issues, positive and negative, about the development of Hong Kong's old street blocks. On the one hand, it demonstrates the sheer physical potential of the district: on the other hand, the particular configuration shows an 'island mentality' that erodes the established functional pattern of the area's street network, for the development's shop fronts do not so much duplicate or extend Mong Kok's street-life but rather transfer it from the flanking Shanghai, Argyle, Portland and Shantung Streets to the internal, and more or less dead-end, 'hill-street'. (See also the following chapter for further discussion and illustrations of Langham Place, p. 128.)

Some streets and districts survive with relatively low buildings (four to twelve storeys), especially in Victoria and Kowloon. But increasingly, most of Hong Kong (Victoria, Kowloon, the New Towns and other settlements) are operating at many times those heights and with public movement across several levels, whether it is to mediate between steeply rising *terra firma* and the upper floors of high buildings, or simply to make possible higher level circulation between buildings. For instance, the extensive deck and bridge systems in Central enable the pedestrian to walk at an upper level across an area almost 2 kilometres in length and over 1 kilometre broad. Both early and later generation new towns support extensive multi-level pedestrian (and vehicle) movement systems, from 'old' Tsuen Wan to new Tsing Yi. And in older city districts such as Mong Kok and Wan Chai, there are also long elevated walkways or 'pediways', conceived on the principle of the elevated motorway principle just to keep pedestrians moving by avoiding the congested ground below: pedestrian flows can reach over 4,000 per hour on a single side of the street in parts of Mong Kok, a district in which several street blocks have densities of more than 3,000 people per hectare and even higher spot densities. Because of its many natural and built levels, Hong Kong has become a stairway, escalator, 'expresscalator' and transparent eleva-

**5.10.** Tsing Yi new town - two rail lines: the Airport Express with limited stops and local Tung Chung line enter the podium at upper levels, one above the other. Residential towers stand tall over the podium.

**5.11.** Tsing Yi new town – multiple movement levels The picture shows complex level relationships between walkways, steps, roads and podium.

tor city. The general visibility of these infrastructure elements plus the views to be gained while riding them, are very important. They enable users to 'read' the city's three-dimensional movement network, the 'legibility' of which is as important as that of the street structure of a conventional city where emphasis is upon the ground plane.

There is an impressive range of 'stacked' and 'sky' phenomena: stacked cemeteries, drive-in multi-level flatted factories, warehouses and port storage: stacked transport depots, multi-level markets and even high-rise horse stables. Likewise, extensive use is made of roof levels for schools, churches, gardens, sports pitches and other cultural and educational facilities, which are as likely to be encountered above buildings as on the ground. The next two chapters will present examples of many of these vertical and volumetric phenomena, including podia- and-tower typologies.

## Never Far from Nature

Given our emphasis on built form, we have said relatively little about the city's relationship to the natural world, and with the number of people packed into Hong Kong's small land area, it would be easy to assume that this is of little consequence; but this is not so. Hong Kong is made up of a large and irregular peninsula and numerous islands of varying size. Hong Kong Island is the place of original settlement, the most populous island and therefore best known but it is not the largest: the superlative applies to Lantau Island (or *Tai Yue Shan*). Also, while reclamation has straightened significant stretches of coastline, most remains highly indented. Altogether, this gives a coast that is extremely long relative to the land areas that it contains. If we add into the equation, the territory's extreme relief, varied geology, and geographical position at the meeting of tropical and temperate zones, plus a predilection for colonial visitors and immigrants to import their own plants and animals, there is a good recipe for diverse habitats with a wide variety of flora and fauna.

On the peaks and hilltops are rocky faces and grasslands; on the hillsides, varieties of scrubland; and on lower slopes and in valleys are thick woodlands. Mangrove forests surround many inlets, and there are mudflats and open beaches as well. These diverse places provide homes to no fewer than 3,000 species of flowering plants, 300 native trees, over 100 amphibians and reptiles, 240 butterfly species, many mammals and an astonishing 450 birds, including 120 breeding species. The butterfly and bird species alone represent fully 15 per cent and one-third, respectively, of all China's species in those categories, although Hong Kong occupies only 0.012 per cent of the national area. There are also diverse marine environments. All this is possible because some three-quarters of this tiny territory's landmass remains as some kind of countryside with about 40 per cent given over to country parks. If Hong Kong's land area was reshaped into a square, the figure would be less than 35 kilometres along each side, yet there are four major country walking trails of between 50 km and 100 km – Hong Kong Island, Lantau Island, McLehose and Wilson Trails – and many lesser ones. In other words, any journey between an older city district and a new town or between new towns is likely to be beneath a ridgeline park of country trails. Thus even the relationship between rail or road travel and walking with nature on a country trail is that of one above the other – or volumetric.

At the same time, the configuration of most of the densely built-up areas is so often a product of curvaceous coast and contours: consequently, 'squeezed', 'narrow', 'linear' and 'contorted' are adjectives that can apply to most Hong Kong districts: 'tall' also applies. The result is small patches and thin strings of intense urbanism cheek-by-jowl with steep slopes, rock face and greenery. As emphasised earlier, Hong Kong residents and nature are rarely far apart, although this is often difficult to appreciate from many of the streets and buildings. Nevertheless, even in the heavily commercialized multi-level Central District there are reminders: one set of signs shows a man and mountain, and guides the way to the outdoor Mid-levels escalator which effectively climbs the slope to green hillsides as well as Mid-levels apartments. Connections may not always be so explicit or made so readily available but the juxtaposition of Hong Kong's concentrated districts of towers and its landscapes of biodiversity is a

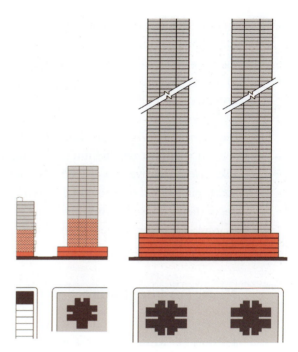

**5.12.** Podia and towers show a quantum change in size towards the end of the Twentieth Century to transform many skylines.

**5.13.** Nature and built form: the city stands tall before a flat sea and immediately beneath a steep and green mountain edge.

**5.14.** Built form and nature: conversely, green hillsides are glimpsed at close range from the city between towers.

condition to which attention is drawn all too rarely. Sadly, the physical opportunities for interplay between the two are not always well developed but a unique potential is present here, and remains one of the city's great opportunities and challenges: greater attention to this relationship would further enhance Hong Kong's reputation as a model of small footprint urbanism – an aspect of Hong Kong life that we will revisit in the Addendum.

# 6 Podium and Tower

In tracing the development of built form in Hong Kong, a constant theme has been the need to increase overall provision of all kinds of living, shopping, working and recreational space while confronting the limitations of available ground space. Importantly, development has not been undertaken without acknowledgment of local conditions: it has been driven less by design or planning theory than by local traditions and society. In one important aspect, the distinctions between public and private space have not been maintained rigidly: this condition, which we have seen earlier, is central to traditional forms of urban habitation such as shop-houses.

As we noted in Chapter 2, the streets and alleyways in Kowloon Walled City were progressively incorporated into private space. Roof surfaces were regularly enclosed to serve as extensions of habitable space or co-opted to serve as access pathways, drying spaces, playgrounds, schools, aviaries, or gardens. The boundaries between private and public were vague and readily renegotiated.

This synthesis of private into public can be readily observed today, for example, in Chungking Mansions, the private development of three towers sharing an interconnected commercial podium on Kowloon's Nathan Road and described in Chapter 2. Famous for its rich mix of budget hostels, restaurants and a wide range of commerce, the boundaries for public and private space at the lower levels are well defined and carefully managed. As one moves to the higher floors it is easy to see the way in which activities in the businesses or dwelling units often encroach into the circulation spaces, ventilation shafts and fire escape routes, although periodically building management and fire authorities work to contain the functions within their limits.

The importance of continuous commercial fabric along the street was recognized in the 1948 Preliminary Planning Report prepared by Patrick Abercrombie in which he acknowledges that a European planner might be tempted to 'condemn the practice … of giving up the entire ground floor of the residential area to shops, workshops, warehouses, stores etc' (Abercrombie, 1948). Extending his observation, he noted that this activity 'has the drawback of creating a narrow fronted dark tenement above'. Debating the alternative of shopping centres and tenement factories, as provided in London, he counselled against 'interfering with a settled method of living and working' provided some controls were in place to limit the nature of the commercial activities to those compatible with the proximity of residences.

We can extend this observation further and postulate that the expansion of private space into public areas is a core part of Hong Kong's spatial culture. Historically the street was the extension of the shop-house where a variety of functions took place, including socializing, cooking, washing, drying and playing. Even the introduction of back lanes in order to provide better ventilation and cooking space away from main streets did not change much the blurring functions of street and domestic or business space. Private domestic life was carried out on the street. These patterns of use of space were acknowledged in the planning and design of early public housing. The location of cooking facilities in the public outdoor passage in the Mark I resettlement housing reflected directly the convention of appropriating the street for domestic use.

Thwarting periodic attempts by the government to enforce regulations in this regard, many buildings in Hong Kong still manifest substantial illegal extensions. With such tight conditions, it is inevitable that attempts are made to claim additional private space, for example by constructing cantilevers from windows or by enclosing balconies and roof space. As planning regulations have developed, a common purpose has been to bring order and regulation to the street whether it is in the name of hygiene, safety or simply modernity. In effect, these regulations have striven to replace the complexity, diversity and adaptability of the traditional heterogeneous street with the clean and orderly image of a prosperous modern city where diversity is replaced with homogeneity and where private is clearly distinguished from public.

Plasticity and ambiguity in temporal ownership of space is well ingrained in Hong Kong's society. The informal and adaptive building form of the traditional shop-house depended upon a flexible definition of the outer edge of the building, allowing for transformation of adjoining space to accommodate changing needs and temporary requirements; always abhorrent to regulators, this flexibility has been confronted by a variety of regulations conceptualized on the compartmentalization of activities and, in more recent times, on high-rise, efficient structures. The manner in which buildings have allowed public access has changed through the urban history of Hong Kong. At some times building façades at the street level have been porous, permitting passers-by to see and venture into the buildings; at other times the prevalent approach has been to create opaque edges that isolate those on the street from the activities within.

With the volumetric approach to city making that had evolved, it was perhaps not surprising that a new urban form emerged which made possible the removal of the pressures from the street by sweeping up the multiplicity of activities that spilled out onto its surface and stack these into floors of public markets. As indicated in Chapters 4 and 5, we saw in the 1960s the emergence of the podium and tower structure as a form that developed over subsequent decades into Hong Kong's signature building type. Before the end of the twentieth century, this building form was thriving in cities as culturally different as Jakarta, Beijing, Hanoi and Manila. It became particularly an Asian strategy, although it had also appeared in Western cities as far spread as Los Angeles, Sydney and London.

Though it emerged strongly in Hong Kong, it should be noted that it is a form that had been foreshadowed in several Modernist schemes in the 1920s. Ludwig Hilbersheimer conceived a 'vertical city' of street-block podia and high slab-blocks in 1924: the ground streets were for traffic and the podia provided a bridge-connected pedestrian 'raised ground' at sixth level (Hilbersheimer,

**6.1.** Hilbersheimer's urban blocks of bridge-connected podia-and-slabs, 1924.

1944). Two years later, Van Eesteren went further with a model that included ground streets, and perimeter block buildings surrounding a raised court: slab-and-tower components rose from both the court and perimeter blocks, and the court levels were connected over the streets at intersections and mid-block (Van Eesteren, 1997). Elbert Peets had earlier proposed a similar scheme to that of van Eesteren in America – albeit for a one-block civic centre within a city (Hegemann and Peets, 1922). In Hong Kong, though, the form emerges from regulatory requirements to provide un-built space on a building lot to ensure ventilation and access to light while accommodating valuable street frontage; and not as a theoretical postulation to separate pedestrians from wheeled traffic. Although it might be perceived as a case of modern urban theory meeting Eastern tradition, the reality once again may be of a pragmatic Hong Kong manifesting a form that has been anticipated in modern utopian models and theory but not consciously derived from them.

In this evolution of the podium as an urban form, we can usefully identify five types:

1.  The regulation allowing 100 per cent coverage of the site at the base for retail activity leads to the initial podium form appearing on a single or adjacent building lots and was inserted into the urban fabric, maintaining a continuity of the street frontage while maximizing the plot ratio. The podium then becomes the base for one or more towers; while the podium is integrated into the line of the street, the tower(s) above break free of the surrounding urban form.

2.  The development of a platform across a site to give a large measure of pedestrian separation.

3.  At the largest scale, multiple interconnected podia become the base for a town or a considerable portion within it.

4.  A rhizomic podium development that acts as a connector, or a magnet, which successfully facilitates pedestrian movement across the urban fabric of which it is a part.

5.  A free standing development that becomes so large, inwardly focused or surrounded by roads and railway lines that it becomes isolated from the wider city – in effect, an urban island or mega-structure conceived as an object that is not intended to function as an integral part of the surrounding city.

These five conditions emerge in a series of overlapping timeframes, each from a different opportunity and each with a distinct lesson that is absorbed into practice in Hong Kong. We will consider each of these in turn.

## Covering the Site

The form of this city has been shaped fundamentally by a constant lack of developable land, very high land prices and an ever increasing population. Events in China, especially an acute lack of food as a result of land-use and industrialization policies, led in 1962 to a massive influx of population. In one twenty-five day period, 70,000 people walked over the border and into Hong Kong.

As the population increased in the years immediately after the mid-century, the blocks of low-rise shop-houses were rapidly replaced with high-rise, high-density tenements, as noted in Chapter 4. As also indicated in Chapter 4, the 1935 Building Ordinance was changed in 1956 to permit substantially higher intensity of land use, resulting in a period of extensive inner-city redevelopment. These changes in the regulations permitted the replacement of three- to five-storey buildings with much higher structures, leading to significant increase in land values and therefore the need to maximize the development potential by all means.

The 1956 legislation controlled plot development by specifying building height in relation to the street, permitting twice the street width in height. Continuing the shop-house tradition of building out over the pavement, new construction techniques using concrete were adopted to permit the buildings to cantilever over the street pavement or sidewalk and then rake back at a maximum of 76 degrees as they rose, to control the nominal building shadow to half the street. This led to potential plot ratios of up to 20 in some spots. Recognizing that these ratios facilitated very large populations in residential neighbourhoods which, in turn, imposed tremendous burdens on infrastructure such as utilities, transport and community spaces, a new regulation was introduced in 1962 (but delayed in implementation until 1966 to allow time for projects underway to be completed) that provided a sliding scale of plot ratio and site coverage with relation to building height and building type. The new regulation was understood to reduce the permitted development area; with the delay in enforcement for four years, there was a rush of construction that effectively flooded the market with residential buildings and slowed development until 1970.

An important aspect of the 1962 legislation was the requirement for 'open space' to be allowed for in domestic buildings, ranging from a quarter to half of the roofed over area depending upon the type of building lot, whether an end lot on a city block, a corner lot or one in the middle of a block as a terrace or through lot. This requirement was introduced to overcome the perceived problem of deep floor plates achieved under the 1956 legislation that resulted in residential spaces with little or no light, or access to ventilation. The legislation permitted, however, the lower floors of the building to be set aside for non-residential uses such as retail, parking or building services, and that these floors be allowed 100 per cent site coverage. While initially only a single floor was permitted at full coverage, this was soon expanded to several floors and so we see a prototype of the podium form emerge.

As a result, developments in the 1960s were characterized by shops aligned at the street level with towers above that responded to regulatory requirements for ventilation. The occupants of these towers continued the old norms of mixed functions, both private and public, occurring through at least part of the structure, including apartments subdivided into cubicles rented by the day or week. In its substantial site coverage, with shop frontage at the street edge and mixed uses above, the activity profile was not dissimilar to that of a shop-house. Thus, the two-part form that emerges is in response to the permitted site coverage at the lower levels and regulations aimed at health above.

As the podia expanded to cover more than one building lot, the opportunity

**6.2, 6.3 and 6.4.** Three example conditions of small podia covering their sites. (top left) Tower over a single-storey podium with the podium roof as 'left-over' space. (top right) A slender tower over a small four-storey podium on a small block. (left) A single level commercial podium and residential tower: however, commercial activities are 'invading' the podium.

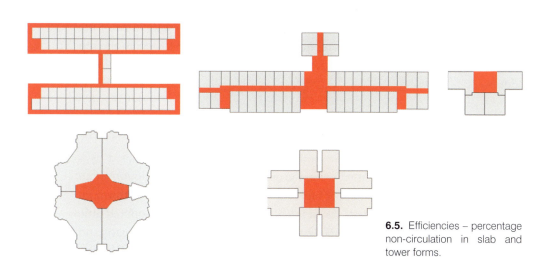

**6.5.** Efficiencies – percentage non-circulation in slab and tower forms.

was realized for larger buildings. As sites were consolidated, larger building masses in the so-called residential portions led to longer access corridors. But as the form developed, the pressure for financial returns led architects to focus their attention on the efficiency of the floor plan. Privately developed residential buildings, in which constraints on the prices of units for sale had to be balanced with costs of development, had difficulty in justifying the additional costs of longer corridors on each floor. The space assigned to circulation was counted in the plot ratio (the gross permitted area) and hence was lost as useable net area, with the additional cost apportioned to each apartment sold. Consideration was then given to the 'net to gross' ratio. Mark I public housing with its perimeter passageway gave an efficiency of 65 per cent but public housing types with a central corridor plan, such as Choi Hung Estate, achieved an efficiency of 77 per cent. This was seen as an improvement in the use of resources at a time when the need for housing was desperate. The private sector was driven yet harder for its return on investment and, without the need to prioritize social needs, developed the first private sector tower block as early as 1962. In this form, the sector was able to achieve an efficiency of 86 per cent.

A significant factor in the efficiency of the floor plate was the requirement that any building with more than six floors provides each floor with two stairs. As the corridor and elevator lobby were reduced in size on each floor, the most space consuming elements in the public areas of each residential floor were the two escape stairs required by law. The proposition of integrating the two within one footprint, in a form known as the scissor stair, was rapidly adopted as a standard solution. As a consequence, tower developments gained popular support as their minimal circulation spaces offered better value for money while also providing better ventilation and views.

As building lots were consolidated and the tower form took precedence, the question of the use of the ground plane came into focus. Where towers rose directly from the ground, the spaces between were seen as wasted. Apartments opening directly onto publicly accessible outdoor space were considered unsafe and undesirable. The space left over was not well used, manifesting none of the liveliness of typical streets. By raising the ground plane for the towers to the top of a podium, both this waste of space and a need for secure access could be addressed.

## Elevating the Site

As towers became the norm, the podium roof came to be considered as a community amenity – as a raised second ground. The podium was no longer an infill between the form of the upper building and the site edges but a platform on which stood one or more towers. As an infill, the roof of the podium offered little to the residents above as it was deemed by the regulations as inaccessible space, and hence was regularly claimed by those whose units immediately abutted the area.

**6.6.** Mei Foo Estate, as viewed from the highway.

Illegal extensions into this space were common, and often monitored closely and removed.

The large development that changed this condition was Mei Foo. Here, we can clearly see the emergence of a new phenomenon in which the platform was largely a translation of the urban street. The development was undertaken on a disused Mobil (formerly Standard Oil) petroleum storage site in Lai Chi Kok, slightly removed from the commercial and business centres of Kowloon. Built between 1965 and 1978, the estate, called Mei Foo Sun Chuen comprised ninety-nine towers, accommodating up to 60,000 people in 13,500 apartments, a massive undertaking for a private development. The name was derived from

**6.7a, 6.7b and 6.7c.** Mei Foo Estate was built over a period of 13 years. This trio of images shows both elevated towers on pilotis and towers with a deck where shopping and commercial services occur at both ground and deck levels (opposite).

*Mei Foo* ('beautiful trustworthy') kerosene lamps intro-duced to China by Standard Oil in the 1890s: as a result, this became then the local name for the oil com-pany, with *Sun Chuen* being New Town in Cantonese (Wordie, 2007).

The form of the typical block in this development shared one important characteristic with the traditional shop-house: residential accommodation was raised above a double level of shops, services and public functions. Residential units were accessed either from the street or from a continuous plat-form, later enhanced by landscape elements, over parking within the street blocks. This mix of func-tions provided some vibrancy at the building base and supported activities which inhabitants found useful and attractive. Thus Mei Foo was attractive to young professionals and others newly able to purchase

**6.8.** Mei Foo Estate. Here, two levels of commerce and two levels of car parking create the podium, from which the towers rise.

property in an attractive and desirable environment outside the city proper. Although initially remote and connected to Hong Kong Island and Kowloon by infrequent ferries and public bus services, the construction of an MTR (Mass Transit Railway) station in 1982 and a KCR (Kowloon-Canton Railway) station in 2003 integrated the community with other parts of Hong Kong.

In our view the importance of the Mei Foo quasi-podium is that it demonstrated that high-rise, high-density residential development was not only possible as a private sector approach, but was also perceived as desirable by the property market. Further, it demonstrated that the provision of communal public space, separated from traffic, was a successful marketing strategy for popular housing. The acceptance of this intense form in which a substantial platform is employed to provide public open space was then fed back to the design of public housing as can be seen in parts of the Wah Fu estate on Hong Kong Island and later in the Trident housing form. The typology of the massive integrated tower estate on a base, when expanded from mere parking provision to include shopping, gained acceptance as a strategy for urban development.

This typology brought with it a corollary benefit for the developer. Where the previous development model for residential buildings allowed for very few, if

**6.9.** Mei Foo 'came of age' with its connection to the rail network in 1982: the sign points to the MTR station.

any, shops at the street level, the provision of the podium spread the development risk between housing and commercial property by permitting a substantial commercial component. Allowing nearly 100 per cent site coverage initially for up to seven floors and later reduced to three with additional floors allowed for transport interchange, shops, parking, mechanical spaces or aesthetic consideration, the model enabled increased plot ratios by providing recreational space on the top of the podium in compensation. For those charged with the development of public housing, the goals were only slightly different. There was no market demand to consider since the shortage of low-cost housing in Hong Kong was consistently a problem. Drawing on the public purse, the efficiency of the development was also critical. Earlier projects had been narrowly utilitarian in their provision of space but as private developments began to exploit the spatial volumes of the city to provide additional benefits, so expectations of public housing began to change too.

## Volumetric Base, Cul de Sac Towers

As the population grew with the continuing influx of refugees throughout the 1960s, discussions in the 1970s turned, in

**6.10 and 6.11.** Old practices persist in modern Mei Foo: eating and shopping continue in open-front premises.

both private and public sector, to projects at a larger scale than piecemeal urban replacement. Property development became a substantial corporate opportunity for any business that had control over a significant land area: it became a primary component of corporate strategy which subsequently led, by the end of the century, to the most substantial portion of the underlying asset value traded on the Hong Kong Stock Exchange being secured by property developments. Development opportunities on major brown field sites were identified, as they had been for Mei Foo Sun Chuen, and government planning turned to discussion of new towns to be developed on green field sites once transportation links could breach the nine dragons peaks which separated Kowloon from the more spacious lands to the north.

In the third quarter of the century, Hong Kong was not the financial power-house it is today and there was little in its history to inspire financial confidence. The 1960s had been marked by political and financial uncertainty. The delayed introduction of the 1962 building regulations led to a surplus of residential construction as developers rushed to take advantage of the more generous earlier provisions; this oversupply undermined stability in the financial sector. A few years later, the Cultural Revolution in China spilled into Hong Kong, leading to political unrest and riots which, in turn, precipitated a stock market crash in 1967. A market boom from 1969 ended in 1973. However, the pressures of population growth continued: in the decade from 1960 to 1970, the registered population grew by one million people and would grow by yet another million in the subsequent decade. The reality of development in this space-constrained context was such that 'every square metre produces a return' (Cuthbert, 1985).

The larger scale urban developments looked to the experience of the British

**6.12.** Multi-volumed commercial terraces and heritage shop-house beneath a tower in Wanchai.

**6.13.** Tai Koo Shing commercial and residential towers.

New Towns for guidance. From this, these developments were framed as comprehensive in nature, providing not only housing but community facilities, recreation and commercial opportunities. As an example of a brown field site development that anticipates the government's green field sites in the New Territories such as Sha Tin, we can consider the Tai Koo Shing development, at the eastern end of Hong Kong Island.

The area was originally used as a dry dock by the Swire (Tai Koo in Cantonese) conglomerate for the construction and repair of ships but, in 1972 Swire Properties Ltd proposed a redevelopment scheme for a new residential community with a shopping and entertainment centre. Tai Koo Shing (in effect, Swire City) covers a total area of 21.4 hectares. The project was completed in 1984 and consists of sixty-one residential blocks of various heights from twenty-two to thirty storeys. Housing occupies a total floor area of 956,000 square metres, producing a domestic plot ratio of about 4.5. There are approximately 48,000 people living in 13,800 apartments. The overall site density is approximately 2,240 people per hectare or 645 apartments per hectare. The heart of the development is the City Plaza, a large commercial project, which includes a shopping mall with restaurants, cafes, fast food centre, ice-skating ring, bowling alley, cinema complex and adjoining office blocks. The complex is connected to the mass transit railway (MTR) below and green recreational space at the waterfront. Open space is provided (103,613 m²) which, although very limited by Western standards, is much more than the 75,000 m² required by Hong Kong regulations: additionally,

**6.14 and 6.15.** Tai Koo Shing: sign and steps to the podium.

**6.16a and 6.16b.** Tai Koo Shing podium landscape: the left view borrows scenery from the distant mountain.

the development offers 13,057 m² of sports facilities. Shops and shopping malls act as connectors to bring all the different parts of the development together. They also link to the MTR station and underground car parking. Tai Koo Shing has many restaurants, which cater for different tastes and budgets. The development functions as an island, independent of the city structure. People can live, work, shop, and entertain themselves without stepping out from the development.

These private developments had shown that purpose could be brought to the podium roof so that it would not be wasted, but the lesson took a

**6.17.** Pedestrian bridges connecting commercial towers over a road in Tai Koo Shing.

while to translate into public sector developments. A pioneering move to provide recreational space in public housing was made in the design of Hung Hom Bay Centre, completed in 1979, in which residents were provided with access to secure landscape areas at the podium level. The cruciform plan tower (with an efficiency of 83 per cent) sprang from this podium, offering the residents lift lobbies and common core areas without any provision for light or ventilation, rendering them unsuitable for social interaction. The podium surface was therefore an opportunity to provide additional facilities for residents, multiplying the surface area of the site by accommodating 100 per cent coverage for retail activities as well as offering a substantial public space on its roof.

## Connecting the Site

By the last quarter of the twentieth century, the podium form had become common in both residential and commercial developments as the means of using a site to the full. It was then adopted as an urban planning strategy to stitch together isolated parts of the urban fabric. As an example of the richest form, the rhizomic podium, we will consider Pacific Place where the topographic and historical challenges had left a gap on the shores of Hong Kong Island. While there are several other well interconnected podia, the particular topographic conditions make for an informative example here.

Very soon after the British arrived, the Armed Forces claimed as their base some 10 hectares on the eastern side of the central district to construct their primary barracks, Victoria Barracks, and ancillary needs. In 1979 the barracks were decommissioned and the major part of the site was converted into Hong Kong Park. The steep edge along Queens Road was designated for commercial and government use. The former emerged as Pacific Place and the latter as the Supreme Court complex. Pacific Place consists of over 1.1 million square metres of retail space and includes three hotels with over 1,500 beds, 240 serviced apartments, and an office tower block of thirty-six storeys. The shopping mall is located on four floors along internal covered streets, with car parking for approximately 650 cars below. The podium level is accessible by road, which passes uphill onto the platform with views of the harbour in between the buildings. From this level one can enter the lobbies of all three hotels and office towers. Access to

**6.18 and 6.19.** Pacific Place from the hill and harbour sides, showing the many built and 'natural' levels.

Hong Kong Park is at a higher level from which the High Court Building and the British Consulate are also accessed. The shopping centre is connected via a pedestrian bridge to the Admiralty and United Centres. Underneath the latter centres there is an MTR station, which can also be accessed from Pacific Place via an underground connection to the adjacent Admiralty Centre where there is a bus terminus. Linked to an elevated pedestrian network, access is provided from Hong Kong Park through to the waterfront and Central. Thus, the complex connects four different parts of the city that otherwise would remain isolated.

Given the site's variable topography, the interfaces between the building's internal levels, external public spaces and 'ground' are particularly complex. 'Street-facing' conditions are to be found on at least three levels. One is at Queens Road, the original public road connecting Central District to Wanchai, a public thoroughfare that traversed the army barracks when it was first established. This has always been unfriendly to pedestrians: it was previously a walk alongside barbed wire topped walls, and has

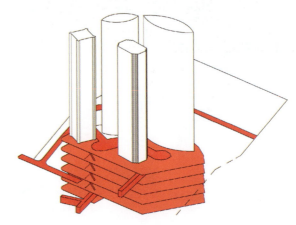

**6.20.** Pacific Place binds routes from Wanchai, Central, Admiralty and Mid-levels.

never acquired a public face. The second street entrance for Pacific Place is a road system built on top of the podium, the skylight of the atrium appearing as a feature in a small park in this system. The third street entrance is at the highest level across the south side of the complex, providing access to the Supreme Court. As a consequence, the tower currently accommodating the Conrad Hotel has three means of entry: directly from the third level of the shopping centre (lowest level), from the podium roof and from the upper street. Where then is the ground floor of this building?

## Isolating the Site

While the podium has demonstrated the capacity to knit elements of the city together, it can also lead to division. As the podium form is scaled up and takes over a whole city block, or several blocks, it can take on an introverted, monolithic form that excludes the surrounding areas and so becomes an urban island. Although this latter form is to be found in new towns in the New Territories, an inner-city example is Olympian City which we see as a mega-structure isolated and in competition with its surroundings.

The site for Olympian City was the result of a public transport infrastructure project, the provision of access to the new airport site on Lantau, developed at the

**6.21.** This advertising, used to sell residences in the Olympian City development, emphasizes the conceptual isolation of the podia.

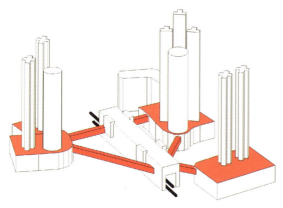

**6.22.** The diagram emphasises the podia and their surfaces as an archipelago and the towers as culs-de-sac.

**6.23.** The edge of one of the Olympian City 'islands'.

end of the 1990s. Two train lines were created, one an express route to the airport, the other part of the slower MTR rail system to the Tung Chung residential neighbourhood created adjacent to the airport. These infrastructure projects leave patches of lost space that are fractures in the urban fabric between the station-related Olympic City and adjacent neighbourhood of Yau Ma Tei.

Conceived as an integrated estate adjacent to Olympic Station, one of the new stations of the MTR network, the development occupies 13.1 ha and was built in three stages. Stage one, Island Harbourview, has nine forty-storey towers and provides 2,314 apartments, estimated to accommodate almost 7,000 residents. Stage two, Central Park, has four fifty-storey towers with 1,344 apartments for some 4,000 residents. Park Avenue, which is stage three, has five fifty-storey towers with 1,592 apartments for close to 4,800 residents. In total the project was planned to accommodate around 15,750 residents. In common with many other private housing developments, the project has its own clubhouse and two shopping malls.

Planning started with the need to provide access and riders to the MTR. The station is located within the complex, which in theory should encourage people to go through the shopping centre, and use the shops on the way home. The shopping centres also provide an air-conditioned environment, which in the Hong Kong climate is considered desirable. The development was placed on newly reclaimed land, much of it just 200–300 metres from the existing old and very dense communities of Yau Ma Tei, and Tai Kok Tsui and little further to Mong Kok. Old districts such as Mong Kok, Yau Ma Tei and Tai Kok Tsui may be crowded and run down but have a vibrant atmosphere. Mong Kok, one of the densest areas in Hong Kong, is extremely popular with young people. Yau Ma Tei is also a popular destination and frequented by tourists who visit the Night Market, Jade Market, or cinema complex. Tai Kok Tsui, does not have anything special to offer but it does have a thriving community and benefits greatly from its location, close to Mong Kok and Yau Ma Tei. By contrast, the monolithic physical form of Olympian City has the image of an isolated island, and movement on foot between the new 'City' and old districts is neither easy nor legible.

## The Ubiquitous Form

The podium form has contributed significantly to the broader success of Hong Kong by facilitating a social tradition of public space. In this evolution of urban form described above, there is some essence of the shop-house carried through to the podium and tower developments, albeit within a different form and at an exploded scale. While the original shop-house had a floor of publicly accessible shopping with a mix of commercial support and residential uses on the few floors above, the podium provided several levels of the publicly accessible space, with shops, services and amenities, and residential towers above. The podium was thus capable of continuing retail activities at street level with porous façades to enliven the street and provide services and employment in the neighbourhood. It also provided a commercial component in a residential development, enhancing the financial formula for a developer.

As the podium was permitted to expand to encompass several floors, a fundamental shift occurred. Activities that had been open to the street, and hence free to engage the street by extending activities onto it, were now subject to tighter oversight by the landlord and the variants of shop front presentation and activity disappeared. The interplay of private and public domain, as manifested by domestic and commercial activities appearing on the 5 foot way or pavement of the shop-house, was no longer possible. Although the immediacy of transition from domestic to public street so typical of the city during the first half of the twentieth century was lost, the residents of the towers above came to consider the inside of the shopping podium as an extension of their residential space. Nevertheless, with the internalization of these activities, streets suffered from reduced vitality.

While the podium emerged as a consequence of allowing complete site coverage at the lower floors for commercial uses or building services, the resultant roof space gained purpose as regulations for the provision of open space came into force. In 1981, the Hong Kong Planning Standards and Guidelines introduced requirements for recreation and open space provisions across the territory. Subsequent refinements of these standards require 2 square metres of open space

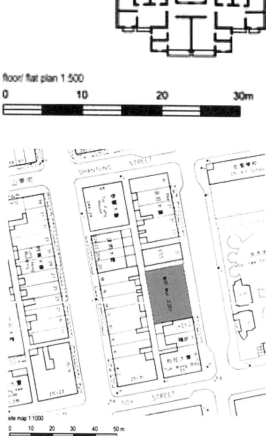

floor/ flat plan 1:500

0          10          20          30m

site map 1:1000

0    10    20    30    40    50 m

**6.24.** An anonymous example of a podium and tower on a tight urban site.

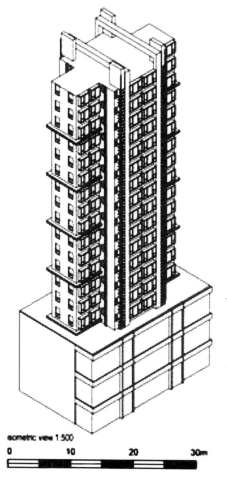

isometric view 1:500

0          10          20          30m

per person, 1 square metre being Local Open Space and an additional square metre per person as District Open Space. Local Open Space can be provided primarily for what is defined as 'passive' use, i.e. children's playgrounds or sitting areas, as distinguished from 'active' space for organized sports. Public and comprehensive residential developments are required to provide the minimum Local Open Space but may do so on a podium, with the proviso that any circulation space under a building is not counted. Although specific requirements have changed over time, the podium and tower form had become the norm for both public and private developments as a strategy to maximize site development potential.

Podium structures were now seen as a solution for much needed recreational and social space. With the roof space satisfying regulatory requirements and the commercial volume providing financial returns, this urban form was firmly established as an effective typology. The podium has gained further favour in recent years as the roof offers additional space for planting as the city strives to become greener. It has been identified as a strategic component in addressing urban noise as the lower levels of the towers can take advantage of the noise shadow from the street.

## The Volumetric Site

At the start of the twenty-first century we see a new urban form emerging as the next evolution of the podium takes the step from being merely a stack of separate floors to a volume in which a variety of functions are linked together. In this manifestation, the large urban structures shed the previous sharp distinction between the base podium and towers above, and evolve to a more seamless integration between the various formal and functional components.

A clear example of this volumetric evolution is Langham Place in Mong Kok, to which we have previously referred. Undertaken as an urban renewal project by the Land Development Corporation with initial site acquisitions starting in 1989, the complex was opened in 2004. This renewal project was targeted at an area known for its prostitution and shady commercial practices, officially perceived as an undesirable and chaotic environment. In its place, the project occupies most of two city blocks, bringing a mixture of exclusive shopping including boutiques for locally-designed fashion (in an area well known for its cheap and plenti-ful shopping opportunities), a five star hotel, an A grade office building with associated range of high to low end food outlets, and a community centre.

Clearly an island, the form is a distinct evolution from the

**6.25.** Street view of Langham Place hotel and office towers, Mong Kok.

**6.26a and 6.26b.** Express escalators move visitors through several levels to higher shopping floors. In the right hand photograph, taken from the vertiginous top shopping level, the lower floors of the office tower may be seen overlooking the vast volume containing several sets of escalators, each rising to a different level.

podium in which, we suggest, the distinctive lessons of Hong Kong's topography have emerged in a powerfully volumetric manner. Here, the hotel tower rises immediately from the street itself, engaging with other parts of the development as it rises. The fifty-nine storey office tower integrates with fifteen levels of shopping mall, not as a podium on which the tower stands but as a single volume in which the two building types are not differentiated. The mall has within it two high-speed escalators to take shoppers up four floors at a time and introduces a spiral of ramps and steps into the volume from the ninth to thirteenth floors. These various modes of movement take visitors up an artificial hillside that is legible and familiar after a century in which the city on Hong Kong Island has dealt with the challenges of steep slopes. In this example we can see that the two towers and the shopping mall have been conceived as a singular whole with a web of interconnected opportunities throughout its vertical form, not simply a collage of two towers standing on a layered plinth.

The tower and podium form has now pervaded most of Asia. Massive urban renewal is occurring in China where the form replaces whole neighbourhoods. In contrast to the use of towers alone, the podium can allow a continuity of street activities, which are characteristic of the Asian city. The experience in Hong Kong is that the podium form can also be successful within urban structures for other reasons, such as providing the three-dimensional nexus by which previously disconnected parts of the city can be joined. The problems, however, are all too obvious: the podium can emerge as an urban island that inverts attention, captures all street activity into an air-conditioned interior, and effectively sucks the life from surrounding streets. As we have observed, even Langham Place, which is a pioneer in its embryonic merging of podia and towers, is more defensive than porous about its street-level edges. As a strategy, therefore, a podium needs to be engaged with the city, not treated as a self-contained entity.

# 7 Emerging Volumetric Components

Vertical expansion and intensification are two processes that have dominated Hong Kong's urban growth. Both follow from the need to survive through adaptation and reconfiguration. Vertical expansion results in ever taller buildings, while intensification brings greater concentration of activities and modes of movement across more levels of the city. Vertical change is something readily apparent – essentially perpendicular extrusions forming new elements in the skyline. Intensification is less obvious, as it is a process concerning use, movement and often the incremental transformation of existing space: above all, it concerns multiple levels and volume. It is therefore easy to appreciate why the popular image of urban Hong Kong is of towers and *verticality*. However, the even more defining characteristic is that of *volumetric intensity* – a condition exemplified in the seething mega-structure of Kowloon's Walled City during its final decade, when some 35,000 people lived and worked in the approximately one million cubic metre volume over its modest 2.7 hectare site (see Chapter 3).

In this section we examine three aspects of Hong Kong's form and function that contribute to building and sustaining a successful volumetric character:

- the several ways in which ground is being redefined;
- the nature of movement on and between these 'new' grounds; and
- the layering of functions on them.

Further, to illustrate each point, we select some example components.

## Redefining Ground

With a shortage of natural land on which to build, Hong Kong has engaged in reclamation from the earliest days of British settlement. Pouring sand into the sea is not, however, the only manner in which additional ground can be created. This section sets out several ways in which usable 'grounds' have been constructed.

### Duplicate Ground

Although it is often repeated that Hong Kong is one of the densest places in the world, specific spot densities in certain neighbourhoods and blocks are well beyond the norm. For example, the spot density in Sham Shui Po is greater than 4,000 people per hectare and in Mong Kok it rises above 6,000 per hectare. These figures are calculated using census data, which reflect residential figures. Any visitor to Mong Kok could assume that the spot density on a busy shopping evening is substantially higher. In many sectors of the city, the population moving through the area can readily overwhelm the capacity of the surface of the streets to carry the flow. An obvious response to this demand is to duplicate the means of access to distribute the population. An early example is the bridge constructed in the early 1990s that carries substantial traffic from Wanchai MTR station to Immigration Tower, a destination that must be visited by everyone obtaining or renewing their Identity Card (carried by every resident of Hong Kong over the age of eleven), visas or Hong Kong travel documents. Adjacent to this tower is Revenue Tower, less frequently visited but, as home to the tax office, also a common destination. The narrow streets that connect the destinations – O'Brien and King Streets – do not have the necessary capacity for the flow of traffic as well as serving neighbourhood needs of vehicular access, shop frontage and local activities. A duplicate ground surface has been created to facilitate the foot traffic across this area, traversing each block as a bridge and connected back to the neighbourhood at every junction.

In a private context and at a smaller scale, we see 'ground' surfaces being reclaimed for individual use. As already noted, flower pots, sheds for additional rooms, washing lines, and the like are common roof-top sights. There are also more unusual ones. An example is the moon-viewing pavilion, which is a traditional Chinese structure for an intellectual. Here, tea or wine can be drunk

**7.1.** Wanchai: duplicate ground in the form of a bridge from the MTR Station to Immigration Tower, from which links are made directly to upper floors of adjacent buildings.

**7.2.** Part of Central's extensive system of duplicate ground, where the edge of the 'balcony street' can be seen as a place that is commonly used for stopping, looking around, meeting and talking. For an indication of the area across which duplicate ground provides upper level movement in Hong Kong's Central and the neighbouring Admiralty and Wan Chai districts, see figures 8.4.

while contemplating the night sky and poetry written. Tucked away in Pokfulam on the western end of Hong Kong Island we find such a moon-viewing pavilion atop a residential building of six floors. Constructed at least as early as the 1950s, this pavilion exists at the time of writing, but the surrounding towers and night light pollution probably obscure the moon on all but a few days of each year.

**7.3a and 7.3b.** Duplicate ground: moon-viewing in Pokfulam (right): roof pavilion in its high-rise context (left).

## *Split Ground*

The topography of Hong Kong poses considerable challenges to a planar understanding of a city but offers some advantages. One of these is the opportunity to create more than one 'front door'. An example of this is Hopewell Centre in Wanchai where the principal 'front door' is located on Queen's Road East but, because the building is located against the hillside, a second access is available directly to Kennedy Road approximately 60 metres higher. These circumstances in effect create a ground plane through Hopewell Centre that includes a seventeen floor vertical translation. Access is granted to the public

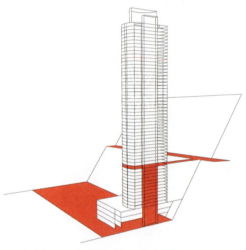

**7.4 and 7.5.** The Hopewell Centre includes the tall cylindrical building on the left of the photograph. It rises on the edge of Wanchai to connect Queens Road East, which once ran along the waterfront, to Kennedy Road, which follows the contour along the hillside some 60m above.

**7.6 and 7.7.** The Centre gives very different impressions at its two entry levels: one may enter or leave in sign-saturated Wanchai or the more salubrious Kennedy Road: seventeen building levels intervene between the two grounds.

who use the elevators in Hopewell Centre to connect the residential towers on Kennedy Road with the shops and offices of Wanchai below. In this example, we find an illustration of ambiguity in the concept of 'the ground floor'.

This is played out to a greater extent in Pacific Place, of which we have written earlier, where the lobby of the Conrad Hotel can be accessed through its primary entrance on Justice Drive, from a lower entrance on Park Avenue (which runs on the roof of the shopping atrium) that gives access to the coffee shop, or directly from level three of Pacific Place shopping centre to the function rooms. While these two examples are the direct result of the topographic conditions, this feature can be created through design. For example, the main entrance to the Sha Tin Town Hall is from the upper podium level while service access is from the street below. This concept of a split ground expands the notion of ground level access, enhancing the porosity of the city not only horizontally but also vertically. While it increases the commercial or operational frontage of a building, it also folds functions that were limited to one plane into a volume of space.

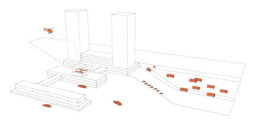

**7.8.** Multiple ground: Shun Tak Centre/ Macau Ferry Pier.

## Multiple Ground

The Shun Tak Centre, departure point for Macau, is a rich mix of activities. The closest example ever built of the aspirations of Futurists and Modernists, this building brings together the transport systems of MTR, tram, ferry, and helicopter with road systems of buses, taxis and cars. Completed in 1984, this pair of towers on a four-storey podium is accessed by underground, surface and above ground links including by air. A similar condition can be found in the complex of buildings at Exchange Square and the International Finance Centre, spanning from the Stock

**7.9 and 7.10.** These fragments of the Sun Tak Centre and Macau Ferry Pier are sufficient to indicate its multiple levels of public circulation - from ground through elevated walkways to multi-storey car park and ferry terminal. The complex and the 'raised grounds' of its immediate surroundings connect trams, buses, mini-buses, taxis, car parks, helicopters, several varieties of ferry, and underground train.

Exchange building to the IFC2 tower between which there are up to six levels of connection, some aligned with the urban road network and others that set up connections in new directions, such as the underground connection that links the Airport Express and MTR lines at Hong Kong Station. In Exchange Square, for example, the main public space of the notional town square is suspended over a substantial bus station that, in turn, sits adjacent to the underground trains noted earlier. In both these examples, we can find functional engagements of a ground floor at multiple levels. Visitors can traverse each of the buildings as if they were walking on the ground plane.

## Borrowed Ground

While reclaiming land by mounding sand onto the seabed is the most obvious way to create additional space, a traditional mode of placing activities on the sea cannot be ignored. Long before the British arrived, boat-based living was common in Hong Kong. Floating communities and structures built over the sea provided accommodation for portions of the populations of those times, most commonly the Tanka people. Today we see remnants of these water-based communities. While the large floating communities that were found in bays such as Aberdeen Harbour (and later moved to constructed locations such as the Causeway Bay Typhoon Shelter) have disappeared, we can still see two distinctive manifestations of borrowed ground. In Tai O, on Lantau Island, the village of housing on stilts over the sea continues; communities such as these can be found throughout Asia. A more colourful alternative is regularly photographed in Aberdeen – the floating restaurants. Developing from a tradition of visiting the floating fishing community to eat seafood on board, purpose built barges were anchored in the harbour by the middle of the twentieth century. In the late 1970s the strategy was

**7.11 and 7.12.** Aberdeen's exuberant restaurants 'borrow' their ground from the sea. – the right photo shows an extensive kitchen annex behind.

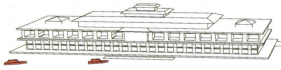

**7.13.** Multi-level floating restaurants at Aberdeen.

developed to an enormous scale and three interconnected two-, three- and four-storey structures were branded as Jumbo Kingdom and located a little outside the main Aberdeen Harbour. These multi-storey immobile vessels are now a common tourist destination, accommodating both Chinese and Western restaurants with, collectively, several thousand seats.

## Movement in Space

Having established new grounds, new modes of movement are needed to access these different grounds.

### Interlocked Ladders

A scissor stair is a set of two interlocking stairways providing two separate paths of egress located within one stairwell enclosure. The stairs wind around each other, and are separated from each other within their enclosures by fire rated construction thus providing two separate but physically intertwined paths of egress. An ingenious device, this stair design satisfies the regulatory requirement for two paths of escape from every floor without duplicating the stair tower, thus achieving the most pressing need in Hong Kong to maximize use of plot area. Apparently used first in Hong Kong in the 1960s, the scissor stair has become ubiquitous in Hong Kong as it facilitates the development of the small plot areas to provide maximum usable space. The device has been credited as a key invention to solving Hong Kong's housing problems (Keynote Speech by David C. Lee, Chairman of the Hong Kong Housing Society, at the Inauguration of the CII-HK, 17 November 2003). So common is it that the scissor stair was chosen to represent Hong Kong in the 2006 Venice Biennale where bamboo scaffolding, giant folding beds and a representation of the Mid Levels escalator complemented an almost full-size scissor stair rising three flights as four symbols of the way space is used

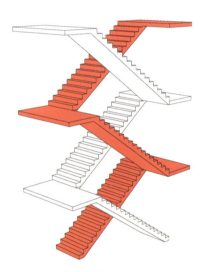

**7.14.** Two interlocking stairs make up the 'scissors' arrangement.

intensively. Scissor stairs have been adopted by other national building agencies as a means of providing more cost effective design for multi-storey structures, for example, in New York City Construction Code Section 1014.2.1 and a modular construction of such stairs subject of US Patent 4930273 issued in 1990. Reputedly, its origins can be traced back to the wooden staircase in the Big Swallow Temple (大雁塔) in Sian China in the Tang Dynasty (618–907 CE); a similar wooden staircase was supposed to be in the Ying Yan (應殷木塔) Temple in Shan Si in the Yuen Dynasty (1291–1368 CE).

## Mechanical Ladders

Data reported for 1998 suggest that Hong Kong has the largest number of escalators per capita in the world, with one escalator for every 1,242 people. Japan, by comparison, had one per 2,801 people and Germany one per 7,017 people. With its topographical challenges and intensity of use, this is not too surprising. What is remarkable is the extent to which such systems have been put to use. Immediately upon establishing their hold on Hong Kong, the British faced the challenge of moving up and down the hillsides. With its highly unstable soils on slopes and typically high rainfall, walking or riding up slopes required some effort to stabilize or surface the slopes. With their extremely steep inclines, many slopes in the new Central District were navigated by means of granite steps, with one coming to be known as Ladder Street with reference to its structure and incline. When technology allowed, such stone ladders were replaced by what we identify as moving ladders, namely escalators. The most famous of these is now the Central to Mid Levels Escalator, which is really a series of eighteen escalators and three travelators (essentially escalators that move up gentle slopes without forming steps) linked by covered walkways and access stairs: the system carried 81,000 people per day in an estimate from 2008. Covering a distance of 800 metres, the system climbs 135 metres. Initiated as a means of reducing vehicular traffic on the congested streets accessing the lower slopes on Hong Kong Island, the project was officially labelled

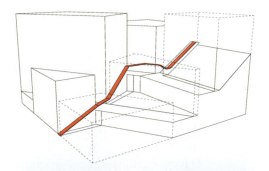

**7.15, 7.16 and 7.17.** The Mid-levels Escalators thread between buildings and over streets to connect the flat ground of the former waterfront and the elevated Mid-levels.

a failure in 1996 by the Hong Kong Government Director of Audit because it overran budgets and there was no discernable reduction in traffic on the roads. This judgment would not appear to be supported by empirical evidence of the escalator's success in regenerating the city, the introduction of a band of vitality through sections of what were difficult to reach areas up the hillside.

The Central to Mid Levels Escalator is the most public example of the way in which this transport technology has redefined Hong Kong. With its open structure, the escalator facilitates the movement of pedestrians through otherwise inaccessible places or through uninviting transitions of contour without the disjuncture of an elevator. By encouraging greater pedestrian traffic, the escalator has increased commercial transactions.

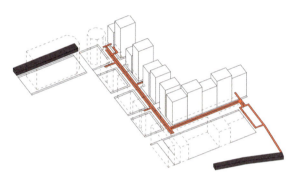

**7.18.** The Mong Kok elevated pediway takes a flat route with right-angle turns between two stations.

## Elevated Pediways

Established surface transportation infrastructure can be categorized by its speed of movement and access facilitated into streets, roads and motorways. Streets afford a locus for community engagement and access. Roads are distinguished by their purpose for traversing a particular site and their primacy in connecting one location to another. These different purposes will be reflected

**7.19, 7.20 and 7.21.** Mong Kok elevated pediway: it has few exit and entry points, allowing large numbers of pedestrians to cross the district at speed, functioning like a human motorway.

in their dimensions, the barriers (or lack of such) used to separate different modes of movement, surfacing and articulation. This then is reflected in their use; streets might be crossed by a pedestrian at any point but a road at indicated controlled crossings, for example. Within this categorization the next level of capacity can be indicated by the motorway, a thoroughfare intended for higher speed traversal between points at longer distances on which a lack of motion is not anticipated nor encouraged. Observing Hong Kong, we can see a similar categorization of movement systems. In describing *duplicate ground* earlier, we illustrated the replication of circulation space by way of the bridge between Wanchai Station and Immigration Tower. This bridge replicates the streets below in all except their building access; on the bridge

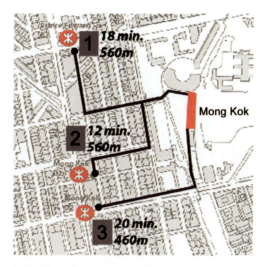

**7.22.** The plan shows walking times between Mong Kok East and three closest MTR stations. The pediway runs between Mong Kok East subway station (No. 2 in the figure) and Mong Kok station to cut the usual ground level walking time by one-third.

it is common to find vendors illegally hawking their wares, acquaintances stopping to speak or people walking slowly as they observe the views within adjacent buildings or along vistas between buildings. This use of the bridge can be contrasted to that which links Mong Kok East station to the Mong Kok MTR station, a distance of 400 metres. In this instance, the bridge provides fewer opportunities to access the ground, running at one point 150 metres without egress. By contrast, the Wanchai pedestrian bridge has regular exits over its 300 metre length. The manner in which the Mong Kok connection is used is akin to that of a motorway, hence we identify it as a *pediway*. Such purposeful high-speed routes can be found across the city where densities are high and distances longer – for example in Central District running from the Shun Tak Centre to Exchange Square.

## Elevated Roadways

Although Hong Kong has a com-paratively low number of vehicles for its population, the need to move these through the congested areas and across challenging topographies has led to inventive solutions. While the original overpasses, or flyovers, were constructed in the 1970s to solve congestion problems at intersections, the capacity to build roadways atop columns has come to be an elegant solution to weaving roads across the topography. Of the several surprising solutions, the most extreme of these can be found taking east bound traffic from Pokfulam Road in Western District (Sai Wan), Hong Kong Island, through the air space above Hill Road and down to the waterfront elevated dual carriageway along

**7.23a and 7.23b.** Elevated roadways are a common sight in Hong Kong. The left hand example is the more common type above a street in an older district: Tai Kok Tsui. The right hand one is unusual in that it is single lane, extremely curvaceous, and steep as it threads its way between buildings to take traffic from the hillside (Pokfulam Road) to the waterfront.

Connaught Road. Traffic using this 600 metre bridge descends through almost 100 m with close-up views into the upper level windows of flanking apartments en route. This prosaic bridge over a congested junction has become a masterful freeform road that appears unconstrained by topography to take traffic through the city on a route freed of any ground constraints.

## Layered Functions

To complement a ground that can be manipulated and multiplied, and access achieved in a variety of ways, functions can be freed from their conventional positions on the ground. Over time a variety of inventive ways have been created to accommodate such functions: here we identify a few.

### *Cubed Civic Centres*

The government has provided Municipal Services Buildings across the territory as centres for the local community. These are composed of a distinctive combination of activities, many of which had previously taken

**7.24.** Sheung Wan Municipal Services Building.

place on the street. There is no consistent provision of functions in the building as these respond to an official reading of the community needs. The Smithfield Municipal Services Building can serve to illustrate the composition. The ground floor houses a meat and wet fish market where it can be hosed out easily and the sometimes pungent materials moved in and out with minimal impact. Rising a floor is the fruit and vegetable market, still able to be hosed but less pungent (if you ignore the durian). The next floor is for cooked food stalls, which have been transported from their original kerbside locations into safer and less polluted surroundings. The activities on these three floors had previously been arranged in the side streets throughout Kennedy Town, which now are freed for traffic. Rising to the next level, the third floor using the British method of

**7.25.** Sai Ying Pun Market. These civic volumes are variations on the Smithfield theme, described in the text. As a volume, the Sai Ying Pun frontage is particularly interesting, since it is really a slab of space with numerous steps, stairs and escalators that offer multiple entrances across several levels.

numbering floors, is the Smithfield Library (in some centres there will be several floors of library), on the fourth floor are administrative offices, a playroom for children, a fitness centre and a study centre for the majority of school students who do not have a quiet space at home. Above these are three more floors of sporting facilities including archery, squash, dance, basketball, and badminton. In many there are also government service centres and offices.

## Stacked Cemeteries

Handling the dead in a city of six million with a limited land area is a delicate matter. While cremation has been heavily encouraged, the strong traditions of earth burial remain. A second tradition of the second burial entails the exhumation of remains after six or seven years (during which the tissue matter has decayed) followed by a cleaning of the bones or cremation of the remains at that time and their internment in an urn in a columbarium. Twice a year, the cemeteries and columbaria are visited on days designated by the traditional cosmological calendar as grave sweeping days, the Ching Ming (in spring) and Chung Yeung (in autumn) festivals. In order to reconcile the need to provide land to support essential cultural activities with the

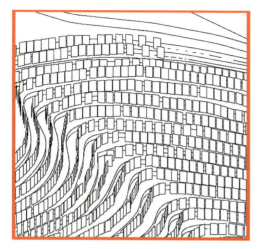

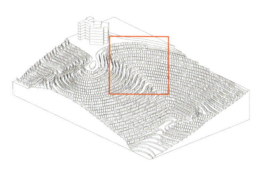

**7.26a and 7.26b.** This cemetery steps very steeply up the Pokfulam hillside.

**7.27.** Note there is a multi-storey columbarium at the top of the cemetery: this can be seen most conspicuously on the drawing (figure 7.26b) in figure 7.26a.

demands of the living for space as well as their distance from the dangers and spirits of the cemetery, the government of Hong Kong quickly identified appropriate places for the cemeteries and columbaria, establishing the pattern of locating them on steep hillsides otherwise unusable. Sited with consideration of the principles of *fungshui*, even in the Christian cemeteries, these are nested into hillsides typically offering views across the sea. Their steep slopes are terraced into narrow access paths along which are aligned headstones, which are assigned for the brief period of ground interment. Graphically describing the contours of the hillside, these paths and the headstones leave little space for plants, which are discouraged as the twice annual sweeping is accompanied by the burning of offerings which can lead to hill fires. The Chinese Christian Cemetery on the western end of Hong Kong Island offers an illustration. With Pokfulam Road delimiting its upper boundary, the cemetery spills down the hillside, has extended across Victoria Road and continues to the bottom of the valley at which point there are several homes for the elderly, hospices and special care institutions. Columbaria have been constructed both on Pokfulam Road and Victoria Road in which to accumulate the urns as the cyclical interment ends.

**7.28.** At the centre of the photograph is another stepped cemetery and multi-storey columbarium in Kwai Chung: it is surrounded by a multi-level vehicle park (to the fore), multi-storey warehouses (behind) and residential towers forming a distinctive stepped skyline (right).

## Flatted Factories

With land such a scarce resource, industrial activities are subject to the same constraints as commercial and residential uses. Land noted for industrial uses has been leased by the government with similarly high plot ratios as residential land – it is common for such land to be leased with an FAR of 15. The leasor developer has therefore the pressure to generate returns by constructing a multi-storey building. In this vertical arrangement of industrial activities a factory may take over all or part of a floor.

The term for these arrangements is 'flatted factories', derived from the British description of an apartment as a 'flat' so the term is used not only in Hong Kong but also Singapore and India. Not all industrial purposes are suitable for such arrangements, obviously, but it is remarkable the extent to which industry is accommodated in this way: printing works, plastics moulding plants for children's toys, food production.

As Hong Kong industrialized after the 1950s, domestic industrial

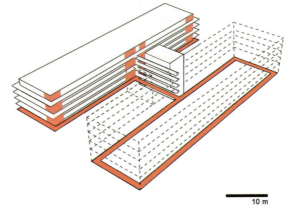

10 m

**7.29.** A flatted H-block factory: although larger in size than the residential H-blocks (see figure 7.32) the form and circulation were similar.

production became a common mode of employment. Subcontracted assembly of products paid on a piece basis supplemented many household incomes in these cottage industries. Manufacturing activities were also established in residential units or in illegal structures in squatter settlements. In the late 1950s,

**7.30 and 7.31.** Flatted factories in Tai Kok Tsui The building in the right figure is in effect an industrial 'massive block' that rises through 16 functional levels, if the first level mezzanine and roof are included.

the government constructed buildings for light industrial uses to provide for these entrepreneurial activities, following the model of their Mark I resettlement housing. The government expanded this capacity by constructing seventeen industrial estates in the late 1970s and early 1980s. Over time, the private sector has taken up the opportunity and constructed large buildings for heavier industries such as printing plants with their very heavy machines. In solving the problems of vertical access and the constraints of freight elevators, especially in the multiple handling of goods that such a form of transport demands, later buildings have included enormous ramps to allow articulated container trucks to drive directly up to the factory door on the higher levels.

By the end of 1996, over 83 per cent of all industrial space was accommodated in such multi-storey facilities, with the private sector providing 17.8 million m² of such space (Tang and Tang, 1999). The problems with such arrangements are several, including: the need for standard floor plates regardless of the various activities on each floor; limited access; limited clear span spaces; difficulty in managing industrial effluents; problems in isolating vibrations from machinery; and complexities in fire safety.

By the end of the 1980s the demand for industrial space began to drop as China opened up and welcomed industrial investments, especially in the areas lying just north of Hong Kong. A decade later, over 50 per cent of the government industrial estates were empty. With more land available, industrial facilities could be constructed with greater ease, customized to particular uses. The reduced demand for flatted factories led to an exploration of other uses, so industrial/office space came to be accepted by the government and slowly regulations were changed to allow such space. The changes, however, were additive such that the buildings had to satisfy both industrial and office requirements which resulted in more expensive space. There are few attempts at the time of writing to create residential spaces from these since the act is illegal, so the loft spaces that are so popular in North America and increasingly in Europe are not feasible in Hong Kong at the time of writing.

## Sky Schools and Churches

As the population grew in the middle of the century, infrastructure investment was concentrated in large part on the creation of adequate housing stock. Much of the population growth consisted of younger people as they had the mobility to cross illegally into Hong Kong; this led to a rapid growth in the population of children and thus the need for schools. The government allowed the establishment of schools on the roof tops of the resettlement estates to supplement the government run schools on the estates which had insufficient capacity. Typically operated by religious organizations, these schools often ran three sessions each day to cope with the demand, one each in the morning, afternoon and evening periods. Without space to assign to educational activities not formally sponsored, these schools were expected to find accommodation where they could. Other associations and organizations promoting ideologies not supported by the government also ran schools, for example the communist workers' unions, and these too were not assigned facilities. Typically these schools occupied a small area and this could be created in small rooms accommodated on the roof of a structure since these were typically flat, the remainder of the roof often being used for physical activities. Once again, official sanction followed from illegal precedent and such roof top schools were formalized and

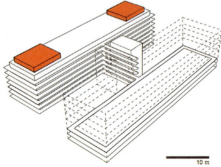

**7.32 and 7.33.** Sky schools on residential H-blocks: school buildings using roofs as 'ground' were a common H-block skyline feature.

purpose built rooms and fencing provided on rooftops of housing estates for this purpose. Although no longer a norm, this convention for the placement of schools

**7.34a, 7.34b, 7.34c and 7.34d.** Another example is the Kau Yan Church on Third Street on Hong Kong Island. Originally built as the Basel Mission church on this site in 1861, it was rebuilt in 1934 and a school added in 1958. In 1995, a substantial redevelopment was undertaken to expand the school and construct a residential tower with a design taking advantage of the hill. The seven-storey school is accessed from the lower boundary on Third Street and a twenty-storey residential tower is accessed from the upper site boundary on High Street.

has now become so accepted that purpose built schools typically employ the roof for a range of activities, typically physical exercise and outdoor activities.

Religious institutions have played a significant role in the development of Hong Kong not only in schooling but in the provision of social infrastructure, allowing the government to focus its resources on other forms of infrastructure such as housing, transportation or services. The British administration had allowed certain denominations to use land for churches; typically built in the English style, these set buildings on the site with space left around them. As the demand for land increased and funding for church activities typically difficult to secure, churches became aware of the opportunities for raising additional income from their land. With regulations allowing churches to use their land for other purposes (e.g. Law No. 55 of 1999) and a practice of multiple uses on a site, churches have taken to redeveloping their land. With typically small sites and a desire to continue the presence of a church on the site, several inventive solutions have been built. One example is the Kau Yan Church on Third Street on Hong Kong

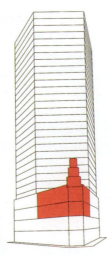

**7.35 and 7.36.** Part of a multi-level development, this church sits above its wedge-shape site between Hennessy and Johnston Roads, Wanchai.

Island. Originally built as the Basel Mission church on this site in 1861, it was rebuilt in 1934 and a school added in 1958. In 1995, a substantial redevelopment was undertaken to expand the school and construct a residential tower with a design taking advantage of the steep slope. The seven-storey school is accessed from the lower boundary on Third Street and a twenty-storey residential tower is accessed from the upper site boundary on Upper Lascar Row. Another example is the Methodist Church located on the triangular site defined by Hennessy Road, Johnston Road and Fenwick Street, a site created by the reclamation of the 1920s. Originally occupied by a church alone, the site is now home to a twenty-eight-storey office tower on which the

**7.37.** Schools, churches and office and/or residential towers occur in various configurations of form and use. Here the school and church are at street level with a tower above the church.

church is presented as perching on the leading edge of the prismatic form, facing towards Central District. This combination of a church in a skyscraper is not unique to Hong Kong, having been used by the Methodist Church in the Chicago Temple Building built in 1924. In this instance, however, the presentation of the church on the second floor and the chapel on the third topped by a symbolic spire presents to the approaching traffic an image that recalls the hillside churches of the Mediterranean, but here the church is perched on a man-made 'hill' of an office building.

## Horses in High-Rise

Under the management of the Hong Kong Jockey Club since 1884, horse racing has become a significant part of community life in Hong Kong. Nothing in Hong

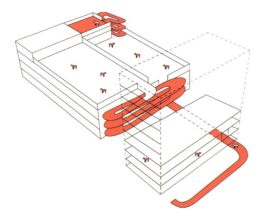

**7.38.** This multi-level composition includes housing for stable hands above the stables in the foreground and exercise facilities for the horses on the roof of the building behind.

Kong is exempt from the need to use land more carefully, not even horses. As racing has become more popular and more horses are kept, the problem of accommodation for the horses has been addressed in the usual manner here – high rise stables. The initial racetrack was built in Happy Valley in 1845 and remained the only course until the Sha Tin course was opened in 1978. With the racetrack itself occupying the only flat land in Happy Valley, space for the stables was to be found on the hillside to the south. From the 1920s onwards, horses were accommodated at the Jockey Club stables on Shan Kwong Road in Happy Valley. By the 1960s the pressure on stabling and concomitant facilities had led to the need for a high-rise solution in this congested part of town. To address these needs, a complex of buildings was erected on the steep slopes with the tallest building providing four levels of stables and seven levels of residences for the stable hands plus recreational space for the families on the roof. In the adjacent buildings linked by ramps were additional stables and roof top exercise paddocks for the horses, providing a total of four paddock areas.

Although not so constrained by space, the new facilities in Sha Tin provide twenty-three stables with accommodation for 1,260 horses, using multi-level stables.

## Tiered Transport

The need for multi-deck transportation in Hong Kong was established soon after the tramways were built. The narrow corridor of traversable flat land along the

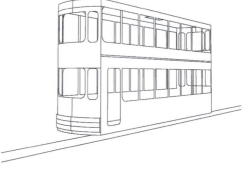

**7.39 and 7.40.** Slim-line double-deck trams. The trams in the photograph are on Des Voeux Road, Sheung Wan.

waterfront ensured that the intensity of transportation needs demanded a high capacity system. Within a decade of starting their service in 1904, single-deck were replaced by double-deck trams, starting in 1910 with all removed by 1912. Although these initial double deck trams were open to the elements on the second level, they were enclosed by 1925. While not the originator of multi-level trams, Hong Kong continues to use this form of transport as a principal and high capacity system along its 13.5 km of track.

Multi-level transportation can be found in other forms. Most obvious on the streets are the double deck buses, introduced in 1949 in Kowloon where the flatter land allowed these heavier vehicles to be used: the bus system today has over 5,000 double deck buses in operation. Multi-deck ferries were introduced before the end of the nineteenth century, for example, the Star Ferry introduced a second level on its ferries. Yaumatei Ferries, later Hong Kong and Yaumatei Ferries, introduced two deck car ferries in the 1960s to carry the increasing number of cars across the harbour. Until the opening of the cross harbour tunnel in 1972 this was the only means for a car to travel from Hong Kong Island to Kowloon and on a busy day, this

**7.41.** Tall buses serve tall buildings.

**7.43.** An iconic double-deck Star Ferry on Victoria Harbour. (Langham Place in Mong Kok is the tall building in the background that breaks the hills skyline.)

**7.42.** Most buses may be double deck but they are still stored in multi-storey parking structures.

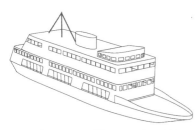

**7.44 and 7.45.** Triple-deck ferry: the one in the photograph is passing Kowloon skyscrapers.

journey could entail a wait of many hours to obtain a space for the vehicle on board. As the population increased and settlements on outer islands began to grow, Hong Kong Yaumatei ferries started with triple deck passenger ferries in the mid 1970s to accommodate the heavy demand on the inter-island routes between Hong Kong and Lantau and Cheung Chau.

Just as scissor stairs enable a single service core to provide twice the functionality, double deck elevators have also been employed in Hong Kong in such buildings as the World Trade Centre and the International Finance Centre. Here, the building's even and odd floors are served by the two different decks in the elevator.

## Sky Gardens

The device of the borrowed view can be found in the Chinese tradition of gardens and is best exemplified in the exquisite urban gardens of Suzhou. These gardens

**7.46.** A transfer floor in a tower, which is required for fire-safety, provides oppor-tunity for a community garden: Manhattan Hill Towers are located in the old industrial area of Lai Chi Kok.

illustrate the manner in which a very small piece of land can be used to create a garden with expansive intentions. The technique expands the experienced view by layering elements within it and bringing distant elements that are often not part of the garden in which you stand into the

**7.47 and 7.48.** Surprisingly large bushes and masses of vegetation are a common sight on the balconies and roofs of many older Hong Kong buildings.

composed view. When this idea is brought into the Hong Kong capacity to layer surfaces to create land in unusual places, the notion of a sky garden emerges. In these, a garden space is provided on elevated planes as a place of refuge from the urban intensity. Gardens such as these have been created by private individuals on accessible roof surfaces, including those with structures such as the moon-viewing pavilion, as noted above. Consistent with the pattern of legitimating individual initiatives by publicly delivering the same end, tower-based housing estates began to manifest sky gardens in the late 1990s. One example was that of Verbena Heights, Tseung Kwan O in the New Territories. In this public housing estate constructed in 1996–1997, the landscaped podium covering the whole site is complemented by small pocket gardens in the tops of the towers. This approach was broadly evident in the submissions to an architectural competition held by the Hong Kong Housing Authority in 2000, 'Public Housing in a New Era', and is current in the urban design language in the region.

### Stacked Warehouses/Folded Portside

The technology of bulk storage demands an ease of access and scale of provision. A common transport technology such as shipping containers, for example, is limited by the structural capacity of the container to be stacked up to eight units maximum. This constraint requires container ports to be surrounded by large areas of land. With one of the busiest container ports in the world and a severe shortage of land, Hong Kong has come up with a remarkable solution of multiplying the container land surface within stacked warehouses. These structures are misleading

to observe since the obvious measure of scale, the access ramp for vehicles, appears to be a familiar circular ramp for a personal car. Instead, these ramps accommodate articulate trucks conveying single containers, a clear height of 4.2 metres and climb several storeys so that a single section of land can accommodate many cargo

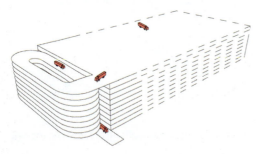

**7.49 and 7.50.** Stacked warehouse with massive drive-up road ramp for articulated trucks: Kerry Cargo Centre Kwai Fuk Road, Kwai Chung Industrial Centre.

handling activities concurrently. Additional floors are accessed by heavy duty lifting equipment, allowing one structure at the Kwai Chung docks to replicate handling facilities across eleven floors.

## Veneered Functions

The association of shop floor area to the value of the activity contained is one that is practised throughout the world. A visit to the grander shops of Manhattan, Paris, London or Hong Kong will provide evidence of this association. A larger area assigned to little or no purpose signifies the importance of the commercial transactions entertained within. Nowhere is that association tested so well as in Hong Kong; the world-renowned brands occupying substantial shop fronts in the grander parts of the city are not that far from shops that transact substantial volumes of commercial business on almost no floor space at all. Throughout the territory can be found commercial businesses in which the vertical surface is more important than the horizontal. News vendors hang their stock on the walls adjacent to a stool on which the 'shopkeeper' sits. Real estate agents paste flyers to external walls and use a mobile phone to run the agency. Relevant paperwork is transported in a box or a briefcase, as mobile as the agents. In these businesses, ground surface is hardly a necessity: the activities can be accreted in remaindered spaces under staircases or on the edges of pavements. The traditions of private claims on public space, commonly used for the hawking of goods or temporary use for a service, are extended to include high-value commercial transactions such as property sales which are given a physical presence by means

Veneer functions are a common sight. **7.51.** An extremely thin estate agency. **7.52.** Books for sale form the 'outside wall' of a small shop. **7.53.** Plants are removed from the shop to form a 'curtain of merchandise between the (stepped) footpath and carriageway.

of a veneer of activity pasted to a building of substance. In addition, there are other businesses that will occupy legitimately the edge of a building or otherwise remaindered space – perhaps occupying a short one metre wide strip: these slip between the sidewalk and the larger interior volume, which is occupied by other business activity, or are tucked under a staircase. High-value small-volume services and merchandise, such as tobacco products, camera or computer accessories and property, are offered from such slim slices of space.

# 8 Conclusion
## Vertical and Volumetric

Hong Kong is often held as a model of *laissez-faire* economics, and much of the official rhetoric that has emerged from the place since its 1841 foundation reinforces this image. Our enquiry suggests that this is but half the story in the urban context: in practice there has been a semi-autocratic government carefully observing trends, often in extreme circumstances, and following with deliberate intervention to enforce control around established trends and channel their potentials. Hong Kong governments have waited, watched and reinforced the forces that have shaped the city's physical growth, building forms and modes of movement within their tiny territory of rugged landforms, against a backcloth of usually rapid population growth and volatile regional politics. Within this context, it has been government as much as 'God' that has created land for city building, and it has been government that has codified and shaped the building forms upon that land – into a succession of dense street-based, and later varied vertical and volumetric forms. Further, it has been government that has controlled, franchised and sometimes owned the companies that have enabled the people of Hong Kong to dwell in their high-density forms and move about them in the great variety of public transport that has come to run on, under and over Hong Kong land and water.

The result is a small footprint city that has not always been tall but always dense – indeed very dense. The main characteristics that have emerged in Hong Kong are each unusual in today's urban world, and together extremely rare. They are

◆ extreme verticality across most of the city in a world that has generally favoured urban spread;
◆ extensive volumetric development when most places have been reluctant to abandon natural ground as the primary plane of reference for city-building; and
◆ continued expansion of public transport when elsewhere, there has been mostly obsession with private vehicles.

Further the small and irregular footprint, usually squeezed between water and rocky heights, means that few amongst its stacked inhabitants live far from the basic elements of earth, water, wood or stone, occasionally fire, and other natural elements.

These extreme conditions, forms and relationships have become the essence of Hong Kong; and offer a window onto a special set of urban phenomena that includes the vertical and volumetric organization of space (form), highly intensive mix of activities (content), diverse but integrated public transport (movement), and the juxtaposition (though not necessarily integration) of all three with nature – all dimensions of urbanism that preoccupy contemporary urban professionals and thinkers, especially those involved in design. We have outlined the context, origins and physical characteristics and dimensions of the most salient forms that have been integrated or simply put together to make Hong Kong into the extraordinary habitat we know today.

Prior to the arrival of the British in Hong Kong, evidence suggests at least 6,000 years of human habitation with only modest interference to the landform. However, following 'possession', it took little more than one-and-a-half centuries for transformation from 'barren rock' and colonial outpost to urban system that is 'home' to over seven million residents and host to more than four times that number of visitors each year. To enable such expansion on its relatively tiny territory, one of the most consistent themes in the city's expansion has been the constant creation of flat land for building and the stacking and squeezing of all manner of activities and links upon it. We usually think of reclamation as solid displacing sea or swamp, and Hong Kong has expanded in this way more than most cities, with artificial land now exceeding the land area of the original island colony. No less artificial has been the massive reshaping of the landform itself. For instance, whatever happened to the great mound once occupied by Kowloon Walled City, Wan Chai's Morrison Hill, and other landmark hills? Here, there may again be strong cultural threads at play, for the readiness to reshape or reclaim the land is rooted in the region's culture. For centuries, in agriculture, tea or rice-growing demanded the reconfiguration of hillsides into terraces. And in other contexts, there has been a tendency to remove or extend hills or build flat platforms (for instance out from city walls) for the placement of religious and official structures: temples, ancestral halls, watch buildings all stand on raised or cut flat ground. Accordingly, modern Hong Kong has built massive structures that offer multiple platforms for activities confined mostly to the ground in other places: for instance the extensive 'layered grounds' for warehousing, factories, wharves, transport interchanges, horse stabling, etc, often served by spiralling roads, plus other forms that have facilitated vertical and volumetric functioning.

Preceding chapters have recorded the rise of the city's forms from precedents that can often be traced to other places. For instance, Chapter 2 notes the tradition of mixed functions and movement across several levels in the walled villages of the region's Hakka people, and the dense occupation of colonnaded shop-houses in the wider Asian region. In Hong Kong multi-level aspects of development tended to become exaggerated by virtue of the territory's topography. Perhaps the most complex, if slightly sinister expression of three-dimensional urbanism was Kowloon's Walled City, which stood as a high-rise feral mass on contested territory – there for all to see, though probably not enter. Certain values embodied in these examples were particularly evident in the built forms that emerged over the two post World War II decades, in which shops, all kinds of services, industries and dwellings co-existed through much of the four to fifteen levels of development – sometimes with informal building-to-building or roof-to-roof connections. And, as shown in Chapter 4, the earliest public housing forms showed the same volumetric values in congested H-block culture, in which the path to education meant a journey to the roof.

Further, this regional strand of cultural heritage was married loosely to that of several Modernist models; for a range of Hong Kong's component buildings bear close resemblance to certain utopian configurations envisaged by prominent architect-cum-urbanists during the inter-War and post-War years of the twentieth century. We saw, for instance, the appearance of forms that may be likened to: Le Corbusier's slab blocks and cruciform towers complete with indentations for increased light and ventilation; Ludwig Hilbersheimer's podia topped by tall residential blocks; and Team X's extensive pedestrian 'second ground' decks above vehicle dominated streets. Between Hong Kong's hills, such ideas were forged into a system of urban forms and movement probably without much explicit reference to theory or models.

In the latter part of the twentieth century (the period covered by Chapters 5 and 6), some of the more clinical aspects of the source models' spatial and functional organization became increasingly evident at the expense of the more inclusive and chaotic strands of local practice: in particular, greater separation of functions and movement advanced at the expense of the previous all-sorts mix. Residential towers reached to greater heights (from thirty to over seventy storeys), management exerted tighter control, and shopping became more of a big box internalized experience in planned shopping and service centres.

Increasingly, dwellings came to occupy identical floor plates in individual and conjoined slabs or, more likely, towers standing beside and above the big-boxes, which are themselves layered with shopping, eating, health and other services – in effect, stratified town centres. Given the 1,000 or even 2,000-plus densities, and proximity of residential towers and commercial boxes, it is all too easy to assume such developments as exemplars of urban intensity but impressions can be misleading. The towers are vertical culs-de-sac, organizationally the stacked equivalent of a Modernist residential neighbourhood often with a single cluster of lifts to connect with the centre below, which is zoned level by level to take several categories of use but not dwellings. Hong Kong has therefore, with its podia-and-towers developments, become more and more an up-ended, albeit concentrated, version of suburbia, and this is especially so in new towns and on some of the newer reclamation sites. Compare the structures in figures 8.1 and 8.2. The former shows Australian architect, Walter Bunning's post World War II model for a small garden city, which is a synthesis of ideas and forms from Ebenezer Howard, Le Corbusier and Clarence Stein. Figure 8.2 depicts a typical podium and tower township. While the former is low-density and horizontal and the latter high-density and vertical, they are topologically similar. Both have a centre, which is retail, commercial and public services and both have single-strand connections to residential neighbourhoods. Between centre and neighbourhoods there are 'green belts', although one is in the form of trees on the ground and the other a garden on raised (podium) ground. In the latter, slim-line residential neighbourhoods are connected by a route (of largely invisible elevators) to a 'town centre' of piled

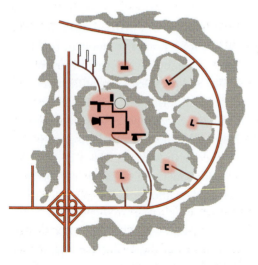

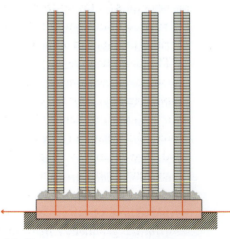

**8.1.** Diagram of Walter Bunning's 1944 model new town, consisting of town centre and single strand connections to residential neighbourhoods, each with its own small centre. Both town centre and neighbourhoods are bounded by a green belt.

**8.2.** Diagram of typical Hong Kong tower and podium consisting of a town centre (podium) and single strand connections to isolated 'tower neighbourhoods' above, in which floors are isolated from each other. Although the respective Bunning and Hong Kong conditions are primarily horizontal and vertical, they are topologically very similar.

rather than areal zoning. In the language of Christopher Alexander or Stephen Marshall both are simple tree structures.

As the photographs of Michael Wolf demonstrate so well, Hong Kong's forests of towers can have their visual drama; and their densities do offer potential efficiencies (see: http://www.photomichaelwolf.com/intro/index.html – especially *Architecture of Density*). They can also offer easier management by way of large land parcels and simple stacks of units. But as elements of urban structure they have the inbuilt weakness that each is a cul-de-sac, which means, by definition, minimal connection. In only a slightly earlier era, the English language would have called them more forthrightly 'dead-ends' – that is, routes that lead to nowhere or, more literally, to lifelessness. Hallmarks of intensity and vitality (the opposite of lifelessness) are multiple connections and rich mixes of things to connect. Hence the taller and slimmer the towers, and the more uses are classified and stretched apart, the more problematic the city becomes.

In 2003, Ken Yeang produced a kind of manifesto on *vertical urban design*: it was a critique of single-use towers with identical mono-use floor plates, and the lift shaft as the depressingly single means of travel. He noted that towers must somehow embrace the essential qualities espoused by design theorists for conventional street oriented cities: high-rise buildings also need walkable and legible connections (as well as lifts), vegetation, public spaces, mixed programmes and mixed schedules throughout their height – *plus* preferably high-level links to other buildings to form true networks. His own analyses and examples are not very convincing: for instance the mismatch in dimensions between his horizontal and vertical analogies (an upended London street-cum-district with a slender skyscraper) is large, and his own tower examples are mostly culs-de-sac. But the implication is sound: that the principles for the horizontal city to be found in the work of writers from Jacobs to Hillier and other major design theorists have somehow to be reinterpreted, rewritten and applied in the vertical and to volume.

The overwhelming implications are that concentrated vertical developments cry out for three-dimensional multi-directional connection, and permeable and legible volumes. Thus the *vertical* rising from a single ground plane is transformed into the *volumetric* served by multiple grounds and connections. For all our expressed criticisms of recent podia and towers, Hong Kong's extreme landforms, rapid growth, and meeting of Eastern and Western cultures have produced an urban setting and lifestyle that is both more volumetric *and* vertical than any other city. We have noted how the formidable geography has sparked a constant search across cultures for urban components that intensify fabric, movement and use, and how this has generated a string of intriguing responses, which include: the design of the Mark I and II squatter resettlement blocks of the 1950s; the widespread adoption of scissor stairs from the 1960s; the introduction of mechanical or escalator streets from the 1990s; drive-up warehouses of up to twenty storeys; the reduction of the sales office to a sliver of space that is little more than a street edge information board, fold-up seats and mobile phone; the continual extension of

Team X-like walkway networks that allow for walking across large parts of the city entirely on 'floating ground'; and many more.

On the Central district's elevated walkway network, it is now possible to walk east–west for 1.3 km (as the crow flies, somewhat longer for a flightless human negotiating an indirect spatial structure) and almost as far north–south. This is a substantial area across which the public can eat, shop or promenade without descent to 'real' ground. Further, this is just one of three walkway clusters that line up almost end-to-end along some 3 km of old Victoria's waterfront, through the districts of Central, Admiralty and Wan Chai. Ironically, all hover not over 'real' but artificial land: it is therefore three cases of double reclamation – from both air and water. The new upper *and* lower grounds are connected via steps, ramps, escalators and lifts, with the upper levels running at points into the hill-slopes immediately behind the original shoreline. And there is an extensive third though more specialized layer: *underground*, to serve three stations. This is the fast expanding pattern of Hong Kong's waterfronts.

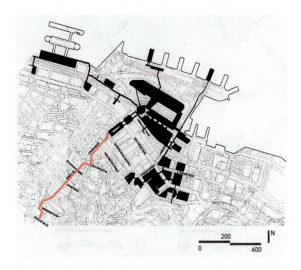

**8.3.** Hong Kong Central – Second Ground. This shows the area of 'Central' across which one can walk at a second or more ground levels. The red line shows the path of the Mid-Levels Escalators as a largely above-ground extension to the hills.

Extending from Central's deck network is the 'mechanical ladder', on which it is possible to climb the hill slope from the original waterfront at Queens Road to the Mid-Levels by a series of escalators and travelators that in some places parallel the pedestrian at street level but, in others, snake contortedly above to negotiate the confines of the streets that were once home to sedan chairs. The University of Hong Kong's main campus in Pok Fu Lam is effectively a volumetric campus and microcosm of the city: barely 400 m from low-level front to high-level back, it is housed in mostly big-box forms that make awkward cuts into an otherwise

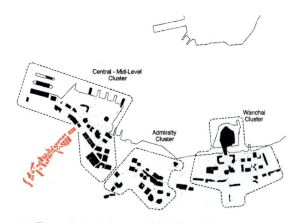

**8.4.** Three distinct clusters of buildings across three adjacent city districts are each connected by 'second grounds' in the form of decks and bridges: the plan also includes the line of buildings between which the series of escalators and walkways rise from Central to the Mid-Levels.

curvaceous hill-slope site that steps through more than 80 m of 'real' ground. Crossing the campus's modest breadth from low to high is nevertheless quite a journey and can involve a tangle of steps, escalators and lifts, entering buildings on one level and leaving from another, switch-back paths, bridges, and inside and outside places: at the same time, it is difficult to avoid pockets of lush cool greenery, birdsong and insect sounds. In new towns such as Sha Tin, residents may leave their tower homes and go to cinema, restaurant, gym and doctor, do a complete round of shopping, and return home without ever touching conventional ground. It is not even necessary to live above a podium centre to do this but simply in a high building with bridge connections. At Tsing Yi new town, not one but two (local and express) train lines, one above the other, crash through the great volume of the centre to meet their passengers at higher levels. And at a larger regional scale it is entirely possible to board and alight from a bus at some altitude within mega-structure centres and travel between the two on the vehicle's top-deck. The list goes on. Hundreds of thousands of Hong Kongers must live their daily lives almost entirely 'in suspension'. Nature's ground is no longer their major point of spatial reference, given their fleeting encounters with it.

As a pile of principles (though not as a set of actual conditions), the complex mass of Kowloon's Walled City is perhaps the best representative of three-dimensional or volumetric urbanism. Hong Kong shop-houses had similar volumetric qualities and intensity. This was certainly the case when the city expanded in the post-war 'industrial era' (1950s and 1960s) with extrusions of the shop-house form and a collective massing of built form on the street blocks. From the 1970s, towers mushroomed and rose to new heights. The most significant addition to this past was the birth of the podia and tower – at first of relatively modest scale, perhaps a box of retail and commercial uses straddling four old shop-house blocks plus a slender tower of perhaps fifteen storeys. But through the 1980s and afterwards, podia inflated to enfold greater volumes and towers extruded to greater heights. In terms of content, towers over podia were endowed with a vertical purity (flats, offices *or* hotel but rarely mixed) and the podia themselves were layered in their uses. In the metropolis as a whole, the layered city advanced while *relatively* the volumetric mix receded. Again, symbolic of the transformation was Kowloon Walled City with its evacuation and demolition between 1988 and 1992.

The volumetric is, however, robust. Even big box layering is partly volumetric, especially where atria offer views and ease of movement between levels; and even more so where connections occur at grade with adjacent spaces (streets) and nearby structures, above-ground via decks and bridges, and below-ground (which are at present by little more than tunnelled passages). Further, in the last few years, there have been instances of the distinction between tower and podia blurring, and of the podium itself morphing into more complex shapes – as in Langham Place (see chapter 6). Although in the same Langham Place, a design dimension that receives scant attention is the street level relationship between the inside and the street: long, blank door-less walls and service openings characterize most of the perimeter. By contrast, the size and configuration of its primary entrance appears to address Portland Street as an oversized suction vent (see figure 5.8): across the street, this people inlet faces the small traffic-free Nelson Street where there is an entrance to Mong Kok MTR Station (see figure 5.7). The station entrance and street crossing between can be hugely crowded, even by Hong Kong's congestion standards, while the rest of the Langham Place perimeter remains almost deserted. It is a case of single point 'tower thinking' taking hold over an otherwise more volumetric concept, to the detriment of the city and probably the centre itself.

Hong Kong remains the quintessential compact metropolis and a prime example of the notion of *IntenCity*, as outlined at the book's beginning. In a world preoccupied by issues of sustainability, discussion turns increasingly towards morphological solutions. Hong Kong's compact components (stacked homes of modest size alongside scissor stairs), and concentrated functions (multi-level mixed activity is the norm) and movement (most people move on public transport) are material objects and conditions that deserve our attention. They bring together some of the vertical characteristics of central New York and Chicago with the volumetric tendencies experienced in many parts of Tokyo and other large Japanese cities, to present an unusual vertical-volumetric combination with a multi-modal and multi-directional transport system that is second-to-none. There is every reason to regard it as a model, especially in East Asia where there are cultural affinities but also beyond where there are massive cultural-demographic, economic and environmental changes bringing morphological change.

However tracing Hong Kong's making also brings weaknesses of urban structure to our attention, and the conditions identified by theory as desirable for conventional cities based on 'natural ground' have to be revisited and reinterpreted for new multi-level forms, the vertical *and* volumetric. It is necessary to develop model approaches and regulations that will bring more mixed activity and three-dimensional multi-directional movement, greater integration between towers and podium, more connection between podia, more links between towers, greater landscape integration between podia and landform, and a far better meeting of city and nature. At a purely pragmatic level, Anthony Wood (2003) suggests that a city of connected towers is also a safer city, for in an emergency it is a simple fact that there are alternative routes for escape.

In the Hong Kong metropolis itself, we cannot ignore the shifting centre of gravity. The dense older districts of Kowloon, Mong Kok and environs, are increasingly the most central, being on the main public transport routes between the old established centre of Victoria and the maturing centres of New Kowloon and New Territories' new towns. There is a strong case for experimenting with super-density in this place (see the Addendum). Such experimentation is not only good for Hong Kong but is also relevant to other world cities where urban intensification is on the agenda. Our exposition here establishes Hong Kong as providing some of the most fertile *grounds* for super densities and design experimentation.

The transformation of cities to more vertical or volumetric configurations is not new: it has captured imaginations for centuries. One of the better-known early examples is Leonardo da Vinci's multi-level city with elegant upper levels for gentlemen, and lower levels for transport, utilities and tradesmen. Over the last century, science fiction has consistently depicted multi-level configurations as characteristic of future urbanism – to be glimpsed in many films, from Fritz Lang's 1927 *Metropolis* to and beyond Tezuka's 2001 animated version of the same title. Sci-fi has tended to portray cities as combinations of soaring vertical structures with high-level activity and movement, plus light-enhanced night skylines, and Hong Kong is known to have influenced several exponents of the genre. Most famously Ridley Scott has said that he wished to film *Blade Runner* in Hong Kong but the budget did not allow this: it nevertheless provided a model and inspiration. Likewise, Oshii Mamoru turned to Hong Kong for part of his *Ghost in the Shell* imagery. Their attention seems to have been drawn to several characteristics of the city: grungy old sign-filled streets and alleys, the left-over spaces surrounding brutal in-frastructure, the stunning night-time signage and skyline, awesome verticality and volumetric move-ment. It is perhaps not surprising that Hong Kong is a place where sci-fi film-makers should feel that they can glimpse the future. At the same time, their references to Hong Kong are confirmation of the place's futuristic tendencies, although it is with some irony that sci-fi is not especially popular there. Perhaps familiarity breeds indifference?

**8.5.** Dim Sum – identical stacking baskets – towers of separated single food types – vertical culinary zoning.

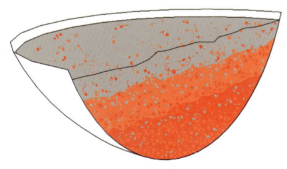

**8.6.** Poon Choi – irregular layers of food in which the juices percolate through the mix to enrich the whole.

Lastly, it seems appropriate to close on a lighter note: by analogy to two popular items of Hong Kong cuisine. Both consist of a great many ingredients and are products of the immediate region. One is *dim sum*, a meal in which items are served separately from steam baskets stacked in tower formations – it is a kind of vertical culinary zoning. The other is *poon choi*, a dish in which the component items are also layered but placed within a large single container (*poon* meaning 'basin'): however the strata are not rigidly separated, and the magic of the dish depends upon the juices from each layer percolating through other levels – a matter of synergy or enrichment through proximity and connection, which is the essence of Hong Kong – a kind of *poon choi urbanism*?

# Addendum

## Exploring the Volumetric on Old District and New Territory Sites

Noted repeatedly in the later chapters of this work is the vital and dominant role of public transport in the life of modern Hong Kong. Over the past two decades, the rail network has been extended to most parts of the New Territories and, as a consequence, Kowloon Peninsula has emerged as the most connected place in the urban system. More specifically, at the centre of Kowloon are Mong Kok and its neighbouring districts, which collectively form an area of enormous intensity.

In 2003, we were asked by the Kowloon & Canton Railway Company (KCRC) to explore new design ideas for station-related urban forms – to which we responded with example proposals for two contrasting settings. The first was for an area of land that lies between the super-dense mixed-use district of Mong Kok and the elevated Mong Kok East Station to the east. The second was for a new town station and new town in the northern New Territories – at Kwu Tung on the Lok Ma Chau Line. Salient points from these studies and proposals are presented below.

# 1. Transforming an Old District: Mong Kok

While very dense, Mong Kok does have some open spaces and community services. Markets are to be found in the streets, which is what the area is known for. There are pocket parks, some big enough for playing basket ball, and other limited sports facilities. There are homes for the elderly, tucked into multi-storey buildings, and some provision of social services. However, these are inadequate for the present population so further development is constrained by planning laws and building regulations, which only allow additional development if it is accompanied by the provision of such services. This can be illustrated most clearly by the regulations for neighbourhood open space. The Metro Plan published in September 1991 specifies the shortfalls in the area. The current provision of 8 hectares of open space needs to be supplemented by an additional 19 hectares to meet regulations. The Metro Plan also identifies the need for twenty-six social centres, three day-care centres, one multi-service centre as well as one indoor recreation centre, two sports complexes, one leisure pool, three youth centres and eighteen post offices.

Mong Kok has been described in earlier chapters where we have remarked on its rich urban fabric and noted how recent developments in the district have been innovatory but disruptive of this fabric. Mong Kok East Station is located to the north-east – on the edge of the vibrant commercial and residential neighbourhood. In contrast to the main neighbourhood, it is zoned for primary government purposes and occupied by schools, government offices, a transport interchange and a small area of commercial activity. In comparison to Mong

**A.1.** Mong Kok East and Kwu Tung (not to scale). Mong Kok's central situation on the Kowloon Peninsula and in the Hong Kong rail network is clear; the location of the proposed new station and new town of Kwu Tung is also shown. (See figure 5.5 for the whole network.)

**A.2.** The Mong Kok site. It is between Mong Kok East Station on the East Rail line and the Mong Kok street grid, and close to two subway stations.

Existing and required public open space in Mong Kok.
**A.3a.** (left) Existing public space.
**A.3b.** (middle) Existing public space as it would appear if consolidated into one area.
**A.3c.** (right) Land required for the district to meet Hong Kong's public space planning requirements.

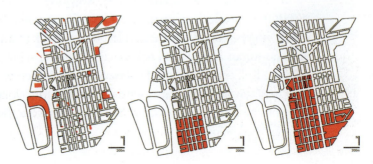

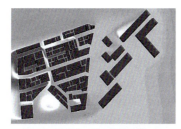

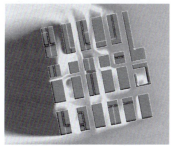

**A.4a** and **A.4b.** Tsim Sha Tsui and Mong Kok showing the effects of prevailing wind through built form illustrating the way pollution is flushed from Tsim Sha Tsui but trapped in Mong Kok. (White indicates stagnant street air.)

**A.5.** Mong Kok site – sections showing alternative building forms and wind flow. The two sections show wind flow with a conventional building mass (top), and a perforated building mass (bottom) on the site beneath the escarpment on which Mong Kok East Station is perched. Perforations result in more air circulation at street level on the left side, while reducing turbulence.

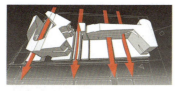

**A.6.** Design strategy: perforating the building mass assists in the ventilation of adjacent spaces.

Kok, it is underused, inaccessible, contributes little to the community and deters use of rail transport by isolating the station. The specific brief for Mong Kok Station was to find a way by which a community centre could be provided and community activities generated in the redevelopment of this heavily (if under-) used public transport node.

One problem that we were quick to recognize in Mong Kok was air quality. The urban fabric of the area has much in common with nearby Tsim Sha Tsui: urban block and building plot sizes are similar, and building heights of older buildings are much the same. However, a comparison of the two shows that Mong Kok's air flow is much reduced and the quality substantially worse than that of Tsim Sha Tsui. A Computational Fluid Dynamics (CFD) model of the two areas supports this empirical evidence. The specific block sizes, orientations and, most importantly, surrounding topographies result in more stagnant air in Mong Kok. That this area is a substantial transport interchange for trains, buses and minibuses linking Hong Kong island and Tsim Sha Tsui to areas north, east and west, means that vehicular pollution is considerable and not easily dissipated. Thus what may look like two similar urban forms give rise to very different environmental conditions.

After an initial site analysis, it became obvious that the current model of urban development creates barriers to wind flow and contributes negatively to the movement of air. If the site is to be developed using the typical podium and tower model, the district's air quality would deteriorate further. In our strategy, the large building masses are perforated, where applicable, to change the airflow and better ventilate the city's spaces.

By breaking the building mass and establishing a landscape strategy based on the identification of negative pressure zones, the proposed structures would create a volumetric 'urban oasis', of buildings and spaces, which is rich in vegetation and with a distinct microclimate – a place of escape from overcrowded Mong Kok. What was previously a harsh barrier along Sai Yi Street is replaced with a stack of greenery that further improves air quality since plants absorb $CO_2$ and release oxygen through photosynthesis.

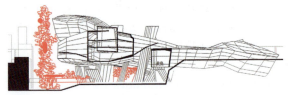

**A.7.** Section from Sai Yi Street to the 'escarp-ment', including the mid-level station close to the escarpment. Through many levels, there are substantial volumes of greenery (red) with significant ecological benefits to the district. (Adapted from studio work of Kai Wah, Uni-versity of Hong Kong, 2005)

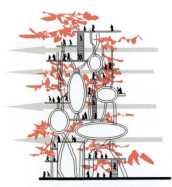

**A.8.** Section through the perforated stack of greenery between Sai Yi Street and the Station – this multi-level oasis is envisaged as a major attractor.

The new structure becomes a major attractor in Mong Kok as well as a rainwater collector. The water is stored in retention ponds within the stack to be used for irrigation and as a source for the evaporative cooling of outdoor spaces.

Community facilities, presently assembled under the Dim Sum approach (as described in Chapter 7 and figures 7.24 and 7.25, in the Conclusion on p. 163 and illustrated in figures 8.5 and A.10.) are reinterpreted to provide a form that is more open and interactive with its environs, and accommodates a greater variety of activity. The oasis houses an aquatic centre with a 50 m x 8 m wide training pool, other pleasure pools, numerous platforms for practising Tai Chi, mini-football fields, tennis courts, basketball courts, cinemas (both indoor and outdoor), a library with a garden for reading, computer facilities for checking e-mail and accessing the web. It also accommodates eating places ranging in scale, quality and cost. Thus, a structure that had been envisioned as a building has been transformed into a permeable green volume of communal open space and facilities.

**A.9.** View along Bute Street to the oasis.

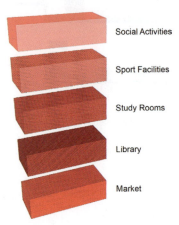

Social Activities

Sport Facilities

Study Rooms

Library

Market

**A.10.** A 'Dim Sum' stack of activities that is typical in a Hong Kong market-cum-community centre – see p. 163.

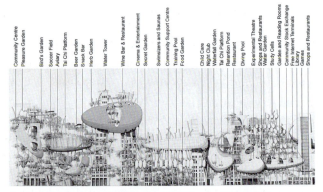

**A.11.** The urban oasis with a 'Poon Choi' mix of ingredients.

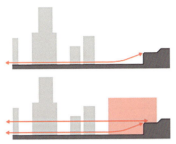

**A.12.** Two-level circulation. The lower section shows the introduction of a higher station-level network.

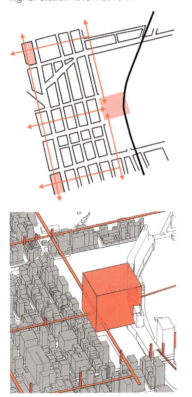

It is also the node from which a green extension over the railway line begins to change the role of the rail corridor from that of a divider to connector – much in the way of New York's High Line. This provision of a 'green corridor' along the line affords pleasant and leisurely pedestrian access through the central part of Kowloon, connecting Mong Kok to Tsim Sha Tsui – in contrast to the neighbourhood's pediway which channels large numbers of people at speed between two stations in a utilitarian manner.

There is another key strategy, which would take advantage of the station's elevated site and extend the volumetric movement and activity from the new station-related developments into Mong Kok itself. It is to extend 'mid-level' movement from the station concourse through and beyond the proposed new development into the neighbourhood by an upper, probably sixth floor, walkway system. Unlike the singular and disconnected route and role of the pediway, this would be a *network* of upper level streets that *connects* with buildings above ground: it would stimulate more activity and circulation to permeate across the levels between ground and sixth floor, and probably higher. Thus, the proposal for a volumetric 'centre' of community-orientated facilities adjacent to the station is a transformation of the idea of 'town square' into 'town cube'.

**A.13.1** and **A.13.2.** An above-ground network for Mong Kok: these plan and volumetric drawings show the beginnings of a mid-level network through the district.

## 2. Creating a New Town: Naturbia at Kwu Tung

The Kwu Tung proposal is for a new town of 200,000 people to be sited in the northern New Territories where a new station had been fore-shadowed. We drew on our analysis of the volumetric richness of Hong Kong as explored in the earlier chapters and proposed a Poon Choi solution.

The well-rehearsed new town strategy in Hong Kong has been that of integrating a transport inter-change into a podium structure. In this model, a bus or train station (sometimes both) is positioned in or under the extensive mass of a shopping podium, which in turn sits beneath a group of tall towers: these include residential and often office or hotel towers. The approach starts with the calculation of the number of passengers required each day to board the trains at a station to justify the infrastructure investment, then extrapolates this into household counts and con-sequent social and community infrastructure. It assumes, however, that employment is located at some other point along the rail line, resulting in the line being overloaded in one direction or the other during rush hours and greatly under-utilized at other times. As the majority of employment in Hong Kong is to be found within a 7.5 km radius of the middle of the harbour, the three-decade strategy of locating residential populations in the New Territories has resulted in 51 per cent of the population living outside this locus of employ-ment. Thus a new settlement becomes 'a new dormitory' in the form of a vertical suburb, rather than a New Town.

Our strategy sought to create a centre of attraction that would generate rail passenger traffic at times other than the morning and evening commuter peaks. To this end, we derived, from our examination of the vibrancy of the older urban neighbourhoods, an approach that turned away from the podium form and looked instead to the fabric of an earlier era, namely small urban blocks with a close network of streets and mixed activities. The block scale of Tsim Sha Tsui and Mong Kok has successfully supported the development of community activity at street level, and includes a wide range of activities and modes of ownership'.

Working from this scale, we used the diagram of courtyard forms to expand the occupiable areas within the blocks. Both Tsim Sha Tsui and Mong Kok have a developed laneway pattern, which can be expanded to bring community activity away from traffic. Using the work of Leslie Martin and Lionel March in the 1960s at the Centre for Land Use and Built Form, at Cambridge University, a town form for 200,000 people was found to be feasible within a radius of 800 metres from the proposed station entrances using buildings of six to twelve floors, instead of

**A.14.** Site for Kwu Tung station: the associated new town will lie between the ridges.

**A.15.** Station site and area within 800 m. Dots indicate places of cultural or landscape interest and the lines represent a network of connecting walking trails – see text for further explanation.

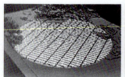 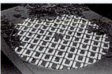 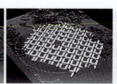 

**A.16.** Exploring urban form. The images show variations of the 'Mong Kok block' to accommodate 200,000 people within an 800 m circle (left), adaptations to a courtyard form (centre left with lower buildings and right with higher) and a morphed version of the taller and double layered courtyard form to fit the place and local climatic conditions (right). The right hand form accommodates the target population with the greatest proportion of outside space with layered and roof top gardens and hiking trails.

**A.17a.** Urban blocks. **A.17b.** Urban structure including high-level walking trails. The trails rise through modest gradients (maximum slopes of 1:12) from points around the new town to a high point over the station.

**A.18.** Naturbia's cityscape.

**A.19.** Courtyard within a block: view from the deck.

the podium with towers of over forty floors as in Tseung Kwan O, a similar development.

A second overarching goal was to integrate the urban fabric with the landscape. The site is located on a flood plain between two ridges. Rather than creating an isolated island on the plain, separate from the landscape, the proposal creates a walkable landscape between the two ridges. As noted earlier, country walking (hiking) is a popular recreational activity in Hong Kong and a successful and essential antidote to the urban intensity.

From the initial formal analysis that established a prototypical town of the appropriate size, the courtyard forms were then manipulated to encourage summer wind flow to ventilate street and other ground level spaces, reducing pollution and providing cooling breezes, and appropriate sun angles to support a range of productive gardening. The landscape is then taken over the buildings to extend the walking paths along the ridges and so connects one side of the valley with the other. The surfaces across the roofs are planted as are portions of the walls and pathways at lower levels. The planted areas support sporting activities, community gardens and productive agriculture with high value crops. This manufactured landscape may support the otherwise illicit community activities found on many hillsides around Hong Kong. Rainwater runoff into the flood plain is reduced as hard surfaces are reduced; water storage voids in the foundation zone also buffer runoff from further up the valley to solve a periodic problem downstream when torrential rains flood more densely inhabited areas. Further, there are micro-climatic benefits from this strategy as it reduces the urban heat island.

This strategy of integrating nature with the urban form, we call *Naturbia*. It brings a train ridership which is counter directional and countercyclical to that of commuters; and avoids a Dim Sum layering to create a Poon Choi mix that encourages activities in both streets and on roofs, harking back to the early urban settlement in Hong Kong where the roof was a duplicate ground. Thus the Naturbia strategy at Kwo Tung demonstrates a new and vibrant volumetric approach with forms derived from both ecological considerations and Hong Kong's particular urban history.

# Bibliography

Abercrombie, Sir Patrick (1948) *Preliminary Planning Report Hong Kong*. Hong Kong: Government Printer.

Alexander, C. (1966) The city is not a tree. *Design*, No. 206, pp. 46–55.

Arida, A. (2002) *Quantum City*. Oxford: Architectural Press.

Ashihara, Y. (1989) *The Hidden Order: Tokyo through the Twentieth Century*. Tokyo: Kodansha International.

Asia Society Galleries/Hong Kong Arts Centre (1997) *Picturing Hong Kong: Photography 1855–1910*. New York: Asia Society Galleries/George Braziller.

Bentley, I., McGlynn, S., Alcock, A., Smith, G. and Murrain, P. (1985) *Responsive Environments: A Manual for Designers*. London: Architectural Press.

Bertaud, A. (1997) Measuring Constraints on Land Supply: The Case of Hong Kong. Available at http://alain-bertaud.com/images/HK_outline4. Accessed 22 January 2010.

Biswas, R.K. (2000) Suzie Wong's revenge, in Biswas, R.K. (ed.) *Metropolis Now! Urban Cultures in Global Cities*. Vienna: Springer.

Boyden, S., Millar, S., Newcombe, K. and O'Neill, B. (1981) *The Ecology of a City and Its People: The Case of Hong Kong*. Canberra: Australian University Press.

Boyd, A.C.H. (1962) *Chinese Architecture and Town Planning: 1500 BC–AD 1911*. Chicago, IL: University of Chicago Press.

Busbea, L. (2007) *Topologies: The Urban Utopia in France 1960–70*. Cambridge, MA: MIT Press.

C40 Large Cities Climate Summit (2009) Seoul Declaration 18–21 May. Available at http://www.c40cities.org/news/news-20090522.jsp. Accessed 22 January 2010.

Capra, F. (1991) *The Tao of Physics*. Boston, MA: Shambhala.

Carroll, J.M. (2007) *A Concise History of Hong Kong*. Lanham, MD: Rowman and Littlefield.

Chadwick, O. (1882) *Mr Chadwick's Report on the Sanitary Condition of Hong Kong: With Appendices and Plans*. London: Colonial Office.

Chadwick, O. and Simpson, W.J. (1902) *Report on the Question of the Housing of the Population of Hong Kong*. Hong Kong.

Chen, P.H. and Toong, P.M. (2003) *A Century of Kowloon Roads and Streets*. Hong Kong: Joint Publishing (HK) Co. Ltd.

Chiu, T.N. and So, C.L. (1986) (eds.) *A Geography of Hong Kong,* 2nd ed. Hong Kong: Oxford University Press.

Choh-Ming, L. (1959) *Economic Development of Communist China*. Berkeley, CA: University of California Press.

Chung, C.J., Inaba, J., Koolhaas, R. and Leong, S.T. (2001) *Harvard Design School Guide to Shopping*. Cologne: Taschen.

Commissioner for Resettlement (1955) *Annual Department Report by the Commissioner for Resettlement for the Financial Year 1954–1955*. Hong Kong: Government Printer.

Commissioner for Resettlement (1956) *Annual Department Report by the Commissioner for Resettlement for the Financial Year 1955–1956*. Hong Kong: Government Printer.

Cuthbert, A.R. (1985) Architecture, society and space: the high-density question re-examined. *Progress in Planning*, **24**(2), pp. 71–160.

Cuthbert, A.R. (1998) Genesis of land-use planning and urban development, in Dimitrou, H.T. and Cook, A.H.S. (1998) *Land-Use/Transport Planning in Hong Kong: The End of an Era. A Review of Principles and Practices*. Aldershot: Ashgate.

Cuthbert, A.R. and McKinnell, K.G. (1997) Ambiguous space, ambiguous rights – corporate power and social control in Hong Kong. *Cities*, **14**(5), pp. 295–311.

Dimitrou, H.T. and Cook, A.H.S. (1998) *Land-Use/Transport Planning in Hong Kong: The End of an Era. A Review of Principles and Practices*. Aldershot: Ashgate.

Dwyer, D.J. (1971) (ed.) *Asian Urbanization: A Hong Kong Casebook*. Aberdeen: Cathay Press.

Dwyer, D.J. (1972) (ed.) *The City as a Centre of Change in Asia*. Hong Kong: Hong Kong University Press.

Empson, H. (1992) *Mapping Hong Kong: A Historical Atlas*. Hong Kong: Government Information Services.

Girard, G. and Lambot, I. (1993) (eds.) *City of Darkness: Life in Kowloon Walled City*. Haslemere: Watermark Publications.

Guitierrez, L. and Portefaix, V. (2001) (eds.) *Mapping Hong Kong*. Hong Kong: Map Book Publishers.

Hadland, B.J. (1978) Land policies in Hong Kong, in Wong, L.S.K. (ed.) *Housing in Hong Kong: A Multi-Disciplinary Study*. Hong Kong: Heinemann.

Han, D.W.T. (1978) Social background of housing in Hong Kong, in Wong, L.S.K. (ed.) *Housing in Hong Kong: A Multi-Disciplinary Study*. Hong Kong: Heinemann.

Hayes, J. (2001) *South China Village Culture*. Oxford: Oxford University Press.

Hays, J. (2008) *China's Earliest Cultures*. Available at http://factsanddetails.com/china.php?itemid=32&catid=2&subcatid=1. Accessed 24 January 2010.

Hegemann, W. and Peets, E. (1922) *The American Vitruvius: An Architects' Handbook of Civic Art*. New York: The Architectural Book Co.

Heisenberg, W. (1958) *Physics and Philosophy*. New York: Harper Torchbooks.

Hilbersheimer, L. (1944) *The New City: Principles of Planning*. Chicago, IL: P. Theobald.

Hillier, B. (1996) *Space is the Machine: A Configurational Theory of Architecture*. Cambridge: Cambridge University Press.

Hillier, B. and Hansen, J. (1984) *The Social Logical Space*. Cambridge: Cambridge University Press.

Hitchcock, Alfred M. (1917) *Over Japan Way*. New York: Henry Holt.

Hong Kong Museum of History (1997) *History Through Maps: an Exhibition of Old Maps of China*. Hong Kong: Provisional Urban Council.

Hopkins, Keith (1972) Public and private housing in Hong Kong, in Dwyer, D. J. (ed.) *The City as a Centre of Change in Asia*. Hong Kong: Hong Kong University Press.

Hoskins, W.G. (1955) *The Making of the English Landscape*. London: Hodder and Stoughton.

Housing Commission (1938) *Report of the Housing Commission 1935*. Hong Kong.

Howard, E. (1965, originally published 1902) *Garden Cities of Tomorrow*. London: Faber.

Hui, S.C.M. (2001) Low energy building design in high density urban cities. *Renewable Energy*, **24**(3–4), pp. 627–640.

Ingham, M. (2007) *Hong Kong: A Cultural and Literary History*. Oxford: Signal Books.

Inwood, S. (2006) *City of Cities: the Birth of Modern London*. London: Pan.

Ip, Iam-chong (2002) The rise of a sanitary city: the colonial formation of Hong Kong's early public housing. *E-Journal on Hong Kong Cultural and Social Studies*, **1**(2), pp. 189–217. Available at: http://www.hku.hk/hkcsp/ccex/ehkcss01/issue2_ar_iic_01.htm. Accessed 22 November 2009.

Ishiwari, H.O. and Wallacker, B.E. (1979) *Chinese Walled Cities: A Collection of Maps from Shina jōkaku no gaiyō*. Hong Kong: Chinese University Press.

Jacobs, J. (1961) *The Death and Life of Great American Cities*. New York: Random House.

Jenks, M. (2009) From the compact city to the defragmented city: another route towards a sustainable urban form? in Radovic, D. (ed.) *Eco-Urbanity*. London: Routledge.

Jenks, M. and Dempsey, N. (2005) (eds.) *Future Forms and Design for Sustainable Cities*. Oxford: Architectural Press.

Jenks, M., Kozak, D. and Takkanon, P. (2008) *World Cities and Urban Form: Fragmented, Polycentric, Sustainable?* London: Routledge.

Jiao, J.J., Leung, C., Chen, K., Huang, J. and Huang, R. (2005) Preliminary studies on physical and chemical processes in the subsurface system in the land reclaimed from the sea. Available at: http://hydro.geo.ua.edu/jiao/research/ FullPaper/JiaoLeungetal.pdf. Accessed 24 January 2010.

Johnson, C., Hu, R. and Abedin, S. (2008) (eds.) *Connecting Cities: Networks: A Research Publication for the 9th World Congress of Metropolis*. Available at: < http://www.metropoliscongress2008.com/images/PDF_languages/ Research%20Publications/Revised/Global%20Networks_Intro.pdf>. Accessed 13 June 2009.

Karakiewicz, J. (2005) The city and the megastructure, in Jenks, M. and Dempsey, N. (eds.) *Future Forms and Design for Sustainable Cities*. Oxford: Architectural Press.

Karakiewicz, J. (2004) Poon Choi, a Multi-layer City: Dealing with Overcrowding by Intensifying the Land Use. Paper to the International Symposium on City Planning, Sapporo.

Kelly and Walsh Ltd (1924) *Hong Kong: a Brief History and Guide of Hong Kong and the New Territories*. Hong Kong: Kelly and Walsh Ltd.

Kenworthy, J. (undated) Transport and Urban Planning for the Post Petroleum Era. Available at: http://www.naturaledgeproject.net/Documents/KenworthyTr ansportPostPetroleum.pdf. Accessed 26 January 2010.

Kenworthy, J. (2001) The Singapore/Hong Kong success stories and their implications for developing cities. *Renewable Energy*, **24**(3–4), pp. 627–640.

Kenworthy, J.R. (2003) Transport Energy Use and Greenhouse Gases in Urban Passenger Transport Systems: A Study of 84 Global Cities. Paper presented to the international Third Conference of the Regional Government Network for Sustainable Development, Notre Dame University, Fremantle, Western Australia. Available at: http://cst.uwinnipeg.ca/documents/Transport_Green house.pdf. Accessed 8 May 2009.

Kenworthy, J. (2008) Urban transport sustainability, in Johnson, C., Hu, R. and Abedin, S. (2008) (eds.) *Connecting Cities: Networks, a Research Publication for the 9th World Congress of Metropolis*. Available at: http://www.metropoliscong ress2008.com/images/PDF_languages/Research%20Publications/Revised/ Global%20Networks_Intro. Accessed 26 January 2010.

Kenworthy, J.R. and Laube, F. with Newman, P., Barter, P., Raad, T., Poborn, C. and Guia, B. Jr. (1999) *An International Sourcebook of Automobile Dependence in Cities 1960–1990*. Boulder, CO: University Press of Colorado.

Klauser, W. (2002) Voyage au pays de la e-epicérie. *L'Architecture d'Aujourd'hui*, No. 338, pp. 32–37.

Klug, S., Hayashi, Y. and Black, J. (2007) Social costs of suburbanization in Europe, Japan and the USA: a literature review. *International Journal of Urban Sciences*, **11**(2), pp. 200–221.

Koolhaas, R. (1978) *Delirious New York*. London: Thames and Hudson.

Lampugnani, V.M. (1993) (ed.) *Hong Kong Architecture: The Aesthetics of Density*. Munich: Prestel.

Lau, A. (1997) Justice catches up with fugitive. *The Standard*, 14 November 1997.

Lau, S., Wang, J., Giridharan, R. and Ganesan, S. (2005) High-density, high-rise and multiple and intensive land use in Hong Kong: a future city form for the new millennium, in Jenks, M. and Dempsey, N. (eds.) *Future Forms and Design for Sustainable Cities*. Oxford: Architectural Press, pp. 153–165.

Le Corbusier (1947) *The City of Tomorrow* (translated from the eighth French edition of *Urbanisme* by Frederick Etchells). London: Architectural Press.

Lee, H.Y. (2003) The Singapore shophouse: an Anglo-Chinese urban vernacular, in Knapp, Ronald G. (ed.) *Asia's Old Dwellings: Tradition, Resilience, and Change*. Oxford: Oxford University Press, pp. 115–134.

Leeds, P.F. (1998) Evolution of urban transport, in Dimitrou, H.T. and Cook, A.H.S. (eds.) *Land-Use/Transport Planning in Hong Kong: The End of an Era: A Review of Principles and Practices*. Aldershot: Ashgate.

Leeming, F. (1977) *Street Studies in Hong Kong: Localities in a Chinese City*. Hong Kong: Oxford University Press.

Leinberger, C.B. (2008) The next slum. *The Atlantic*, March. Available at: http://www.theatlantic.com/doc/200803/subprime. Accessed 26 January 2010.

Leung, W.T. (1983) 'The New Towns Programme' in Chiu, T.N. and So, C.L. (eds.) *A Geography of Hong Kong*, 2nd ed. Hong Kong: Oxford University Press.

Li, C.M. (1959) *Economic Development of Communist China: An Appraisal of the First Five Years of Industrialization*. Berkeley, CA: University of California Press.

Liauw, L. (1998) Kowloon walled city density study 1995, in Maas, W. and Van Rijs, J. (eds.) *MVRDV, Excursions in Density*. Rotterdam: 010 Publishers.

Lim, B, and Nutt, T. (2003) Planning and locational aspects, in Yueng, Y.M. and Wong, T.K.Y. (2003) (eds.) *Fifty Years of Public Housing in Hong Kong: A Golden Jubilee Review and Appraisal*. Hong Kong: Chinese University Press.

Lim, Jon S.H. (1993) The Shophouse Rafflesia: an outline of its Malaysian pedigree and its subsequent diffusion in Asia. *Journal of the Malaysian Branch of the Royal Asiatic Society*, **66**(1), pp. 47–66.

Lo, C.P. (1992) *Hong Kong*. London: Belhaven.

Lockhart, J.H.S. (1899) *Report on the New Territory. Sessional Papers for the Year 1898*. Hong Kong: Government Printer.

Lung, D. and Friedman, A. (1995) Hong Kong's Wai: defensive architecture of the New Territories, in Hase, P.H. and Sinn, Y.-Y.E. (eds.) *Beyond the Metropolis: Villages in Hong Kong*. Hong Kong: Joint Publishing, pp. 67–75.

Lynch, K. (1960) *The Image of the City*. Cambridge, MA: MIT Press.

Maas, W. and Van Rijs, J. (1998) *MVRDV, Excursions in Density*. Rotterdam: 010 Publishers.

Mahtab-uz-Zaman, Q.M. (2003) Hong Kong: a review of density, urban form and sustainable development. *Journal of Research in Architecture & Planning* (NED University of Engineering and Technology, Karachi), **2**. Available at: http://www.neduet.edu.pk/ARCH-JOURNAL/JRAP-2003/WebJRAP%202003%20page3.pdf. Accessed 1 Jan 2010.

Maki, F. (1964) *Investigations in Collective Form*. St. Louis, MI: The School of Architecture, Washington University.

Marshall, S. (2005) *Streets and Patterns*. London: Spon.

Maunder, W.F. (1969) *Hong Kong Urban Rents and Housing*. Hong Kong: Centre for Asian Studies Series, Hong Kong University Press.

Maunder, W.F. and Szczepanik, E.F. (1958) Hong Kong housing survey 1957, in *Final Report of the Special Committee on Housing 1956–58*. Hong Kong: Government Printer.

Morris, J. (1988) *Epilogue to an Empire*. London: Penguin.

Morris, J. (2008, 1985) *Among the Cities*. London: Faber.

McDonogh, G. and Wong, C. (2005) *Global Hong Kong*. London: Routledge.

O'Brien, R. (1984) Julian Tenison Woods in Hong Kong. *Journal of the Hong Kong Branch of the Royal Asiatic Society*, 24, pp. 288–294. Online. Available at: sunzi1.lib.hku.hk/hkjo/view/44/4401561. Accessed 17 September 2009.

Ohno, H. (1992) (ed.) Hong Kong: alternative metropolis. *SD* (Special Issue), No. 330, pp. 5–78.

Owen, B. and Shaw, R. (2007) *Hong Kong Landscapes: Shaping the Barren Rock*. Hong Kong: Hong Kong University Press.

Pearson, V. and Gao, T. (2008) *A Sense of Place: Hong Kong West of Pottinger Street*. Hong Kong: Joint Publishing.

Popham, P. (1993) Introduction, in Girard, G. and Lambot, I. (eds.) *City of Darkness: Life in the Kowloon Walled City*. Haslemere: Watermark Publications, pp. 9–13.

Prescott, J.A. (1971) Hong Kong: the form and significance of a high density urban development, in Dwyer, D.J. (ed.) *Asian Urbanization: A Hong Kong Casebook*. Hong Kong: Cathay Press, pp. 11–19.

Pryor, E.G. (1972) A historical review of housing conditions in Hong Kong. *Journal of the Hong Kong Branch of the Royal Asiatic Society*, **12**, pp. 89–129. Available at: sunzi1.lib.hku.hk/hkjo/view/44/4401232. Accessed 17 November 2009.

Pryor, E.G. (1983) *Housing in Hong Kong*, 2nd ed. Hong Kong: Oxford University Press.

Pryor, E.G. and Pau, S.H. (1993) The growth of a city: a historical review, in Lampugnani, V.M. (1993) (ed.) *Hong Kong Architecture: The Aesthetics of Density*. Munich: Prestel.

Pryor, E.G. (1998) Parallel development of strategic land-use and transport planning: the case of Territorial Development Strategy, in Dimitrou, H.T. and

Cook, A.H.S. (eds.) *Land-Use/Transport Planning in Hong Kong: The End of an Era: A Review of Principles and Practices*. Aldershot: Ashgate.

Pun, K.S. (1983) Urban renewal and urban planning, in *Architecture, Building, Urban Design and Urban Planning in Hong Kong*. Hong Kong: Appointments Board, University of Hong Kong.

Rooney, N. (2003) *At Home with Density*. Hong Kong: Hong Kong University Press.

Rowe, P.G. (2005) *East Asia Modern: Shaping the Contemporary City*. London: Reaktion Books.

Runnacles, T.V. (1998) Public transport network and land-use impacts, in Dimitrou, H.T. and Cook, A.H.S. (1998) *Land-Use/Transport Planning in Hong Kong: The End of an Era: A Review of Principles and Practices*. Aldershot: Ashgate.

Salingaros, N.A. (2005) *Principles of Urban Structure*. Amsterdam: Techne.

Schmitt, R.C. (1963) Implications of density in Hong Kong. *Journal of American Planners*, **29**(3), pp. 210–216.

Sears, R. (2003) *Chinese Etymology*. Available at: http://www.chineseetymology.org/. Accessed 26 January 2010.

Shirakawa, S. (1999, originally published in Japanese 1978) *Kanji: Hyakuwa*. Tokyo: Chuo Koronsha.

Sidel, R. (1974) *Families of Fengsheng: Urban Life in China*. Harmondsworth: Penguin.

Skyscraper Museum Exhibition (undated) *Vertical Cities: Hong Kong /New York*. Available at: http://wwww.skyscraper.org/EXHIBITIONS/VERTICAL_CITIES/vc-pr. Accessed 26 January 2010.

Smart, A. (2006) *The Shek Kip Mei Myth: Squatters, Fires and Colonial Rule in Hong Kong, 1950–1963*. Hong Kong: Hong Kong University Press.

Stein, C. (1958) *Towards New Towns for America*. Liverpool: Liverpool University Press.

Tang, B. and Tang, R.M. (1999) Industrial property, market initiative and planning policy: restructuring obsolete industrial properties in Hong Kong. *Property Management*, **17**(2), pp. 157–168.

Taylor, P.J. 'World City Network', in Johnson, C., Hu, R. and Abedin, S. (2008) (eds) *Connecting Cities: Networks, a Research Publication for the 9th World Congress of Metropolis*. Available at: http://www.metropoliscongress2008.com/images/PDF_languages/Research%20Publications/Revised/Global%20Networks_Intro. Accessed 26 January 2010.

Tjoa-Bonatz, M.L. (1998) Ordering of housing and the urbanization process: shophouses in colonial Penang. *Journal of the Malaysian Branch of the Royal Asiatic Society*, **71**(2), pp. 123–136.

Tong, C.O. and Wong, S.C. (1997) Advantages of a high density, mixed land use, linear urban development, *Transportation*, **24**(3), pp. 295–307.

Tregear, T.R. (1959) *The Development of Hong Kong and Kowloon as told in Maps*. Hong Kong: Hong Kong University Press.

University of Hong Kong (Department of Architecture) (2005) *Linear City: A Morphological Approach*. Unpublished research report in three volumes.

Van Eesteren, C. (1997) *The Idea of the Functional City: A Lecture with Slides 1928* (Introduction by Vincent van Rossem). Rotterdam/The Hague: NAi Publishers/EFL Publications.

Van Rijs, J. (1998) Far East, Hong Kong tower typology 1998, in Maas, W. and Van Rijs, J. with Koek, R.(eds.) *FARMAX: Excursions on Density*. Rotterdam: 010 publishers.

Vijoen, A., Bohn, K. and Howe, J. (2005) *Continuous Productive Urban Landscapes: Designing Urban Agriculture for Sustainable Cities*. Oxford: Architectural Press.

Vittachi, Nuri (2002) Mysterious Properties, in the *Feng Shui Detective*. Hong Kong: Chameleon Press.

Walker, A. and Rowlinson, S.M. (1990) *The Building of Hong Kong*. Hong Kong:, Hong Kong University Press.

Wang, W. (1998) Axial inversion – the transformation of the spatial structure and its ritual axis in Hong Kong's walled villages. *Hong Kong Papers in Design and Development*, **1**, pp. 26–33.

Wellington, A.R. (1930) *Public Health in Hong Kong*. Report to the Hong Kong Government, CO 129/531. Hong Kong: Government Printer.

Welsh, F. (1994) *A History of Hong Kong*. London: Harper Collins.

Will, B.F. (1978) Housing design and construction methods, in Wong, L.S.K. (ed.) *Housing in Hong Kong: A Multi-Disciplinary Study*. Hong Kong: Heinemann Educational Books (Asia).

Wong, L.S.K. (1978*a*) The squatter problem, in Wong, L.S.K. (ed.) *Housing in Hong Kong: A Multi-Disciplinary Study*. Hong Kong: Heinemann Educational Books (Asia).

Wong, L.S.K. (ed.) (1978*b*) *Housing in Hong Kong: A Multi-Disciplinary Study*. Hong Kong: Heinemann Educational Books (Asia).

Wood, A. (2003) Pavements in the sky: the skybridge in tall buildings. *arq*, **7**(3/4), pp. 325–332.

Wordie, J. (2007) *Streets: Exploring Kowloon*. Hong Kong: Hong Kong University Press.

Wright, F.L. (1958) *The Living City*. New York: Horizon Press.

Wright, F.L. (2000, originally published 1935) Broadacre City: a new community plan, in Legates, R.T. and Stout, F. (eds.) *The City Reader*, 2nd ed. London: Routledge, pp. 344–349.

Xu Xi (2005) The yellow line, in *History's Fiction: Stories from the City of Hong Kong*. Hong Kong: Chameleon Press.

Yeang, K. (2002) *Reinventing the Skyscraper: a Vertical Theory of Urban Design*. Chichester: Wiley.

Yuen, B. (2005) Romancing the high-rise in Singapore. *Cities*, **22**(1), pp. 3–13.

Yueng, Y.M. and Nutt, T.K. (2003) (eds.) Planning and locational aspects, in Yueng, Y. M. and Wong, T.K.Y. (2003) (eds.) *Fifty Years of Public Housing in Hong Kong*. Hong Kong: Chinese University Press.

Zaman Q, Lau, S.S.Y. and So, H.M. (2000) The compact city of Hong Kong, a sustainable model for Asia? in Jenks, M. and Burgess, B., (eds.) *Compact Cities: Sustainable Urban Forms for Developing Countries*. London: Spon, pp. 255–268.

# Index